I'll Go and Do More

I'll Go
Annie Dodge Wauneka
and Do
Navajo Leader and Activist
More

Carolyn Niethammer

UNIVERSITY OF NEBRASKA PRESS : LINCOLN AND LONDON

© 2001 by Carolyn Niethammer
Manufactured in the United States
of America ∞
Library of Congress Cataloging-in-
Publication Data
Niethammer, Carolyn J.
I'll go and do more : Annie Dodge Wauneka,
Navajo leader and activist / Carolyn Niethammer.
p. cm. — (American Indian lives)
Includes bibliographical references and index.
ISBN 0-8032-3345-0 (cloth : alk. paper)
1. Wauneka, Annie Dodge, 1918–1997. 2. Navajo
Indians—Biography. 3. Navajo Indians—Politics
and government. 4. Navajo Indians—Health and
hygiene. 5. Indians of North America—Medical
care. I. Title. II. Series.
E99.N3 W385 2001
979.1'004972'0092—dc21
[B]   00-064924

for Ford

Contents

Illustrations

Acknowledgments

TO GIVE A FULL ACCOUNT of a life as full and complex as that of Annie Dodge Wauneka requires the cooperation of many people: her family, her friends, her professional associates, and those who wrote parts of her story during various stages of her life. I am deeply grateful to people in each of these categories who have been generous with their time and their memories.

My thanks go especially to Annie Wauneka's daughter, Irma Bluehouse, her husband, Milton Bluehouse, Annie's grandson, Milton Bluehouse Jr., and her sister, Ann Shirley, for sharing family memories. I am grateful to Irma Bluehouse for sharing copies of family photos and to Dianne Bret Harte and the Southwestern Foundation for a grant to cover the cost of prints and reproduction rights to those and other photographs.

Others who generously gave of their time for interviews include Marie Allen, Claudine Bates Arthur, Malvina Begay, Sister Louise Beneke, Robert Bergman, George and Harriet Bock, Bill Cousins, Sam Day III, Dennis DeConcini, Ellouise De Groat, Pal Evans, Ron Faich, Irvy Goosen, Marlene Haffner, Albert Hale, John Hubbard Jr., Lawrence Huerta, Jerrold Levy, Martin Link, Bill Malone, Charles McKammon, Taylor McKenzie, Howard McKinley, Alan Menapace, Mary Caroll Nelson, Louise Nelson, Katie Noe, Ginny Notah, Warren Perkins, Sister Maria Sardo, Sally Lippincott Wagner, Lydia Whiterock, and Peterson Zah.

Although I was not able to interview Annie Wauneka, I had access to many of her reminiscences through a long interview conducted by Abe and Mildred Chanin. Their offer of the use of their unpublished manuscript was an extraordinary gesture.

My friend Martha Blue was the godmother of this book: she suggested the topic, was a fountain of knowledge based on her long association with the Navajos, introduced me to friends, and shared documents that she had uncovered in work on her own books.

Patricia Etter, curator of the Labriola National American Indian Data Center at Arizona State University, has been an enthusiastic supporter of this project and has provided unstinting research assistance over many days. Joe Wilder of the Southwest Center at the University of Arizona gave early encouragement, and Audris Joe helped locate biographical material. I am also grateful for assistance from the staffs at the Navajo Tribal Records Office, the Navajo Tribal Museum, the John F. Kennedy Library, the Gerald Ford Library, the Lyndon B. Johnson Library, Special Collections at the University of Arizona, and the libraries of the Arizona Historical Society and the Museum of Northern Arizona.

Margaret Rand gave me the loan of her luxurious recreational vehicle so that I'd have a place to live while I conducted research on the Navajo Reservation. The late Father Simon at St. Michael's Mission, a few miles outside of Window Rock, gave me permission to park the RV in an open area beside their compound and even let me run a line to their electric source.

Martha Blue, Kate Cloud, Claudine Bates Arthur, Wade Davies, and Sally Barlow read early drafts of the book and gave much useful advice.

My husband, Ford Burkhart, has been a continuing source of help and encouragement, from driving the RV to the reservation over mountainous highways to offering research help to reading early drafts of the manuscript.

Introduction

ANNIE DODGE WAUNEKA, the longest-serving woman in Navajo politics, was loved—and feared, disdained, and venerated. During her lifetime, she gathered so many honors and awards that, after her death, a special show was mounted to display them all. Usually when making her acceptance speech after receiving an award, Annie would reassure the presenters that having received this recognition would not lead her to rest on her accomplishments. She'd conclude her speech with some version of "When I get up tomorrow morning, I'll say 'I have to go and do more.'" Her accomplishments continue to be recognized; in the fall of 2000 she was inducted into the National Women's Hall of Fame.

As a Navajo woman, Annie Dodge Wauneka was both typical and unique. Like most other Navajo women of her generation, she spent many of her childhood years herding sheep, and she continued to raise livestock—both sheep and cattle—well into her old age, managing her herds well. She married young and raised a large family; she was a faithful daughter, a good cook, a thrifty housewife, and a concerned mother. She attended traditional Navajo healing ceremonies for her clan relatives and friends and contributed sheep or cash to the considerable cost of the events. It is no contradiction that alongside her struggle to bring modern medicine to her people, she also respected the traditional medical practitioners and consulted them on spiritual matters. These are the attributes that define an upstanding and admired Navajo woman.

However, in many ways her life differed from that of other Navajo girls born in 1910. She was the daughter of Chee Dodge, the most revered Navajo leader and an important historical figure, and the importance of this cannot be overemphasized.

Most Navajo family units, consisting of a mother and father and their married daughters and their families, live far separated from other people. Especially in the early part of the century when Annie was growing up, for the typical Navajo an occasional trip to the trading post or a gathering for a ceremonial was the only social activity that involved more than family members. Chee Dodge's home, on the other hand, was a hub of coming and going as both Navajos and whites traveled to discuss events with him or to seek his advice. After her first year of life, spent in her mother's hogan, Annie moved to her father's home and grew up in one of the few real houses on the reservation—a house with rugs and curtains and a big front porch. Although she did not receive the expensive private schooling of her three older half-siblings, she was sent to school and completed the eleventh grade. She also learned to speak English well. Most of her contemporaries, even those with a bit of schooling, never learned to read beyond the basics nor speak English fluently.

Because of the interaction of these influences—being the daughter of a charismatic leader, having more education than most Navajo women her age, and being blessed with her own un-usual drive—she became a leader, not only in her tribe but also on the national stage, in the areas of Indian health care and edu-cation. Other Navajo women were active in local politics in the chapters, the grazing committees, or the school boards, but, ex-cept for a few individuals, they tended to be somewhat younger. Only Annie served term after term on the Navajo Tribal Coun-cil from 1951 to 1978 and had the ability to position herself to act effectively and to interact cross-culturally in a dynamic way.

I first heard of Annie Dodge Wauneka in the early 1970s when I was writing *Daughters of the Earth: The Lives and Legends of Indian Women*. She was then a powerful figure in the Navajo tribe, known for leading the battle against tuberculosis and fearlessly challeng-ing federal policies that she felt were unfair to her people. She was also known to be extremely outspoken and opinionated.

I was a young writer, and I found her reputation intimidat-ing. Eventually, my book turned into an exploration of the role of Native American women prior to the twentieth century, rather than in modern times, so I did not pursue an interview with Annie Wauneka at that time.

Years later when I was searching for a compelling subject for a biography, I was considering a number of historical and contemporary women who had been instrumental in the development of the West, the area where I had lived most of my life and about which I had written extensively. My friend Martha Blue, a former attorney living in Flagstaff, Arizona, who has spent decades working with the Navajo both on and off the reservation, mentioned that no major work had been written about Annie Wauneka. With a few phone calls, I learned that Annie was in a nursing home and that Irma Bluehouse, one of her daughters, was handling her affairs. I wrote a letter to the family describing the project I had in mind, and about six weeks later I received a phone call indicating that they were interested in cooperating in the research that would lead to a biography.

PLANNING THE PROJECT

In June 1995, I went to Ganado on the Navajo Reservation to discuss the scope of the project further with Mrs. Bluehouse and one of her sons, Milton Jr., formerly a Marine and currently a university student, who was interested in seeing a book written about his grandmother, to whom he was particularly close. Irma was proud of her mother and anxious for the details of Annie Wauneka's remarkable life to be collected into a book. She was gracious enough to spend the day with me, driving around the reservation and visiting the ranches established by her maternal grandfather, legendary leader Chee Dodge. In order to make good time on the highway, I had driven our rather low-slung sports car—a vehicle eminently unsuitable to the rutted, ungraded back roads leading to the remote sites we visited. We scrapped bottom more than a few times, but we made it in to the places we wanted to visit and back out to the highway.

During that trip and later, Irma introduced me to several of her mother's closest friends and associates. Visiting the Tanner Springs ranch and the Navajo Tribal Council chambers and other places that were important to Annie Wauneka and meeting her family and associates increased my enthusiasm for the project. However, before I could begin my research on the reservation I needed to secure permission from the Navajo Tribe's Historic Preservation Office. Claudine Bates Arthur, a friend and clan daughter of Annie Wauneka's and at the time the chief legislative counsel for the tribe, was an early supporter of the project and wrote a letter on my behalf to the Preservation Committee, which must approve all research conducted on the reservation.

Housing is tight in the Window Rock area where I began my research, and I was fortunate to have the loan of a spacious recreational vehicle that I parked on the grounds of St. Michael's Mission, where Annie Wauneka and her father Chee Dodge had long affiliation.

The mission grounds proved an excellent spot to live, convenient to Window Rock yet quiet, safe, and rural enough that flocks of sheep and small herds of cattle regularly wandered by. One of the brothers at the mission cultivated a very large vegetable garden, and I frequently spent the twilight hours in the fresh coolness of the garden, helping him to pull weeds. I also tried to volunteer a little help to the running of the mission by assisting with the weekend bingo games held in the church hall and attended by hundreds of Navajos.

FINDING RESOURCES ON THE RESERVATION

Obviously, the best way to gain insight into a individual's life is to conduct lengthy interviews with the subject. However, by the time I began the book, Annie Wauneka's once quick mind had been dimmed by Alzheimer's Disease, and so it was necessary for me to approach my research in another way. Fortunately, Annie's life, more than that of any other Navajo woman, had been lived in public. Since she was the daughter of a famous leader, many of the details of his life and thus her heritage had already been studied and published. From the time of her first term as a delegate to the Navajo Tribal Council in 1951 when she was forty-one, much of her life and words had been documented in newspaper articles and other readily accessible sources.

Most of my initial seven weeks on the Navajo Reservation

were spent scanning the transcripts of the Tribal Council sessions covering the twenty-six years that Annie Wauneka served on that body. All of the council's proceedings have been recorded, transcribed, translated into English, and stored on microfiche. The transcripts enabled me to look back into history to learn what issues were being discussed in the council during her long tenure and to read Annie's contributions to the debates. I didn't have to search far before I began finding interesting material. On her very first day on the council she rose to give an impassioned speech decrying the fact that the director of the local office of the Bureau of Indian Affairs office was sitting next to the tribal chairman, whispering in his ear, and making the chairman look like a BIA puppet. In most legislative bodies, the freshman delegates usually wait a while to speak out so pointedly; they watch the more experienced members before taking the floor. But for Annie, there was to be no such hesitation.

As I searched through the microfiche day after day, the transcripts of her numerous speeches showed her to be eloquent, informed, opinionated, and persistent. She was usually one of the voices to urge caution and reason, but during the first term of Chairman Raymond Nakai, a political opponent, she appeared to lead the charge against him. In month after month of contentious council sessions she challenged numerous issues, some of them minor, until she herself was challenged by a few council members and constituents and blamed for holding up the business of the council.

The staff in the tribal records office was helpful, and when it became apparent that I would be appearing every morning at 8:30, they set me up with my own microfiche reader in an air-conditioned room.

I also interviewed Annie Wauneka's friends and associates —as many as I could locate. They included both Navajos and whites. Setting the appointments was not always easy as many Navajos living in remote areas still do not have telephones. But when arrangements were concluded and I did get to sit down and talk to the interviewees, they had colorful and almost universally pleasant memories of their association with Annie. I tape-recorded and transcribed their interviews. Most of these people had a wealth of stories about Annie. She had done a great deal of traveling in car pools to meetings and conferences during her years on the Tribal Council and in the years following that when she worked for the tribe. Distances in that part of the country are vast, and a trip to the state capitals of Phoenix or Santa Fe meant long car rides of three to five hours. She was a great story-teller, and people were always interested in her activities and her memories of her illustrious father. Her entertaining tales made the long miles go faster. I could tell which of the stories were Annie's favorites, for they were repeated to me by several of her friends.

During those weeks on the reservation when I was not work-ing, and my eyes needed a rest, I drove around the reservation, as Annie had loved to do, trying to look at it through her eyes, as she saw it as a child herding sheep and as an adult working for the betterment of her people. Once, while Annie's friend Lydia Whiterock, who had lived on the Tanner Springs ranch as a child, was showing me around a remote section of the ranch, my Bronco stopped dead on the faint trail we were following through the dry grass on the range. An attempt to restart it brought only silence from the engine. The late afternoon sky stretched from mesa to mountain range in a deep blue bowl over our heads, and in all di-rections, for miles and miles, there was no sign of human habita-tion, not even a power line. It was miles back to the ranch house, where there was no phone, and many more miles to the highway, where the nearest phone was still miles distant. As we pondered our situation, I thought of the hundreds of thousands of miles Annie had traveled, frequently alone, over the back roads of the reservation as she spread the messages of modern medicine and the need for better sanitation in the remote hogans. She got stuck in sand and mud and snow, and with no phone to call a tow truck, she would dig out her pickup with a shovel. As for my own situa-tion, after about a half hour during which we lifted the hood and stared uncomprehendingly at the motor and a web of wires and hoses, whatever was wrong with the Bronco righted itself, and the engine started again. That was the end of the exploration for the day, however.

Irma Bluehouse continued to be helpful, although we never conducted a formal interview. Her recollections were usually offered when we were driving somewhere together or sharing a meal. She still raises some sheep on the ranch at Tanner Springs, and in the summer following my original research, I made another trip to the reservation to see her, planning to spend some time herding sheep and gaining more insights into Annie's life. When I arrived at Ganado, I found the plans had been changed. Instead, we were scheduled to prepare a Navajo feast for some Native American university students in a special summer school session. It wasn't yet dawn when we headed to the ranch in Irma's pickup. After driving several miles past the ranch house on a road that was no more than tracks through the grass, we found her shepherd living in an old trailer next to a corral. We singled out the one unlucky sheep, and as the small herd ran round and round the edge of the corral in nervous confusion, the shepherd lassoed the chosen animal; we tied it up and put it in the back of the pickup. Then it was back to Ganado to the home of an elderly Navajo medicine man who was also the neighborhood butcher. He put the animal on its side under a gnarled juniper tree, lovingly and calmly stroked the wool, then quickly slit its throat, catching the blood in an enameled basin. It was the most spiritual death I have ever witnessed. I knelt there in the sandy red dirt beside the medicine man, helping as best I could as he proceeded with butchering. He spoke only Navajo, but he was able to indicate if he wanted me to hold a leg of the carcass or help to peel back the pelt. When we were finished, I sat back and looked around, trying to memorize the details of the moment. In front of me stretched a vast buff-colored plain dotted by the occasional deep green pinyon or juniper tree and bordered by deep blue mesas on the horizon. Some flat clouds shimmered in the distance in an otherwise clear sky. The air smelled of dust and sheep. It was a scene typically Navajo—one that could occur nowhere else on earth.

After the meat was cut, Irma and I spent the rest of the day cooking it into blood sausage and stew and roasted ribs and a snack made of pencil-thin intestines that we twisted together and baked. As we chopped and mixed, she told me how she had learned these recipes from her mother and how she had been taught to use every part of the animal.

Writing a biography of someone means looking at the most intimate aspect of a subject's life, and I don't think that Irma was ever prepared for the depth of my curiosity. It is an intrusive occupation, and even people who have made a career of writing about others have become rattled when the spotlight was turned on them. Writer Janet Malcolm has called biographers "professional burglars" plundering the lives of their subjects. But the part of a life that biographical subjects or their families wish to keep unexamined often proves to be important, and an unwillingness on the part of the author to go beyond what is easy can result in an incomplete story. Despite the tensions engendered by my questions, Irma and Milton Jr. and I have become friends. While Milton was attending college in the city where I lived, both of his parents stayed with me while visiting him at school. I would have liked to talk to Annie's other children, but they either declined to be interviewed when contacted or sent word through Irma that they did not care to participate.

USING EARLIER INTERVIEWS

Although I was not able to interview Annie Wauneka directly, I was fortunate to have access to earlier interviews done by other writers. The first was an extensive unpublished interview that the writers Abe and Mildred Chanin conducted with Annie in the mid-1970s for a book on old-timers who had contributed to the West. It was only through dogged persistence that they had finally tracked her down. The Chanins had scheduled an appointment with Annie in Window Rock, but when they drove up to the Navajo Reservation from their home in Tucson, she was not in town. They called around and were able to learn that she was attending a conference in Phoenix. When they reached her by phone, she said she was flying home the next day. If they'd meet her at the Gallup airport, about thirty miles from Window Rock, they could talk. The Chanins stayed over and drove to Gallup the next day, but Annie did not get off the plane from Phoenix. A call back to the conference hotel got them connected with a doctor attending the event who said that Annie had a bad cold, and he had advised her to go rest up at her brother's house in nearby Scottsdale. When they called there, Annie agreed that if they would come to Scottsdale, she would talk to them. They packed up the tape recorder and drove back down to the desert. Eventually, after grilling the Chanins about their intentions, Annie talked for several hours, providing stories and insights about her life. It was invaluable to have this resource, as Abe asked most of the questions that I would have asked had I had the opportunity. They used only a small part of the interview for their book *This Land, These Voices* and generously allowed me to use the rest.

Also helpful was the biography of Annie Wauneka published in 1972 by Mary Carroll Nelson as part of a series on Indian women written for young people. Nelson was able to read her manuscript to Annie, after which Annie offered some new information about her youth. Chapters on both Chee Dodge and Annie Dodge Wauneka appear in the two-volume *Navajo Biographies* published by Rough Rock Demonstration School on the Navajo Reservation.

In the University of Arizona library, I found a scratchy black-and-white film of a 1965 *Twentieth Century* program hosted by Walter Cronkite on Annie Wauneka. This gave me an opportunity to see her in action, visiting people in their hogans as she inquired about their health and inspecting one of the new pumps and wells for which she had lobbied so hard. The Bluehouse family had made a videotape of the testimonial birthday dinner the tribe threw for Annie on her seventy-fourth birthday. This provided me with several stories I had not encountered elsewhere. I also found a transcript of an interview conducted for the *New York Times* Oral History Project called "Listening to Indians," which provided an insightful segment on her work on the women's commission.

MINING LIBRARY RESOURCES

I found rich resources on both Annie Wauneka and Navajo events before and during her tenure in libraries in Arizona and New Mexico. The public libraries in Gallup and Window Rock and the library of the Museum of Northern Arizona in Flagstaff provided both published and primary materials. The University of Arizona library in Tucson has an extensive collection of books on Navajos as well as a collection of historical papers from the Franciscan Fathers of St. Michael's Mission, which includes a great deal of material on Chee Dodge, who relied on the priests and brothers to help him with his correspondence. It was there I also found microfiche copies of all the two dozen speeches Annie Wauneka gave in Washington before congressional committees. At Arizona State University in Tempe, I found the papers of Tom Dodge, Annie's brother, in the Arizona collection, other materials in the Labriola Indian Data Center, and a number of interesting letters in the Barry Goldwater collection. I did most of the writing of the book away from the West. Surprisingly, the Montclair State University in Montclair, New Jersey, has an excellent collection of books and materials on Navajos, which I used for researching related details.

The John F. Kennedy Library, the Lyndon B. Johnson Library and Museum, and the Gerald R. Ford Library provided letters and photographs. Since Annie had met President Johnson when he presented her with the Medal of Freedom, she considered him a personal acquaintance and wrote to him whenever she thought a federal official with responsibility for Indian affairs was not performing properly.

LIFE THEMES

The Father's Daughter

As I began to learn more about Annie Wauneka's life through her own words and the reminiscences of her friends and associates, I began to see several themes running through her life. The first and most complicated is her lifelong identification with her charismatic father, Chee Dodge. Although Annie idolized her father from the time she was a small child, it appears he did not recognize her potential until she was a married adult, managing, along with her husband George, one of Chee's ranches and traveling with him throughout the reservation as he explained the federal government's policies. When Chee Dodge, on his deathbed, pleaded with his children to carry on his legacy, both Annie and her brother Ben ran for the Navajo Tribal Council in the next election and won seats representing their chapters. (Ben's early death ended his political career.) During her tenure on the Tribal Council, Annie frequently referred to lessons her father had taught her or trips they had taken together. At the tribal award ceremony on her seventy-fourth birthday, she wept when she described how, during difficult negotiations in the tribal chamber, she had always looked to the picture of Chee Dodge on a mural depicting the history of the tribe, hoping for advice from him on what to say or how to vote.

I became aware of the psychoanalytic concept of the "father's daughter" during a program meeting of a group of New York City–area women biographers called "Women Writing Women's Lives." As I listened to writer and psychoanalyst Polly Howells describe her subject's identification and devotion to her own famous and powerful father, I recognized this as very similar to the situation of Annie Wauneka.

Jungian analyst Marion Woodman discusses the father's daughter in her book *Leaving My Father's House.* According to Woodman, the father and the daughter are mutually admiring. As a father's daughter comes into adulthood, her life energy circles around men; she is driven to please by upholding patriarchal standards. She is empowered by her relationships with the outer world, rather than gaining most of her meaning from her life in her home. The total available energy of her psyche is in the father complex. Generally such daughters have a diminished relationship with their mothers, and this was certainly the case with Annie, who was taken from her own mother at about the age of one and raised by an aunt who she was led to believe was her mother.

According to Howells, in the best of circumstances, the father's daughter takes the attentions her father shows her, both his admiring her as a woman and his believing in her as a capable human being, and integrates these attentions to fashion an independent life, with satisfying work and fulfilling relationships.[1]

Any attempt to lay the pattern of the classic father's daughter on Annie Wauneka's life must be tempered by the fact that as a Navajo, she had a world view that was different from that of the women studied by Jung and Freud. Among Navajos, the feminine principle is not subordinate to the male but has great strength of its own. Changing Woman, as a sort of Earth Mother, is the Navajo holy person through whose successive womb-worlds human beings emerged from the underworld to the surface of the earth. Changing Woman is an immortal woman, continually self-renewing in an ageless cycle of death and rebirth.

Not being a psychoanalyst myself and not having spent a great deal of time with Annie Wauneka while she was alive, I cannot presume to say whether she fits the classic mold of the father's daughter in all aspects. But I do suggest this concept as one possibility for analyzing, in the general sense of the word, the reasons for some of her life choices.

Advancing Health Care and Education

When opportunities for becoming involved with health care were thrust upon Annie Wauneka, she embraced these chances to serve, always doing much more than might have been expected of her. The first was when, as a child during the great flu epidemic of 1918, she found herself at the Bureau of Indian Affairs School in Fort Defiance. When she recovered from a mild case of flu herself, she helped the matron in charge by feeding and tending to the other sick children.

Decades later, during her first term on the Tribal Council, she was appointed to head up the new Health Committee and was charged with trying to educate the other Navajos about the tuberculosis that was infecting so many of them. She could have done this in a minimalist way without censure, but instead she embraced the challenge with her entire force of personality and made it the focus of her life for many years. Concurrently, she worked on reducing infant mortality, not just by talking about it, but also by seeing that money was appropriated for layettes for new babies and sponsoring a baby contest during the tribal fair so that mothers would bring their children in to be checked over by doctors.

When, as the result of her educational efforts and new drugs, tuberculosis was under control, she turned her efforts to eradicating alcoholism, which was equally damaging to the Navajo people. Unfortunately, despite her best efforts, she was not as successful in this endeavor.

From the beginning of her tenure on the Tribal Council, Annie Wauneka was also a vocal advocate of the importance of education. Chee Dodge, although having had little education himself, had been one of the leading proponents of the value of schooling, and Annie continued to carry the message of the importance of education wherever she went on the reservation. During her years as a tribal delegate, Annie frequently visited school functions and supported the students, lobbied for more day schools so small children could remain at home, and was a vocal proponent of local Navajo control of the schools. She even fought hard for the establishment of a medical school on the Navajo Reservation.

A Cultural Bridge

Like her father before her, Annie Wauneka spent much of her life helping to bridge the chasm between Navajo and white culture. Beginning with a volunteer job as a translator during the difficult years when the agricultural agents were preaching the necessity of stock reduction, she worked at helping the agents and the Navajo stock owners understand one another. It wasn't only language that she translated, but thoughts and ideas as well. While encouraging the tribal medicine men to refer their patients with tuberculosis to the white doctors, she also tried to educate the government doctors on the importance of the sacred ceremonies in the healing process for sick Navajos.

BIOGRAPHICAL WORKS ON NATIVE AMERICAN WOMEN

This book joins a growing body of biographical and autobiographical work on the lives of contemporary Native American women. In my earlier book, I relied primarily on information about the traditional lives of Native American women; however, I also used some biographical material about women whose lives reflected both traditional and modern customs. These books included *A Pima Past* (1974) by Anna Moore Shaw and two books by Hopi women, Helen Sekaquaptewa's story *Me and Mine* (1969), written with Louise Udall, and Polingaysi Qoyawayma's life history *No Turning Back* (1964), as told to Vada Carlson. These women were just ten or twenty years older than Annie Wauneka and struggled with some of the same issues as she did.

Glenda Riley writes in her essay in *Rethinking American Indian History* (1997) that historians of the West neglected women and particularly women of color until the 1970s. Then, starting in the mid-1980s, more books on Western women and multiculturalism appeared. Although surveys and studies of groups of women could analyze patterns, biographies were needed to reveal personal differences and private motivations.

Riley writes: "Thanks to several generations of women's historians, including biographers, scholars can place individual Western women in the context of American women's history and raise such issues as how did gender shape the subject's life and work, what female values did she accept or reject, how did women's culture affect her work or causes, were her actions feminist in tone and result, why might she have supported or disavowed feminism, why might she have adopted or ignored other causes of the era, what kind of a role model did she provide, and did she dissemble, that is hide her true feelings and emotions?"[2]

Over the last two decades, dozens of books on contemporary Native American women have become available. What is particularly interesting is how many of these women have managed to maintain what is most important to them of their Native American cultural inheritance while making their way in mainstream American life. In *Mankiller: A Chief and Her People* (1993), Cherokee Wilma Mankiller writes of both her early life and her tenure as the leader of the Cherokee nation. *Essie's Story: The Life and Legacy of a Shoshone Teacher* (1998) by Esther Burnett Horne and Sally McBeth tells the story of a Native American woman who, like Annie Wauneka, chose to have a career. Like many of the other women highlighted in these books, they were both working mothers during an era when that was unusual anywhere in the United States. Irene Stewart's life is told in her book *A Voice in Her Tribe: A Navajo Woman's Own Story* (1980). When Stewart, who was active in local politics, ran unsuccessfully for the Navajo Tribal Council, Annie Wauneka gave her encouragement during her campaign.

In *As Long as the Rivers Flow* (1996) Paula Gunn Allen and Patricia Clark Smith present the lives of nine Native Americans, including the notable writer Louise Erdrich and ballerina Maria Tallchief. *Native American Women: A Biographical Dictionary* (1993) by Gretchen Bataille contains short biographies of 240 women, including Daisy Hooe Nampeyo, a Tewa-Hopi potter; Beatrice Medicine, a Lakota anthropologist, teacher, and writer; and Ada Deer, a Menominee activist and assistant secretary of the interior for Indian affairs. In *Messengers of the Wind: Native American Women Tell Their Stories* (1995), edited by Jane Katz, twenty-five women relate details of their lives growing up and recognizing what being Native American means to them. Among the stories is that of Ramona Bennett, who served as head of the Puyallup Tribe. Although she and Annie came from different tribes and different generations and had widely different personalities, a close reading of their lives shows a similarity in their willingness to knock on every door in Washington DC to exact from the federal government all that was due their people.

THE BIOGRAPHICAL ART

Another of my colleagues in the Women Writing Women's Lives seminar, Dona Munker, has written that "a burning desire to write seriously and at length about the life of another is the product of enchantment." It is the term she uses for "that intense, curious, insidious form of possession that besets writers" who are called to write biography.[3] It is a form of partial madness recognized by anyone who has ventured into the genre. Even the novelist A. S. Byatt has called her story about two English biographers *Possession*, aptly enough. It is true that at times over the last three years while scratching endlessly for the smallest details or for understanding, I have at times felt possessed.

I believe that this book answers, at least in part and certainly to the best of my ability, the questions on women's lives that Riley poses. However, despite my devotion to the project, there can be no doubt that the book I have produced on the life of Annie Wauneka reflects the fact that I am not a Navajo. Some of the people I interviewed may have edited what they remembered or withheld certain information that they might have considered inappropriate to discuss with a non-Navajo. I sincerely hope that because I am writing about a woman from another culture, I have not inadvertently distorted or misrepresented any elements of her life. Any shortcomings remain to be dealt with in the future by a Navajo writer, perhaps some young woman who today excels in a high school composition class or college anthropology or history program.[4]

Born in a hogan, raised to be a sheepherder—Annie Wauneka, had she accepted her apparent destiny, could have led a productive life, respected by her family and neighbors. But propelled by a desire to please and emulate her father and by her own strength of personality, at midlife she chose to embrace the entire Navajo Nation as her family. This is her story.

ll Go
d Do
More

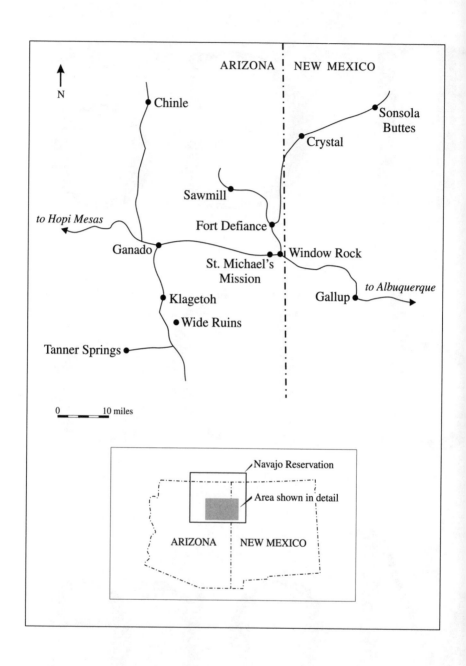

Map 1. The Navajo Reservation and surrounding areas

I

Father and Daughter

1

An Illustrious Father

BY THE SPRING OF 1910, the spotty winter rains and light snow on the Navajo Reservation meant there would be just enough grass for the sheep that year. The grazing lands were still recovering from the drought that had gripped the northern part of Arizona Territory in the earlier years of the century. Patches of dry gray snow remained under the shade of the tall pines and cedars on the Defiance Plateau when Annie Dodge was born on April 11 in a dirt-floored hogan near the settlement of Sawmill.

During the birth, Annie's mother, Kee'hanabah, was attended by her female relatives. Because spring days are cool and the nights are chilly there, most likely a stove burned in the center of the floor, warming the log hogan, a traditional Navajo eight-sided dome. An opening in the top of the dome let out the smoke from the wood stove, and as in all hogans, the small door faced east to greet the morning sun.

When Annie entered the world, she not only became a part of her immediate and extended family, but she also acquired a wide circle of clan relatives. The clan affiliation is an essential part of every Navajo's identity throughout life and marks forever the complex degree of relationship to hundreds of other Navajos in affiliated clans. Annie was born into the Tsenijikini clan (Honeycombed Rock or Cliff-Dwelling People) through her mother and the Coyote Pass People through her father.

The timing and amount of the rain and snow were of utmost importance to Annie's family, for they, like most Navajos of the time, were sheepherders. For them, early April was one of the busiest times of the year, the middle of the lambing season. Although sheep provided food, bedding, wool for weaving rugs, and income for Navajo families, they were far more than an economic asset. During those days, the herds were at the center of the culture, dictating summer and winter moves to optimum grazing and giving a sense of worth to both men and women.

This interrelationship with sheep began for every Navajo a few moments after birth. Newborn Navajo babies in those days were tied in a sheephide until they were about a month old and then put into a cradleboard.[1] No doubt this was the case with Kee'hanabah's daughter. Although Annie eventually rose to national prominence and gained political power, she continued to raise sheep and cattle herself and understood on the deepest level the importance of the sheepherding tradition to the people she governed.

FROM THE HOGAN TO SONSOLA BUTTES

The modest circumstances of Annie's birth did not reflect the full extent of her family situation. Annie's father, Henry Chee Dodge, was not present at her birth. Kee'hanabah had apparently been drafted by her family as a fill-in wife for Dodge when her two cousins, both his wives, had left him temporarily. When the cousins returned to Chee, Kee'hanabah fled Chee's big house at the first opportunity and went back to her hogan at Sawmill, even though she was pregnant.

As Annie grew to adulthood and spent decades serving her people, she would become one of the most powerful and influential of Indian leaders in modern times and gather a string of national honors. She traveled to Washington DC to testify before congressional committees so often that senators, representatives, and their staffs would come into the halls to greet her. But she never lost sight of where she came from. "Pure dirt hogan," she called her first home.

She was not to stay in the hogan long. In fact, by the time Annie was a year old, her father and his wife Nanabah had ridden up to the mountains at Sawmill and taken Annie to Chee's fine home at Sonsola Buttes, near Crystal. There she was raised with her half sister and two half brothers.

At the time Chee Dodge added Annie to his household, he was fifty years old, a wealthy stock owner and businessman, and extremely active in tribal affairs. His large home was a scene of much activity, with a constant stream of both Navajo and white visitors and lengthy discussions of political events ranging from interfamily personal squabbles to concerns over grazing permits to national-level policies that affected the Navajos.

In those days there were few roads on the Navajo Reservation and fewer cars. People covered the long distances between their homes on horseback or in wagons. Frequently the discussions at the Dodge home went on so long that it was too late for the guests to return home, and they were invited to stay overnight. The little girl fell asleep many evenings to the lull of adult voices assessing the meaning of this or that new government policy and how it might affect the Navajos. No one, least of all her father, would have guessed at the seed of political awareness and public service that was being planted as Annie lay bundled in her blankets.

But it was this relationship with her father—indirectly as a child and more intensely as a young adult—that nurtured the growth of her ideals and her desire to work for her people. Although Chee Dodge treated Annie less well than his other children when she was small, it seems he began to recognize her strengths as she matured. When she was in her twenties and thirties, he urged her to get involved in local politics, took her with him as he traveled the reservation, and ultimately passed his legacy for leadership to her on his deathbed. It is impossible to understand her life without knowing about his.

CHEE'S EARLY YEARS

It is unclear where Chee Dodge got his own bent for leadership. Historians admit to confusion over his history. Details like birth records, even memories of dates and times, become lost and twisted in times of crisis and upheaval, and the mid-1800s were such a time for the Navajos. According to the most credible story, Chee was born in the middle of a major clash between Navajos and whites. Historians are still undecided on whether his true father was a white army officer or a Mexican who worked as a Spanish translator for the U.S. Army.

The U.S. Army built Fort Defiance in 1852 on Navajo lands in the north of Arizona Territory, choosing one of the most desirable spots in this dry land—a meadow beside a flowing stream. Navajos called it Green Place in the Rocks and used to pasture their flocks there.[2] Soldiers were stationed at the fort to keep the Navajos from crossing into what is now New Mexico. The goal was to protect the white settlers in the area and also to keep the peace between the Navajos and the Native people of the New Mexico territory, who launched frequent raids against each other. Reports estimate that the Navajos appropriated more than 800,000 head of sheep and cattle belonging to other stockholders during their raiding years, and their neighbors took Navajo animals when they had the chance. Frequently people were part of the booty; records show that thousands of Indians were held captive in New Mexico Territory and Colorado.[3]

Throughout the West, the U.S. government commitment to subduing the raiding Navajos was substantial, what with establishing forts, sending in sufficient staff, and keeping the forts supplied. The Western movies that have given Americans most of their knowledge of this period have misrepresented history, however, for they show the army as always and easily victorious. By the government's own estimates in 1870, it cost approximately one million dollars for every Indian killed.[4]

Government officials found it difficult to negotiate any agreements with the Navajos because no one leader spoke for all of the Diné, the name the Navajos use when speaking of themselves, a term that means "The People," and that differentiates them from the birds and animals. The Navajos were a loose affiliation of clans, each led by a headman who held his position by virtue of personal prestige. Furthermore, no Navajo at that time could speak English, and no Euro-American could speak Navajo.[5] All communication had to go from Navajo to Spanish to English.

In the fall of 1859, problems came to a head when the commander of the army post slaughtered Indian cattle he found on a lush range where he wanted to graze army stock. These were cattle that belonged to Manuelito, one of the Navajo headmen who was grazing them on land he considered his own. The Navajos living there decided that they had put up with enough of the army's arrogance and retaliated with a bloody raid.

The major in charge of the fort was frustrated because he did not understand enough about the Navajos to know what was going to happen next. What was worse, the Mexican who was his translator had been seen riding with the Navajos during the latest raid. This man was Juan Cocinas, who was sometimes called Aneas or Anaya. Showing more arrogance than sense, the officer sent some soldiers out to arrest Cocinas.

Cocinas's wife, Bisnayanchi, who was part Navajo and part Jemez Pueblo, was pregnant and close to delivery. When Cocinas refused to leave her, the soldiers brought her in, too, and locked them both in the stockade.[6]

Juan and his brother Torivio were Mexicans of Spanish blood who had been captured by the Navajos as small children. As adults, they continued to make their homes with the Navajos, although they would have been free to return to their own people. Juan had worked as a translator for Captain Henry Linn Dodge, an army officer who served as the Navajo agent from 1853 to 1856. He was the son of Senator Henry Dodge of Wisconsin and brother of Senator Augustus Caesar Dodge of Iowa. Captain Dodge had been a compassionate officer and reportedly had taken a Navajo wife although he had another wife back East. Because he truly liked the Navajos, he had insisted on living among them at a place called Sheep Springs rather than in official quarters at Fort Defiance. Unfortunately for the Navajos he served so well, he was killed in 1856 by what most accounts say was an Apache. After Captain Dodge's death, Juan Cocinas had continued assisting the U.S. Army—at least so long as it was working for peace. But when Manuelito's cattle were killed, he switched allegiances, teaming up with the Navajos.

Juan Cocinas and his wife, Bisnayanchi, were held for a number of weeks in the stockade, where very early on the morning of February 22, 1860, their baby was born. They named him Henry Dodge after the Indian agent who had been Cocinas's friend and called him Askii Lichii or Red Boy, Chee for short, after the reddish color of his skin. Through his mother he was a member of the Coyote Pass People. Shortly after his birth, the little family was allowed to leave the fort.[7]

Another, less likely, possibility is that Bisnayanchi was carrying Captain Dodge's child when the captain was killed and that Cocinas had then married her. That would have made Chee's birth about three years earlier since Dodge was killed in 1856.[8] As we see later, Chee himself at times claimed Cocinas as his father and other times said he was Dodge's son.

At any rate, hostilities continued between the Navajos and the army, and one morning while on a trip working as a translator, Cocinas was shot in the leg and bled to death, leaving his wife alone with young Chee.

THE REMOVAL

By 1863, the U.S. government decided that the only way to have peace in that region was to remove the Navajos. Kit Carson was sent to round them up and move them to Fort Sumner near Bosque Redondo on the banks of the Pecos River in New Mexico. The Navajos were expected to walk all the way, a distance of 300 to 400 miles, depending on where they started. In March 1864, about 2,400 Navajos, 400 horses, and 3,000 sheep and goats had begun the Long Walk, marching about 15 miles a day. In April, another 1,200 Navajos and their stock began their trek.[9] Families who resisted had their sheep confiscated, their homes and crops burned, and their menfolk shot. Kit Carson enlisted the aid of some Utes and Comanches who were delighted to have official sanction to kill all the Navajos they could find.

To escape the soldiers, any Navajos who could flee did so, hoping to find a place to hide in their vast land. Chee's mother and her sisters joined a group heading west—the opposite direction from Bosque Redondo—hoping to make it to the Grand Canyon, where there would be room to hide out. They traveled slowly, mostly in the dark of night, hiding during the day in canyons or among the rocks and shrubs in the arroyos to avoid the soldiers. They had taken little food, hoping to find some along the way, but all they found were burned fields and other families as desperate as they were. The little band had traveled only as far as First Mesa in Hopi country when their supplies ran out. Chee's mother left her small son with her sisters and decided to go to Walpi, one of the Hopi villages, to ask for corn.[10]

Although the Hopis, who were Pueblo farmers, and the Navajos had been neighbors for several centuries, they were unrelated people. Some Hopi and Navajo families traded goods and lived cordially side by side for years, but among others there was a great deal of animosity, and for years the Navajos had raided Walpi. Bisnayanchi knew that it was possible she might receive a hostile reception, but she was probably desperate to find food for her son. She never returned from the Hopi village, and Chee's aunts decided that the only way they could ensure the child's survival was to give him to another family who had more food. The orphaned boy, probably four years old, but possibly a smallish, malnourished seven-year-old, traveled with one family and then another until he finally hooked up with a young girl he called Shádí ("older sister" in Navajo), who was traveling with her elderly grandfather.

Eventually the soldiers found them and convinced them to surrender in exchange for food and clothing. They led the group back to Fort Defiance, with one of the soldiers taking young Chee on his horse. From there, they joined other Navajos in the Long Walk that took them to Fort Sumner. Eventually around 8,500 Navajos were imprisoned at Bosque Redondo.

The four years the Navajos spent there were miserable for them. Beginning with the Long Walk and during their confinement they were issued white flour, salted bacon, and coffee beans. These commodities were foreign to the Navajos, and at first they were stymied on how to turn these things into food. Imagine encountering a coffee bean if you had never seen one before. Navajos tried the obvious action—attempting to boil them like other dried beans—but they never did get soft. Many of the already weakened Navajos died from malnutrition during the learning period and later as supplies for the Navajos were stolen or sold by traders and unscrupulous army personnel.

Once they were settled at Bosque Redondo, the crops they were forced to plant in an effort to make them farmers failed due to drought, hail, and worms. Beyond lacking the mere elements of survival, the Navajos missed the vast beauty of their traditional home—the pungent smell of the sagebrush, the sandy red earth, the layers of blue and purple mesas on the horizon. Their land was the essence of their survival, inextricably woven into their legends and religion.

Despite his difficult life, young Chee showed signs of the intelligence and engaging personality that would mark his life. He became a favorite of the soldiers, running errands and picking up some English during banter with them.

Meanwhile, the Navajo homelands sat silent and empty, populated mainly by coyotes, prairie dogs, and rabbits. Those Navajos who had managed to evade the soldiers retained their freedom by staying hidden, easily swallowed up in the canyons and vast stretches of wilderness. Eventually, government officials realized that not only was the Navajo internment scheme failing to provide the hoped for utopia, but it was also expensive. The first twenty months of the experiment cost the War Department $1,114,981.70, and the average cost of rations between 1863 and 1868 was $750,000 per year, even though much of it wasn't even getting to the Navajos.[11] Since the Bosque Redondo site wasn't working out, the officials in charge thought maybe they should send the Navajos to Oklahoma. The Navajos may have gotten an inkling that the government was beginning to consider relocating them, for in 1868, the Navajo leaders went together to the U.S. Army officers, pleading with them to be allowed to go home. Barboncito, one of the leaders, spoke for his people, telling the government agents that First Woman had told the Navajos after the Creation that they should never move beyond the area bounded by the four sacred mountains. By that time officials agreed that the experiment in trying to move the Navajos had been a failure, and the Navajos were told they could return to their former area if they promised to stop raiding their white and Indian neighbors. On June 1, 1868, they signed a treaty promising never to fight again, to work and irrigate the soil, and to send their children to school. On June 18, those Navajos who hadn't already slipped away singly started for home.

BACK ON THE RESERVATION

The reservation that was set up for them was about four million acres, only a tenth of their former territory, straddling the northern reaches of what is now the Arizona–New Mexico border. Most of the Navajos returned to the homes where they had been living before, unaware and uncaring whether that area lay within the boundaries of the new reservation. As far as they were concerned, it all belonged to them. They were happy to be back and, for the most part, gave up raiding their white neighbors. They got through the first winter on government rations. The next spring those who lived close enough to water planted gardens, and in the fall the government distributed 14,000 sheep and 1,000 goats.[12]

Looking back, Chee would confide to his children, "I didn't even know who or what I was going back to. All I knew was the soldiers and these Mexican scouts." For most of his young life he had lived as either a fugitive or a captive.

The summer of their return, Chee and Shádí continued to live with the grandfather. Chee was probably about eight years old. When they each received two sheep and a goat, they kept them instead of eating them. The government was still passing out rations of corn, flour, and beef, which the family supplemented with small game and wild plant foods. Chee's animals would form the beginning of what would grow into extensive herds.

Then one day Chee unexpectedly found his aunt. After leaving him behind, she and her sisters had joined another band and had hidden in the Gray Mountain area, where they had stayed throughout the exile. She told him that she was married to Perry Williams, a white man who worked as an issue clerk at Fort Defiance.

CHEE BEGINS INTERPRETING

Sometime during this period, Chee was taken to a Presbyterian mission school where he studied for two or three months, perfecting his English and learning other basic school subjects. Since Chee spoke both English and Spanish, Perry Williams hired the boy to work with him at the store and help translate for the Navajos who came in. English speakers found it difficult to learn Navajo since the language involves use of voice muscles not needed in English. Also, Navajo is a singing language in three tones—and words spoken in different tones may have different meanings. The two languages also differ in ways other than just sounds, with grammar, sentence arrangement, and worldview all contributing to make direct translation impossible. Translators must reformulate the message to convey the speaker's meaning when moving between English and Navajo.[13]

An additional difficulty was that the Navajo material world was of an earlier, simpler era. Chee illustrated this with a favorite story about the match. Although the soldiers used matches, the Indians were still making fire in the old-fashioned way by producing a spark with two sticks or a rock. After they watched the white men light their cigarettes by scraping a match along the seat of their pants to produce fire, the Navajos took to calling the match "fire on the pants" or "he scratches his buttocks."[14]

Somehow, Chee managed to negotiate these linguistic pitfalls and byways. His facility at translation was an early indication of his considerable mental agility, considering his limited education. People began to call him Ashkihih Diitsi, the Boy Interpreter.

Years later, his eldest son wrote that when Navajo leaders came to the agency to discuss tribal and other matters with officials of the government, they frequently threatened the young boy with a beating with a heavy stick if he made any mistake in interpreting for them. Often Chee had to interpret long and involved discussions, and on such occasions he genuinely feared misinterpretation and the consequent thrashing it might bring.[15]

Chee worked as a messenger boy and office interpreter at Fort Defiance for three years, earning $5 a week. From there, he went to work handling mules and cargo for the supply wagon train from Santa Fe to Fort Defiance. This was apparently a hard time for him, as years later he reminisced that sometimes his only food was the corn that the mules didn't eat.

CONFUSION OVER CHEE'S PARENTAGE

Chee's difficult life was apparently evident to others, because early in 1875, the commissioner of Indian affairs in Washington DC received a letter from Senator Augustus C. Dodge, brother of Chee's namesake, the late Henry Dodge, saying that he had received a report from a friend who was recently back from an official tour of New Mexico Territory. The friend had encountered a youth named Henry Dodge, who was talented in languages but who was working as a herder and being treated cruelly. This friend believed that the youth was the son of Senator Dodge's late brother and his Navajo wife. Augustus Dodge requested that W. F. M. Arny, at that time the agent at Fort Defiance, look into the matter and perhaps retain young Henry Dodge as an interpreter.[16]

The photographs of Chee, both as a young man and as he aged, do not show typical Navajo features.[17] One businessman who remembers him said he looked "just like a Welshman." In testimony that Chee gave in 1888 on an unrelated matter, he said that he was about thirty years old and the son of a white army officer and a Navajo woman. However, he referred to "my people" and indicated that he considered himself Navajo.[18]

In an insightful essay on Chee Dodge, anthropologist David Brugge gives an analysis of Chee's rare transcultural perspective: "Obviously while still a young man, he had the opportunity to know and learn from the tribe's leaders in a way provided to no other person of his generation. He also was able to observe from the vantage point of an insider all the details of intercultural interaction on the highest levels. He undoubtedly had identity problems. It can be assumed that most whites viewed him as a 'half-breed' and that his acceptance in white society was limited in many ways."[19]

At any rate, whether because of Arny's intervention or some other reason, about this time Chee returned to school for three months in Albuquerque, picking up what was to be the last of his formal education. Much later, he told his daughter Annie that he would have stayed in school longer, but the older Navajo leaders wanted him to come back to the reservation so they could have an interpreter that they trusted. At this time there were only a very few men who could speak both Navajo and English, and all of the official Navajo and federal government business was funneled through them.[20]

MORE OFFICIAL DUTIES

At the age of twenty, Chee was named official interpreter for the Navajo people, a U.S. government job. He also acquired the job of chief herder. The interpretation job paid $720 a year plus $3 a day for expenses.[21]

In 1882, Denis Riordan was appointed Navajo agent, and he and Chee worked well together. Chee later told Richard Van Valkenburgh, "He [Riordan] was the man who gave me my start. He gave me every chance. Without doubt, he was the best agent the Navajo ever had."[22] Riordan, for his part, had great confidence in Chee: "His life and mine were more than once at stake on his coolness and good judgment and tact. I relied on him implicitly."[23] Chee could not have been older than his mid-twenties at this time.

During these years, as the Navajo population was growing and expanding into unused territory, the U.S. government began adding additional parcels to the reservation the Navajos had been granted in the original treaty. However, in 1882, unbeknownst to the Navajos, the U.S. government established under an executive order a rectangle of land in the western part of the reservation for the exclusive use of the Hopis "and such other Indians as the Secretary of the Interior may see fit to settle thereon." The Hopis, a Pueblo tribe descended from much earlier residents of the area, called the Anasazis, were already living on a very small part of this area—and had been for centuries. The granting of reservation status legitimized their use and occupancy of their ancestral lands. But there were Navajo homesteads there, too. The Hopis did not immediately occupy all of the land they were "given" because they are village dwellers and farmers, and so they remained clustered in their towns—dense villages perched on the edges of steep-sided mesas. There were no marked boundaries to either reservation, and the Navajos continued to occupy the range and their ancestral homes. It looked like their land, and with no one else living on it, there was no reason to believe it was not Navajo land. One hundred years later the problems this caused are still being thrashed out in the tribal councils and the U.S. Congress and would eventually consume a great deal of Annie Wauneka's energy.

Also in this year, the U.S. government maintained it was short on money. Chee's salary dwindled to $300 a year, and he took on other work to make up the difference. Chee spent much of 1883 helping Dr. Washington Matthews, the post surgeon at Fort Wingate, write his now-famous works on the life and customs of the Navajos—*Navajo Legends* and *Night Chant*. It was also through Dr. Matthews that he was sent as an escort for three elderly medicine men on a journey to Washington DC to meet President Chester A. Arthur. In *Navajo Biographies,* we read: "On this trip he had to interpret not only the language, but the social niceties as well. At a state dinner, he puzzled for some minutes over the strange behavior of the medicine man seated beside him, until he discovered that the old man was simply trying to sharpen his fork on the side of his leather boot! Chee was in the delicate position of politely having to reverse Navajo tradition to teach a much older man the 'right' way of doing things." [24]

CHEE BECOMES HEAD CHIEF

In 1884, Navajo agent Riordan was having several disputes with the aging Manuelito, who had been serving as Navajo spokesman. Some accounts indicate that Manuelito was frequently drunk. So, with the concurrence of Manuelito and both the U.S. secretary of the interior and the commissioner of Indian affairs, Riordan appointed the twenty-four-year-old Chee as head chief of the Navajos at a salary of $600 a year. About this same time he was also appointed chief of police and was in charge of hiring and distributing the Native officers to posts around the reservation.[25] Surely there was some Navajo opposition to the appointment of someone to this position who was not only very young but only half Navajo as well, but whatever antagonism existed never appeared in written history, probably because those in disagreement with the appointment didn't speak English and had no one to translate their position.

Manuelito continued to advise his young successor as Chee prepared to lead his people into the twentieth century. Anthropologist Ruth Underhill, who did much work with the Navajos, wrote that two or three days before his death Manuelito said to Chee, "My grandchild, the whites have many things which we Navajo need. But we cannot get them. It is as though the whites were in a grassy canyon and there they have wagons, plows and plenty of food. We Navajo are up on the dry mesa. We can hear them talking, but we cannot get to them. My grandchild, education is the ladder. Tell our people to take it." [26]

Some time in the mid-1880s, Chee claimed a large section of well-watered grassy land near Crystal in the Chuksa Mountains and moved what stock he had out there. The lower elevations are around 7,500 feet, and precipitation is around twelve or more inches a year.

CHEE TAKES UP RANCHING

In a deposition Chee gave regarding a land dispute among his neighbors, he told about his own beginnings in the livestock business, a fascinating glimpse into how a penniless orphan began his road to wealth: "During the time that I was interpreter, I managed to save $1500. When I gave up my government job, I invested $500 of my savings in Mexican cattle, which were then quite cheap. The cattle that I bought numbered about 50 heads. At that time the Navajos, or some of them, had very little livestock of any kind and whatever stock they did have were mostly horses and very few sheep and cattle. For the cattle that I acquired, I found a grazing range around Whiskey Creek and in the neighborhood of Washington Pass." [27]

The area Chee claimed offers some of the best grazing on the entire reservation. He located his home next to two volcanic features called Sonsola Buttes, in Navajo meaning "stars laid down" or "stars they sit." It is a spot of stunning beauty, with a view of dark, densely wooded canyons of the Chuksa Mountains to the east and to the west the soaring sandstone cliffs and cathedral-shaped buttes. Some of the surfaces are rounded, others sharply vertical; all are a rosy buff color with striations of deeper rose, chocolate, and gold. Whiskey Creek flows to the west and into the deep gorges of Canyon de Chelly. He fenced off some of the fields, a practice not followed by any other Navajos but typical of Chee, who throughout his life tried new ways. He also gave up his interpreting job since he found he could make more money as a rancher. Genealogical work done in the Navajo census records at St. Michael's Mission indicates that through this time Chee had short-term alliances with several wives, but none of them produced children.

Life was not without its setbacks, however. Snowfall in the Sonsola Buttes area ranges from sixty to one hundred inches a year, and subzero temperatures are common in winter. In 1891, Chee lost 500 sheep in a deep snowfall during an especially cold winter. About this time, possibly as a reaction to this unfortunate event, he located a lovely spot south of Klagetoh called Tanner Springs. Its elevation was lower and winters milder than Sonsola Buttes, which was on the side of the Chuksa Mountains. Native Americans had found it a pleasant place to live and hunt for millennia. Folsom points—carefully carved flint blades from the Pleistocene Epoch, a million years ago—have been found in the area. This grassy range was not part of the reservation, but Chee borrowed the money to buy it from a white friend, put a trusted Navajo associate in charge of the operation, and soon paid off the loan.[28]

As his livestock holdings increased in volume and profits, Chee decided to diversify his business by acquiring a part interest with Stephen H. Aldrich in a trading post at Round Rock, north of Chinle, Arizona. He appears to be the first Navajo to enter the trading business. Chee became the manager of the new store and hired as his clerk Charlie Hubbell, brother of John Lorenzo Hubbell, who later became famous as the trader at Ganado.

CHEE ARRANGES A TRUCE
In 1892 an incident occurred that showed how Chee's cool head earned him growing respect from both the whites and other Na-

vajos. In the Treaty of 1868, the U.S. government had agreed to provide schooling for the Navajo youngsters, with a teacher for every thirty Indian children. It was many decades before this came to pass, but it did not matter because most Navajos did not want to send their children to school anyway. The government officials, who were interested in assimilating the Navajos, wanted the children, at least some of them, in the classroom. That fall, Indian agent Dana L. Shipley obtained the promises of several parents in the Round Rock area to send their children to the government school at Fort Defiance. Brugge gives a succinct version of what must have been a grueling week for both the Navajos and the officials.

In October [Chee] accompanied Shipley and several other agency employees on a trip to the northern part of the reservation to collect the children. The small group split into three parties. Dodge and Shipley, along with three agency policemen, one of whom was a brother-in-law of Dodge, went to Round Rock, while others went variously to Canyon de Chelly and the Carrizo Mountains. A prominent leader in the Carrizo region, Black Horse, concerned because of reports of mistreatment of students at the Fort Defiance School, gathered a number of followers and proceeded to Round Rock to confront the agent. They found him in the trading post, and after some arguing, they grabbed him, dragged him from the building and beat him severely, breaking his nose. With Dodge and Hubbell leading the three policemen, they were able to rescue Shipley. They brought him back into the post and barricaded the doors and windows.[29]

Outside, Black Horse and his followers threatened to kill those taking refuge in the store. A messenger, Chee's brother-in-law, was then sent to obtain the help of a detachment of U.S. Army troops twenty-five miles away in Tsaile. He was given Chee's horse because it was the fastest one available. With this horse, he was able to outrun three of Black Horse's men and to notify the troops. Meanwhile, Chee and the others barricaded in the trading post were grateful that a rare thunderstorm drenched the trading post, making it unlikely that Black Horse's followers could burn it down.[30]

For three days the Navajos attacked the trading post, and when Chee and the others had just about run out of ammunition, the soldiers arrived. Brugge concludes: "Dodge interpreted during a tense meeting between the military and the Black Horse faction. His skillful handling of this situation—including his adroit use of kinship terms, addressing Black Horse as 'older brother,' and providing food from his store to feed the crowd once an agreement had been reached—contributed significantly to the success of the army in arranging a truce and in escorting the agency personnel back to Fort Defiance without further violence."[31]

Chee had a more pleasant official duty in 1893 when he accompanied eighteen other Navajo headmen to the Chicago Exposition. The government wanted to expose them to the white world and modern ways of living. They rode the elevated train and went to the stockyards to see cattle slaughtered and processed.[32]

CHEE DIVORCES, REMARRIES

All of this activity meant that Chee was frequently away from his home at Sonsola. He was relying on his wife to watch over his affairs, but that was not the case. In Navajo households, particularly wealthy ones such as Chee's, the household makeup is fluid, with relatives and friends frequently coming to stay for long periods. Chee's wife had become friends with one of his old aunts. Chee kept them well supplied with coffee, sugar, flour, and whatever else they needed, but they seemed to consume these goods faster than could be reasonably expected. Eventually, one of the men who worked for him clued him in on the fact that while he was away, his place was the scene of exuberant parties during which his wife was gambling away the household stores and not tending to his business.

Apparently this was not much of an emotional trauma for Chee—reportedly he had already decided on his next wife. While visiting his adopted sister Shádí, he noticed her daughter, Nanabah. When one of the elders in Shádí's household refused to consider giving Nanabah to Chee because he was already married, Chee rode back to his ranch and divorced his wife. This was accomplished quite simply by asking her to leave. In Navajo custom, either party could dissolve a marriage when mutual obligations fell out of balance and either saw the relationship as without merit.

A bigger problem was that Nanabah had been promised to another man, who had already sent twelve Appaloosa ponies and some silver jewelry to the family to affirm his intentions. The wedding was imminent. While arranging affairs at his own place, Chee sent a trusted friend to stop the wedding. Guests were assembled and events were getting underway when Chee's friend ran in at the very last minute, crying to the crowd, "She is already another's." The young girl ran from the hogan crying, and Chee's friend presented his proposal to the family and the rest of the group. Learning that Chee was single now, the old man of the family reconsidered, and the wedding preparations began anew. We can assume the original groom was unhappy with the turn of events, but he had no choice but to take his horses and leave.[33]

Eventually Chee arrived, driving a dozen sleek horses and bringing silver jewelry and $200 in cash. This customary provision of goods, livestock, and cash was considered a gift rather than a purchase price. The marriage took place, but Nanabah stayed with her mother for another two years, maturing and learning to manage a household. This was understandable. Navajo daughters usually brought their husbands to live in a hogan they would build near her mother's place. It was an easy transition from being a daughter to being a wife, and a large extended household was formed, with the daughters and their children spending much of their time at the older's woman's hogan. Although this was the typical pattern, it was not unknown for a young couple to join the husband's family's outfit or to strike out on their own.

SETTING UP A HOUSEHOLD

In this case, Chee's independence and adventurousness coupled with his extraordinarily fine land made setting up house at Sonsola Buttes the most reasonable course. During the time Nanabah was maturing, Chee prepared for her arrival by hiring a German architect in Flagstaff to design a home and began quarrying fine white sandstone block near the building site.[34]

The house was still under construction when Chee brought Nanabah and her younger sister Asza Yaze to live with him. The custom of marrying sisters was part of Navajo culture. Second and third wives from a family were usually added to the first without ceremony, the family bonds having already been established through the initial marriage.[35] Asza Yaze conceived first, bearing Tom, Chee's first child, in 1899. In two years, Nanabah's son, Ben, followed.

By 1903 the elegant new house was ready, and Nanabah's second child, Mary, was born. The new home had a center hall, four rooms including a modern kitchen, and a shady porch stretching across the front. Soon curtains hung at the windows, and furniture, books, and photographs filled the rooms. Nanabah carefully managed Chee's wealth, looked after her own flocks of sheep, and wove rugs, many of which graced the wooden floors of the home. This was a most atypical Navajo dwelling.

During these years Chee managed to prosper, although six of the ten years between 1893 and 1902 drought and poor crops.[36] Chee not only had his stock businesses and his growing family to worry about, but he continued to advise the tribe and act as an intercessor between them and the white culture. In November 1905 he told a Navajo crowd gathered for a traditional ceremony that he had promised Manuelito that he would advise the Navajos to conduct themselves so that they would not be destroyed by fighting the government. The president of the United States, narrated Chee, gave the Navajos a long rope to graze where they pleased, like a person would a good horse, "but if he has a mean horse he gives him a short rope with his head tied close to a post so he can get but little feed." Chee told them that the president had a figurative rope on every one of them, and "if you try to make trouble, he will pull on all the ropes and draw you fellows all together to a tight place. . . . You will lose your stock, you will be afoot, you will be nothing, you will be wiped out and will be guarded by troops, and everybody will laugh at you and say: 'See what a large tribe this was, and this is all that is left of them.' "[37]

ANNIE IS BORN

About this time, something happened to cause great antagonism between Chee and Nanabah. The falling out was so great that she and her sister took their sheep and cattle and went back to their family. There they stayed for four years. Because Chee was not only the most important man in the tribe but the wealthiest as well, Nanabah's family wanted to keep him happy. They sent him a young woman of the clan named Kee'hanabah. The mothers of Kee'hanabah and Nanabah were sisters and co-wives of a man named Bichai Bikis, making the younger women both first cousins and half sisters.

There is some indication that Kee'hanabah did not go willingly to either Chee's household or his bed. Years later one of her children would tell a friend that their sexual relationship was more akin to rape. Kee'hanabah had just become pregnant when whatever disagreement had occurred was ironed out, and Nanabah and her sister returned to Chee and the beautiful house at Sonsola. Kee'hanabah was allowed to return to her home at Sawmill, with the understanding that she would turn over the baby after it was born.

The ties that bind Navajo mothers to their children are intense and lifelong. It is not unusual for a mother to allow a child to be raised by a relative, but that is frequently when one woman has many children and the relative has none or few. We can reasonably assume that Kee'hanabah was deeply attached to her firstborn daughter. But when the little girl who became known as Annie was about eight months old, Chee took her to his home.[38]

2

The Family Sheepherder

ANNIE WAS ABSORBED into Chee Dodge's household, the youngest of his four children living there. It was a dramatic change for the child to leave her mother and the rest of her extended family and the dark, snug hogan where all activity took place around the central fire. Her new house was large enough to be divided into rooms and there was a separate kitchen for cooking. The family ate at a table rather than squatting on the ground and the floors were wood rather than dirt. Large glass windows let light into every corner.

MULTIPLE WIVES AND THE LAW

Behind the big house were two other smaller homes, and a stream of relatives and friends came and went. The atmosphere was somewhat like a feudal estate, with clan relatives and family retainers tramping in and out and women fixing and serving food.

In many ways, Chee Dodge straddled the Navajo world and the white world, with his house, his livelihood, and his family makeup. Federal law, under which the Navajos had to live, forbade multiple wives, and occasionally the law was enforced. In September 1913, the three wives of a man named Little Singer were arrested and placed in the Shiprock jail. When Little Singer returned and found his wives missing, he, his father, and nine companions overpowered one of the policemen and liberated the women from jail. They all went to the top of Beautiful Mountain and refused to surrender. Chee joined several other leading Navajos, the Franciscan Fathers from St. Michael's Mission, a raft of U.S. officials, and four troops of cavalry who tried to get Little Singer to come down. It wasn't until the end of November that the family surrendered, with some of them having to spend thirty days in jail. Little Singer was a respected religious leader and was living well within his culture's norms, but the white officials ignored all of this. It must have caused Chee some discomfort to realize that it could have been him in jail.[1]

An undated note exists from Hataty Yazzie telling Chee that he had been arrested for having more than one wife and was being held on $2,000 bond and asking Chee to put up the money to get him out of jail.[2] Chee's response did not survive, although he was known to be generous in lending money, taking interest payments in sheep or cattle. It would be most interesting to know what position Chee took during any of these negotiations on multiple wives since it was widely known that he himself had not limited himself to one at a time.

ANNIE'S SIBLINGS GO TO SCHOOL

True to his advice from Manuelito and his own experience, Chee was a strong proponent of education throughout his life and saw that most of his children went to top institutions. Despite his own limited time in school, he was able to add long columns of figures in his head and expected his children to apply themselves and do well. When his sons Tom and Ben were in their teens, he enrolled them in All Hallow's College, a private Catholic boys' school in Salt Lake City. They were sent there to get an education in the white world, and apparently there was no general knowledge at the school that they were Navajos. In the summer of 1912, the head of the school had written to Chee's close friend Father Anselm Weber of St. Michael's Mission, thanking him for securing Tom and Ben for the school. "It need not be known at all during their stay here that they are part Indian and I will ask them on their arrival here to withhold any information to that effect from the other boys."[3] As for the part of the boys' heritage that was not Indian, it is likely that the All Hallow's administrator thought or was told that the boys were part white, since at that time being part Mexican would have been as detrimental as being Navajo. Apparently Father Anselm had presented Chee Dodge as the son of Captain Dodge rather than translator Juan Cocinas. Whether the other students knew or cared about the boys' heritage is not known. In photographs Tom appears to have white features very much like his father, whereas Ben is darker.

In January 1914, when Chee's daughter Mary (also called Antoinette) was ten, Chee took her and Nanabah on a train trip through California and on to Salt Lake City. Annie, a young child of only three, was left at home. Chee sent Father Anselm Weber at St. Michael's Mission a postcard from Los Angeles's Chinatown saying that they had stayed there five days. He was amazed at the mild weather, writing "no snow, just like summer." The following year, Mary joined her brothers in school in Salt Lake City, attending St. Mary's Academy.

ANNIE BEGINS HERDING

Even as a very young child, Annie's attention was consumed by the details of sheep raising. When Annie was about five, she began making a contribution to the economic life of the household by taking a small herd of sheep out in the morning. Chee and Nanabah and other relatives living in the household had vast herds of sheep, far too many for a small child to supervise. The numerous herders in the extended household could no doubt have handled the lot, but all Navajo children are expected to learn to herd, and Chee wanted his children to learn the value of work as well as the value of education.

It appears, however, that Annie was given more work than the other children. Every morning she was awakened at dawn and sent to take a small flock from the corral to a grassy area nearby. Some of the sheep were her own, for in the Navajo tradition, her father added to her private flock every year at lambing time. She could recognize them by their special earmark.

She drove the herd to water and then watched after them while they grazed. At midmorning, she took them back to the corral and returned to the house for a late breakfast—usually fry bread and coffee—with the family. Then it was back out to the range with the sheep, carrying a packet of cold fry bread and a bottle of water for lunch.

COMBINING WORK AND PLAY

Although Annie had considerable responsibility watching over the little flock, she was still a child and liked to play. Her toys and pastimes reflected her experience. While the sheep were grazing, she devised games for herself. In one of these diversions a collection of small white stones spread on the ground represented sheep. A black stone stood for the wily coyote, creeping up on the unsuspecting lambs. Another of the games involved setting up ant battles. By transporting groups of black ants to red ant-hills and vice versa, she entertained herself by watching the ensuing interaction as the resident ants joined forces to repel the invaders.[4]

Annie was large and strong for her age. Although a well-trained group of sheep behave by bunching and staying near to each other, they can occasionally scatter on a whim. Sometimes they would run up the sloping backside of a bluff, leaving Annie trudging after them down below. Eventually she discovered a way to outwit them. She attached a rope to the front side of the bluff where it ended in a cliff. Using the rope, she could scramble to the top of the bluff, saving herself a long walk. Years later as an old woman being taken for a drive by her daughter, she wondered if the remnants of that rope might still be there.

We see an early indication of her independence and willingness to take risks in an incident in which she decided to imitate the butchering activities she had seen so often around her house. Since she was away from home for a large part of the day without supervision, she had plenty of time to carry out her plan. While out herding, she chose one of her lambs and killed it, no doubt by the customary Navajo method of slitting its neck. Afterwards, she skinned it and roasted part of it over a fire she had built. This time she got to eat the choice parts—the roasted ribs—rather than the liver she'd been served at home. When she'd completed her meal, she tied a rope around the rest of the carcass and hung it from a tree limb to save it for another meal.[5]

As an adult, she looked back on those days with pleasure. She told a reporter, "It was a good time back then. Those animals never did talk back to you!"[6]

Although Annie's days were spent much like those of children in more traditional Navajo families, she was getting an indirect exposure to the outside world through all the political activity that swirled around her father. The most troublesome questions, mainly those concerning the interactions of the Navajos and the federal government, would persist for decades. Years later, she would think back to those discussions and wonder what her father would say as she sat as delegate to the Navajo Tribal Council trying to make sense of some regulations.

SCHOOL AND INFLUENZA

In the fall of 1918, when Annie was eight, Chee decided that it was time she went to school. However, she was sent to the government boarding school at Fort Defiance, rather than the private schools where her half-siblings were. Perhaps it was because her family wanted her close enough to return to help with lambing. Before then she had probably been no farther from home than the nearest trading post at Crystal. During that first year at Fort Defiance boarding school, she was baptized in the Catholic Church and made her first communion.

However, within a matter of months after her arrival at school, her lessons were interrupted when a terrible epidemic of what came to be called Spanish influenza swept through the country. Chee responded by sending for Tom, Ben, and Mary, who were attending Loretto Heights School in Denver that year. Getting them back home quickly would not have been a simple procedure. Chee would have had to travel by horse or buckboard from Sonsola Buttes either thirty miles to Fort Defiance or seventy miles to Gallup over roads that were little more than tracks to send a telegraph or letter requesting that they return home. The process would have had to be reversed to receive an answer. Then a buckboard would have had to make the slow trip over the rough dirt path to the railhead in Gallup to pick up the children and all their luggage.

The influenza epidemic was worldwide, spread throughout the United States by the movement of American troops to Europe and back to fight in World War I. The disease was unlike any flu anyone had ever seen. Highly contagious, it was spread through coughs and sneezes sending droplets through the air. A single sneeze might distribute more than 85 million organisms that could remain suspended in the air for half an hour to be inhaled by someone else.[7]

Once the three youngsters were home, Chee locked the lower gate in an effort to protect his family from the deadly virus and let no one onto the property. Annie, however, was left at school in Fort Defiance. The disease appeared at the school when an infected Navajo laborer who had been visiting in Zuni mingled with the children. Ten days later 250 pupils and 20 employees had the flu.[8] Annie became ill, but perhaps because of her strong constitution, she had a mild case and soon recovered.

That was not the case with the rest of the student body. Many of the students became very ill, and the school was quarantined. There was only one nurse, Mrs. Domatilda Showalter, to look after them. Even her assistants fell ill. Annie, used to taking responsibility and working hard, was drafted to help. The hospital was without electricity, so every day Annie was given the kerosene lanterns to clean and fill. "I remember that little wooden hospital there," she said, looking back on this seminal episode in her childhood. "There were lots and lots of sick students, there were hundreds of students. These students were full-grown adults, men and boys, big fellows that went to school. At first one or two died, pretty soon they're just dying like flies. And I just wonder what in the devil is goin' on.

"She [Domatilda] would call me and say 'Would you wash these lanterns and make them bright and shiny? And that was my job. And I would see them sick. Just come into the hospital. They hemorrhaged, every one of them hemorrhaged, and they were sick about a day or two. They were gone the next day. And the hospital was packed. The superintendent says to me, 'Will you give water to the sick, will you give food to the sick?' "[9]

So Annie spoon-fed soup to students too weak to feed themselves. Decades later the memory was still fresh of one day when she was feeding students. One boy who had just been fed coughed and coughed, eventually spitting up the soup along with lots of blood. The student was soon dead. He was dressed and put into a wood coffin, but soon, with more and more students dying every day, there was no one to build coffins or help with the burials.[10]

Annie recalled, "They'd just wrap them up in a sheet and pile them on top of each other, just pile them. And in the school buildings, the boy's dormitory and the girl's dormitory—they're huge big buildings—five or ten died each night. And corpses were sitting in the hall. There were horse-driven wagons and they used to just pile them up like a bunch of wood and haul them away."[11]

The nasal hemorrhage was typical of the Spanish influenza and marked the crisis point of the disease. Something in the virus interfered with the passage of blood from the heart's right ventricle to the lungs. When doctors performed autopsies on the bodies, they would find that the lungs contained up to six times the normal weight of blood.[12] Also typical of this particular virus was the death of the young, such as the Navajo students. Usually influenza takes the old and the weak, but this time it was vigorous, robust people in their twenties who felt the brunt of the disease.

Showalter used to hitch her horse to her buggy to check on some of the hogans scattered on the reservation, helping to treat those who were ill. She would bring the sickest into the hospital to give them better treatment. Most of them died anyhow. Eventually all the bodies were buried in a mass grave.

Disposing of the bodies was no doubt made more difficult by the traditional Navajo aversion to having anything to do with dead bodies. Since illness was thought to be a result of evil supernatural influences, they feared being close to whatever had caused the death.[13] Times have changed, of course, but typically when a Navajo was about to die, the patient was moved from the hogan to another structure. If the patient died in the hogan, it had to be destroyed. If the family could not talk a non-Navajo into burying the body for them, they all needed to undergo a special cleansing ceremony. Family members watching over very sick relatives were probably all too happy to have Showalter take over the final nursing and burial responsibilities.

Throughout the world, more than twenty-one million people

died, and it was estimated that more than a billion people were affected. Few other events in human history could compare to this plague, other than the Black Death, which is estimated to have slain twenty-five million Europeans between 1347 and 1350. As many as 2,500 people died on the reservation from the Spanish influenza.[14] The widely separated living conditions of the Navajos probably saved many of them.

When spring came, school was closed. Those students who had survived went back to their hogans, and Annie returned to Sonsola Buttes. "There was everybody back from private schools," she remembered. "They didn't get sick, as I understand. At least I'd done something to help which I guess they didn't."[15] The experience heightened her growing suspicion that there was some reason she was being treated differently than her sister and brothers.

MORE SCHOOL INTERRUPTIONS

Annie was always expected to leave school in the spring, whether classes were in session or not, to help with the lambing. Watching over the pregnant ewes and caring for the newborn lambs were labor intensive, and she was needed to work along with the rest of the family and hired help. Years later, her brother Tom would remark, "Annie was always considered the family sheepherder."

When Annie was in fourth grade at Fort Defiance, her education was again interrupted when an epidemic of trachoma hit the school. Trachoma is a rampantly contagious infection of the eyelids in which granular bumps form on the inside of the eyelid. It is spread by hands touching an infected eye and then touching something that will be touched by others, the use of common towels, or even by shaking hands. It is difficult to keep children from touching their eyes since the roughened eyelids itch. Trachoma can lead to blindness when the eye itself is scratched and a thick white tissue grows to cover the cornea.

To protect the students who were not infected, Annie among them, officials transferred them temporarily to St. Michael's, a Catholic mission school about ten miles from Fort Defiance. The school at Fort Defiance was turned into a trachoma treatment center.

At that time, and until 1938 when sulfanilamide was discovered, trachoma was treated by a method used since the time of the ancient Egyptians called *grattage* in which the granules were cut off with a special surgical instrument. The infected surface was then rubbed with a copper-sulfate pencil.[16] Since this procedure was effective only when repeated at frequent intervals over long periods of time, it was mainly confined to the children in the boarding schools.

While being taught by the nuns at St. Michael's, Annie received more religious instruction and was confirmed in the church. Her father had had a long association with the priests and brothers at St. Michael's. He and two other headmen, Charlie Mitchell and Silversmith, paved the way for the Franciscan fathers to set up their mission near a spring in the Black River valley ten miles south of Fort Defiance. He had helped the fathers write the first English-Navajo dictionary and was particularly useful in helping to devise translations of religious words that would be used in teaching the catechism. The priests found him always anxious to find the exact words to express a concept. He used an English dictionary to help translate the thoughts and meanings into the exact English idiom. They gave him great credit for being discriminating in his choice of words.[17] One of the Franciscan priests wrote: "Words like 'immortality,' 'original sin,' and others were very difficult to render in Navajo. Chee helped here and gave accurate readings for these words. Even the word for 'God' had to be invented. The Fathers were using the word 'do datsahi,' meaning 'one that doesn't die.' Chee said the words could be used for that purpose, but the Navajos might think that a person could be talking about someone who goes by that name. So Chee said he would think the matter over and after much discussion with the head men of the tribe Chee introduced the word 'diyin ayoitei,' which means The Great Holy One." [18]

In addition to translating specific words, Chee helped with making the translations reflective of Navajo speech. Once, after checking over some prayers and catechisms that had been rendered into Navajo, he said that although the words were right, the prose sounded as clipped and terse to a Navajo as a telegram would to speakers of English.[19]

Chee continued to be a frequent visitor and guest at St. Michael's, and a room was kept for him at the mission so he could stay there whenever he wished.

After Annie had been at St. Michael's about a year and a half, the trachoma epidemic was contained, and she returned to school at Fort Defiance. About that time Mary thought she had had enough of being away from home, and her father allowed her to return from Denver and go to school at Fort Defiance as well.

A SISTER PLANTS SUSPICIONS

Mary's return home meant that she and Annie were together more than they had been for many years. Annie was a bright child, and with the events surrounding the flu epidemic and her heavier workload, she began to wonder why it was that she was treated differently than her siblings. Her concerns were compounded when Mary, with whom she had always had a difficult relationship, would taunt her, saying, "You don't belong here. You're from another family."

Annie would then go to Nanabah and ask, "Are you my real mother?" Receiving an affirmative answer from Nanabah, she'd resort to the typical childhood retort, "Well, Mary said . . ."

"Don't listen to her," she was told. "She's just a troublemaker." Eventually reassured, Annie grew up thinking Nanabah was her mother.[20]

A photograph of Chee's four children as adults shows physical traits that must have been apparent when they were children. Tom and Annie, the offspring of Nanabah and Kee'hanabah, respectively, have their father's broad nose and a square, chunky build, while Asza Yaze's children, Ben and Mary, have narrow noses and thin, wiry frames. Despite the close relationship of the three mothers, their offspring reflected quite different traits.

The conspiracy of silence on the matter must have been complete, for Annie would occasionally go to visit her real mother, who she thought was her aunt. By this time Kee'hanabah had other children who were born after she had returned to Sawmill and married a man named Hastiin Klah. Annie's sister Ann remembers those visits well.

"My mother used to stock up on material before Annie came to visit," she recalls. "Annie was a really good seamstress and she would sew for all of us little ones when she came." Annie's Navajo name meant "going in-between," and it was used during these visits. Ann maintains that all the children on her side of the family knew about Annie's real parentage, but apparently they did not tell. The subterfuge may have been helped by the fact that Navajo children call both their mother and their mother's sisters by the same name: *Shimá,* translated as "my mother." [21]

TO ALBUQUERQUE INDIAN SCHOOL

By the time Annie had completed the fifth grade, the Albuquerque Indian School was opened to all Indian students. Annie had been getting good grades, and Chee decided to send both Annie and Mary to school there. The trip—Annie's first train ride—turned into something of an adventure.

The children were taken to Gallup in wagons so they could board a train heading for Albuquerque. During the trip, about evening of the first day, the train stopped near Laguna Pueblo to pick up some local children. Annie was wide-eyed, looking out the window at the sights and all the new children about to get on the train. Then there was commotion, the few adults were rushing up and down the car, telling the children to run to the front of the train. Another train was coming on the same track and about to crash into them. Many of the children did not speak English well and did not understand what they were being told to do, but they did begin running. Annie recalled, "So I was running too and heard this great big locomotive—the head just plowed into the back of our train, derailed some of it, and all of us just fell on top of each other. Some of the students jumped from the windows and broke their hips and their arms. We just fell on top of each other in this big train."

Afterward, someone herded the children up and told them all to sit under a big tree. Annie knew no one but Mary. Although

Mary had been told to look after her little sister, instead she told Annie to watch their luggage while she went off with some of the older girls. Night came and the moon rose, and there Annie sat all alone, guarding the luggage and with nothing to eat or drink. The next morning the tracks were cleared, and another train was sent to pick up the youngsters and take them on to school.[22]

The Albuquerque Indian School was run by the Bureau of Indian Affairs. Since one of the purposes of Indian education was to prepare the students for assimilation into broader society, it was important that the students all spoke English. Annie had known some English before, but her facility with the language improved quickly after her arrival in Albuquerque.

She made friends with girls of other tribes, particularly those from some of the New Mexico pueblos. Since her own grandmother, Chee Dodge's mother, was part Jemez Pueblo, she felt an affinity with them.

Years later when asked how she acquired such a good command of English, she said, "When I went to elementary school on the reservation, the speaking of Navajo in or at the school was forbidden. And when I went to high school at the Albuquerque Indian School, the speaking of Navajo was still prohibited. So I and many of my Pueblo friends decided that we were going to speak the very best English that we could. It was very unfortunate that I had to forsake my Navajo friends and not enjoy the privilege of speaking my native language. But it probably turned out better this way."[23]

In addition to a curriculum more rigorous than that at the Fort Defiance school, the Albuquerque school offered music and sports—and Annie did especially well in tennis. Years later when a white friend working on the reservation confessed that she missed hearing Mozart, Annie told her that she did not know that composer, but that she was fond of Beethoven.

CHEE'S WORK EXPANDS

During all the years that Annie was growing up, her father was extremely active in tribal business. Sonsola Buttes was remote from any population centers, and many hours away from even the railroad, but officials in Washington knew where to find Chee when they wanted to know what was going on with the Navajos.

In 1914 Franklin K. Lane, secretary of the interior, wrote him asking three questions: 1) Do you think it would be a good thing for you to have your property and be entirely free from the Indian Bureau? 2) What reasons have you for thinking as you do? And 3) Is there any one thing that the government of the United States should do for the Indians of the country that it is not now doing?

Chee answered that he was among the very few members of the tribe who could get along if they owned their property outright and were independent of the Indian Bureau. His reasons were that there were fewer than four hundred members of the whole tribe of about twenty-five thousand who spoke English and that they were largely uneducated. He felt that without federal help the Navajos would never get enough schools. He also asked for trade schools and expanded irrigation projects. He concluded with a plea for the expansion of the reservation, saying that the Navajos were willing to pay for more land by selling their ripe timber.[24]

Three years later, in early 1917, Chee led a delegation of eastern Navajos to Washington to report that the tribe was in need of additional land. The secretary of the interior followed up by requesting a report, and the commissioner of Indian affairs agreed that the Indians could use additional territory. But by that time the white ranchers had begun moving onto the margins of the reservation, and because they had more political power, their needs won out. The weeks before and after his trip must have seen many strategy meetings in the big house at Sonsola Buttes.

Federal government officials also called in Chee when they needed help with the important negotiations. Around 1920, prospectors began looking for oil around Shiprock in the northern part of the reservation. Chee interpreted for a meeting between the Shiprock Navajos and oil companies wanting leases on the reservation. Apparently he did more than interpret—he advised the Navajos from that area to grant the leases. This led to rumors that he had been bribed by the subsidiaries of Standard Oil, which seems unlikely given his personal wealth. At any rate, this set up friction between him and his tribesmen of the Shiprock area that persisted for decades.

Eventually, the federal government wanted a body that could do business for the Navajo Tribe as a whole. In 1922, either the secretary of the interior or the commissioner of Indian affairs appointed a business council consisting of Chee Dodge, Charley Mitchell, and another man called Red Mustache's Brother. By July of the following year, the secretary of the interior, who had ultimate jurisdiction over all Indian reservations, issued a directive that oil leases were to be approved by a council elected to represent all the Navajos. The Tribal Council was to be made up of one delegate and one alternate from six districts, as well as a chair and vice chair to be chosen from outside the council membership. Chee Dodge was elected as chairman by the other delegates. Although this might appear highly democratic on the surface, in fact the council was to meet only when the newly appointed government commissioner to the Navajos called a meeting, and it could not convene without him in attendance. Furthermore, the secretary of the interior reserved the right to remove any delegate "for cause."

Nevertheless, on July 7, 1923, the delegates assembled for the first time, gathering in Toadlena, New Mexico. Although we can assume Chee and some of the other delegates were savvy enough to feel manipulated, they were told that only if they cooperated would they have any chance of the government providing them with badly needed new lands.[25]

Though in some sense the new council had been set up as a convenience for the U.S. government, the delegates believed that they had been elected to serve, and they began to work together to lead their people into the modern era. Between the years of 1923 and 1929, while Chee Dodge was heading the council, the Navajos negotiated more than $700,000 in oil bonuses and royalties. The council used part of this money to buy additional land to add to the reservation.[26]

Meanwhile, Annie was studying hard at Albuquerque Indian School and was in the audience when her father and some other Navajo leaders came to speak at the school, urging the students to study hard and complete their educations to prepare themselves for a future in which the tribe would be more involved in events of the outside world.

ANNIE DOES WELL AT SCHOOL

At the Albuquerque Indian School, Annie did indeed study hard. Her grades of A's and some B's led to her quick promotion, and she covered two grades each school year. One reason that she moved ahead so quickly might have been that for once she did not miss large blocks of lessons each year because of spring lambing; she stayed at the school all year except for summer vacation.[27]

Mary, however, did not like the school and convinced her father to let her return home, where he put her to work in the family store behind the house. Mary began to live the life of a traditional Navajo young woman. After her first menses she was given a Kinaaldá ceremony, the four-night traditional puberty rite. She was also taken to squaw dances, which are part of the Enemy Way ceremony, an important healing ritual and social event. The women and girls ask the men and boys to dance, which gives the young people the opportunity to get acquainted.

The summer breaks were anything but vacations for Annie. "Every time I went home during the summer vacation, all I did was sheepherding," she recalled. "Every time I come home there'd be a batch of sheep sittin'. The next morning I had to get going."[28]

Her oldest brother, Tom, meanwhile, was going to St. Louis University Law School, fulfilling his father's plans for him. Annie remembered her father frequently saying, "Tom has to have the best." Ben was at home, acting as his father's chauffeur.

Although Annie was not given a Kinaaldá ceremony, one summer when she was home from school, Nanabah and her father decided to take her to an Enemy Way ceremony. There was no explanation of what was to transpire, but in the late morning she was called in from her herding duties and told to wash. Nanabah presented her with some lovely new clothing, much nicer than any she had ever worn before. She was also allowed to wear some pieces from her father's extensive collection of silver and turquoise jewelry, and she was presented with a large shawl. At an Enemy Way ceremony, when the women ask the men to dance, they stand next to each other with the shawl over both their backs and dance to the drum beat, with all the couples moving in the same direction around the dance area.

As Annie told the story to Mary Carrol Nelson, Chee and Nanabah took her by wagon to an Enemy Way ceremony being given by their neighbors, the Tsosies. All the way as the wagon bumped over the uneven road, Annie wondered what would happen, who they would see. Because Enemy Way ceremonies, of which the squaw dance is a part, are expensive events to put on, all the guests bring food to share with the others attending. The Dodge contribution was large bags of bread, and when they arrived, Chee told Annie to take the bread to the host family. Annie stood next to the wagon holding the bread and looked out at the large crowd of people, some sitting in their own wagons and others milling about. It was more people than she had ever seen in one place, and she was terrified. Since she had never been included in social affairs, she did not know how to dance. Clutching her new shawl, she ran back to the wagon and climbed under the seat. Chee had to pick up the bread and take it to the Tsosies himself. Through the long night, Annie stayed in the wagon, only peeking out from her hiding spot now and then to watch the others having a good time.[29]

Chee and Nanabah were irritated at her behavior but did not force her to participate. Neither did they make any effort to explain the process to her or take her to any more social occasions of that kind. Navajo parents usually do not coerce their children to do something unless it is a matter of safety, and Chee and Nanabah apparently figured that her participation or lack of it was up to her.

AN ATHLETE NAMED GEORGE

Back at school, because she was moving ahead of her age mates, Annie ended up in a class with a young Navajo man named George Wauneka. He was from Blue Canyon, just north of Fort Defiance. George was several years older than she, and he was handsome and an accomplished athlete. Apparently with George, Annie's shyness vanished. Many years later when she was going through accumulated belongings, she called her grandson in to see an old clipping. "That's Pa," she said with pride, showing him a photo of George in a sweater with a big letter A on it. The headline read, "George Wauneka Scores the Big Win. Albuquerque Indian School Takes Title."[30]

BACK TO THE SHEEP AT SONSOLA BUTTES

When Annie had finished eleventh grade in 1928, Nanabah told her that she was needed back home. Although Chee's duties as head of the Tribal Council ended that year, he continued to be involved in tribal affairs. Chee was fulfilling a traditional local leadership role that Navajos call a *na'tanii*, meaning "one who talks well." The authority of the role comes solely from the people —his relatives and neighbors—who are willing to listen to his advice when he speaks at ceremonies or other gatherings. Although most men who had this informal title had influence only in their area, Chee's reputation was not confined to the Crystal chapter. Because of this, his travels around the vast reservation kept him away from home a great deal.

By this time, Chee had bought his first car. He was one of only a handful of Navajos to have a car at that time. With hardly any roads on the reservation fit for cars, wagons would continue to be more appropriate for transportation for many years. Although Chee owned many cars over his lifetime, he never drove himself, always having a retainer—or later, his son Ben—drive him around while he sat in the back seat.

At any rate, with Chee gone so much, Nanabah thought she needed help with the thousands of sheep and goats and the cattle that required looking after. So Annie left school and returned to Sonsola Buttes. The young scholar's life settled into another routine—taking the sheep out in the morning, watching to see that they drank water and did not eat any poisonous weeds, and bringing them back in the evening.

She also continued her training in the art of running a large Navajo household under the watch of Nanabah and Asza Yaze. This included basic doctoring of children and animals, sewing, butchering, cooking various stews and meat dishes, making flour tortillas, and baking. With the large number of people who ate at the Dodge household and the skill necessary to turn basic ingredients into tasty meals, this was an involved process. Nanabah, Asza Yaze, and her mother Kee'hanabah in Sawmill were also all accomplished rug weavers. Although Annie received training in all the steps from processing the wool to weaving, she found she had neither skill nor interest in producing rugs.

Meanwhile, Annie's sister Mary had married a local boy named Carl Peshlakai. Because so much of her life had been spent in Catholic boarding schools, she wanted to be married by a priest. After the wedding, which was a large social occasion, Chee sent the newlyweds to watch over his cattle ranch at Tanner Springs.

ANNIE AND GEORGE MARRY

At some point in this year, Annie told her father that she and George Wauneka, the handsome athlete she had met at Albuquerque Indian School, wanted to marry. Although it was more usual during those days for a family to choose a husband for their daughters, Chee and Nanabah acceded to Annie's wishes. Annie and George were married in a traditional Navajo ceremony in October 1929 at the ranch at Tanner Springs.

An old-fashioned Navajo wedding was usually held at the woman's hogan. The couple would sit on the west side of the hogan floor with a small pot of water with a gourd ladle and a basket filled with unflavored corn mush in front of them. All the relatives would be there except the bride's mother because Navajo women and their sons-in-law avoid looking at each other or being in each other's presence as much as is practical. The bride's uncle or a medicine man marks the basket of mush with a line of white pollen and a line of yellow pollen and addresses the couple, urging the woman to be a good wife and the man to be an industrious worker. After the bride and groom pour water from the pot over each other's hands with the ladle, they then each eat a fingerful of mush from the east, south, west, north, and center of the basket. Whatever mush is left is eaten by the wedding guests.[31]

For her wedding Annie wore a printed tiered cotton skirt and a long-sleeved velvet blouse. Her hair was tightly pulled back and tied with white yarn into a *chonga*, or double bun. Her dark brown hair was thick and glossy, and the style emphasized her high forehead. She was adorned with several pieces of Chee's extensive collection of silver and turquoise jewelry—a necklace, several bracelets, and large rings with exquisite stones. Her wedding picture and other early photos show that even at nineteen years of age she was a large woman, capable of wearing with dignity belts with silver *conchos*, or ornaments, three or four inches wide. Throughout her life, Annie was never seen without her jewelry, whether she was addressing a classroom of children or walking the halls of Congress in Washington DC. The wedding photographs show that George wore a long-sleeved muslin shirt and a silver squash blossom necklace. The wedding was a major regional event and attracted a large crowd of guests since Chee was such a celebrity.[32]

SETTING UP HOUSEKEEPING AT TANNER SPRINGS

Annie and George went to live at Sonsola Buttes, while Mary and Carl continued to represent Chee at Tanner Springs. Chee liked George and put him in charge of all of his sheep. Annie admitted that they were "just actually his hands," but the young couple worked hard and won Chee's trust. On the other hand, Mary was unhappy at the remote Tanner Springs ranch, so she and Carl returned to Sonsola Buttes, where she could live a more traditional life, close to her mother and other relatives. In their place, Annie and George were sent to watch over the Tanner Springs enterprise with its vast herds of cattle. In the late autumn, both Chee and Nanabah sent their flocks of sheep to Tanner Springs along with their herders to winter in the milder climate. Annie had been given her own sheep since she was a child, so she and George also took their own flocks to the ranch to be raised with Chee's larger herd.

The rolling plain area around Tanner Springs offered fine grazing land. Grasses, sagebrush, Russian thistle, sunflower, and lambsquarter grow in abundance here, but the canyons, valleys, and fields are also infested with several plants that are poisonous to sheep, so sheepherders need to keep a close watch on their animals. The elevation varies from 6,500 feet to 2,800 feet. On the south Tanner Springs is bordered by the La Pinta Mesa and slopes gently southwest into what is known as the Painted Desert. The area receives an average of 10.2 inches of rain, which come mainly during July, August, and early September.

Near the spring, Chee had built a stone house similar to the one at Sonsola Buttes, but smaller, and had constructed a log cabin somewhat closer to the main road, where he intended to stay during his retirement. Somehow, under circumstances not widely discussed and still hotly debated, his former herder Arthur Chester and his family ended up living in the stone house, while Annie and George lived in the cabin. They also built a hogan, which eventually burned down.[33]

Overseeing the ranch at Tanner Springs was a major undertaking, and Chee was a stern taskmaster. He gave explicit instructions to the young couple about how he wanted the place run and expected Annie and George to carry out his orders to the letter. "He comes around and leaves instructions for us," Annie recalled. "I want this thing to be done in this fashion. I want the cattle sale on this date. And I want the calves branded on this day. And I'll be here on this day and I want the report from you on this day. He'll go away again and he'll come back, sure enough he'll come back."[34]

The conditions were primitive and lonely, and the work was strenuous, but Annie had been brought up to value hard work. She remembered it as an interesting job and said she had enjoyed the work with the livestock. She adored her charismatic father, and by pleasing him, she strove to win the affection she had missed earlier in her childhood. One of the most taxing jobs was caring for the bulls, which were kept in a fenced pasture six or seven miles away from the house where the young couple lived. Every day, whether the sun was beating mercilessly down or whether a winter storm brought biting winds and snow, she made the long walk on a path though the sagebrush to pump water for the animals and then walked back to take up her other tasks. The bulls were ill-tempered and rambunctious, and every day Annie had to summon up the courage to open the gate, enter the enclosure, and pump the water so that her father's prize breeding stock would be properly cared for.[35]

Alan Menapace, whose father, Rico, bought Chee's cattle and sold him his cars, remembers going on cattle-buying trips with his father in the 1930s. They would start at Chee's place at Sonsola Buttes and slowly drive whatever cattle they picked up there south toward Tanner Springs. The sixty-mile trip took about two weeks, and along the way other Navajos would bring in small groups of two to twenty head of cattle. Frequently the small-time ranchers who brought in their cattle would have nothing else to do, so they'd hire on as herders and ride along. Rico Menapace hired a cook, usually a woman, and she'd bring several of her sisters or daughters. There was plenty of work on the cattle drive. Sometimes they would have to butcher a cow every day to feed everyone.

By the time they arrived at Tanner Springs, Annie was ready for them. "When we got to Annie's, she'd have made tortillas," Menapace remembers. "She had a little old rolling pin and she'd pull up her skirt and roll them on her leg. She'd start making those things early in the morning. We'd eat tortillas all day long and when we got ready to leave, she'd give us a big stack to take with us. She was a real good cook; she always had stew and chili and beans for us and all of her help. She had quite a bit of help. Her husband George, he was the cowboy of the outfit. But Annie was the boss." [36]

HER POLITICAL TRAINING BEGINS

Not only was Annie learning to run a large ranching operation, but she was also learning the political game through Chee's continued involvement in tribal politics. After a stop at the ranch to check on his affairs, he would take Annie and George to the local chapter meetings at Klagetoh or Wide Ruins. Since the Navajos live in widely separated encampments, there were no political centers. Instead, the reservation was divided into chapters, like counties, with locally elected officials, so that neighbors could deal with local issues and vote on delegates to represent their interests in the Navajo Tribal Council. At that time there was as yet no chapter house. People rode in on horseback or drove their wagons there, and the meeting was held under a big tree.

Arriving at Chee's side was a heady experience for the young couple. He was probably the leading Navajo celebrity of his day. Annie recalled, "The Navajos would come up and say, 'Here's Mr. Dodge, The Interpreter is coming, our great leader is coming.' The way he jokes, the way he opens the meetings, it's marvelous how he did it. So I just sit there watching him, watched how these people reacted to all of this. And he advises the Navajo people what to do and what not to do and he talks about livestock improvement . . . told them to get better rams, better bulls, better horses."

Annie was not there just to bask in his light—she was intrigued by what she saw, and her curiosity grew. Afterward, she would question Chee on why he was holding the meetings. "These Navajos need attention," she remembered him telling her. "They need care, they need to be educated. Now you go out to those hogans, see what you see."

Occasionally, Chee would call a meeting at Tanner Springs. He would send George out on horseback to let people know Chee would be around on a certain day and expected them to show up.

"I asked him, 'Why are they here?' All these big scary medicine men. He would say, 'Daughter, now you get some mutton stew and have some coffee ready. We're going to sit and talk all night.' And I thought, 'What in the devil are they going to talk about all night? I need the sleep.' He'd say, 'You stay on your two feet.' He was in command. So there he comes with the men."

Chee was to learn that he couldn't lead Annie into the thick of the political life and then expect her to retreat to the kitchen during the next gathering. "After I'm through with my dishes, I would come in and sit in the corner and he would say, 'What do you want to do here?' And I'd say, 'I want to listen to what you're going to talk about.' 'Um, you'd better boil some coffee.' I say, 'I have it on the stove.' So I would sit there and he talked about what's going to happen to the Navajos, what the government is going to offer." [37]

In fact, what the government was planning for the Navajos was something none of the people in those meetings could have anticipated. In the 1930s, Washington policymakers, a continent away from the reservation, made a decision that brought the greatest crisis to the Navajo Tribe since the Long Walk. It pierced the heart of Navajo identity—their herds of sheep. There were too many animals for the available range, and the Navajos were going to have to cut their flocks drastically. Dealing with the effects of this massive mandated stock reduction would consume the energies of Chee and Annie, as well as other Navajo leaders, for decades.

3
The Agonies of Stock Reduction

BY THE 1930S, CHEE DODGE and the other Navajos had been back in their homeland for sixty-five years. Chee, a homeless orphan when he returned, had become the richest Navajo ever and the leader of his tribe. His livestock numbered in the thousands—sheep, cattle, horses—divided between the high green pastures at Sonsola Buttes and the warmer, drier range at Tanner Springs. Perhaps Chee's memory of his mother's ill-fated hunt for food and his own need to scrounge for corn that dropped to the stable floor after the mules had eaten fueled his determination to prosper on a scale that would ensure he would never lack for anything again.

THE DARK SIDE OF PROSPERITY
Although there was a great deal of poverty on the reservation, other Navajos had done well also and increased their flocks. Stock raising was the major economic activity of a typical Navajo household. Sheep and goats provided food, and their pelts were used for bedding. Lambs were sold to the trader for cash or goods.

But the sheep, goats, and horses were more than assets; they were the center around which life was organized, physically and emotionally. Life revolved around the requirements of the flock, which every day needed to be driven to grass and water and every night had to be returned to the safety of a corral, either next to the hogan or in a more remote sheep camp. Each member of a family owned sheep individually and knew which of the wooly creatures belonged to whom, although the animals might be herded together. Everyone pitched in on the herding, from the most senior matriarch to the youngsters. Children were given animals at a young age so that when they became adults, they would have a herd. Periods when increased labor was needed—such as shearing, lambing, castrating, or the seasonal moving of animals from one pasture to another—brought together as many members of the family as could make it to the homestead and provided a sort of focused family solidarity. Although individual family members could do as they wished with their animals—sell them, keep them, or slaughter them—the decision was usually made for the benefit of the entire family.

Livestock was important even in religion. During ceremonies, the medicine man was paid in sheep, and sheep were butchered to feed those who attended the gathering. When there were long ceremonies where people had to be fed for many days, this involved a considerable number of sheep, and guests who could afford it would donate a sheep for the event.

Social status was determined by how much stock a family owned. Thrift and industriousness were Navajo cultural values, and a substantial flock of sheep attested to these qualities in a man or woman.

From the time the Navajos returned from Bosque Redondo and received two ewes each, Navajo stock had multiplied from roughly 15,000 sheep and 2,000 goats to a combined number of 1,300,000 sheep and goats. Similar to other Americans who talk about how a grandparent arrived from Europe with only a few possessions and founded a business from nothing, Navajos would recount how a relative had returned from Bosque Redondo and developed a fine herd of sheep from an original allotment of two animals. More than 75,000 horses also shared the range.[1] One drawback to this increasing affluence was that there were few spots of lush vegetation on the reservation to support the growing herds. The animals had to scramble for scattered patches of grass.

In the earlier years, as the population of people and animals increased, additional lands were annexed to the reservation to accommodate the growth, but by 1915 most of the land was already claimed by other tribes and the white ranchers who were running essentially subsidized operations on federally owned Bureau of Land Management lands. But the number of animals continued to grow. Various agricultural agents and regional officials saw clear evidence that the land was becoming seriously overgrazed, but their warnings were dismissed. Interior Department bureaucrats figured that the more animals the Indians had, the less likely they would be to need government rations.

As for the horses, who were eating grass that should have been available for the sheep, the Navajos were firm about keeping them. A certain number were needed for transportation, but many families owned far more animals than were required to pull their wagons. As anthropologist Ruth Underhill explained it: "Horses were their way of proving wealth and dignity, and no self-respecting man could give them up. A white man may show wealth by having a large house and grounds, with many rooms he does not use. The Navajo had a tiny house with no furniture, but he showed his wealth by owning many horses." [2]

But the sharp hooves of all those animals were beating the land to dust. Chee and the members of the Navajo Tribal Council were made aware of the problem by the federal agents who placed it on the agenda. As early as November 1928, an agenda item labeled "The question of eventually limiting the number of sheep, horses, goats and cattle for any one Indian, so that benefits of the range may be more equitably distributed among all Navajos" led to lengthy and concerned debate. Eventually the delegates voted to impose a tax of eleven cents a head on all sheep in excess of 1000 owned by one family, but since it could always be argued that parts of large flocks were owned by various relatives, the issue was more or less ignored for a while.

Because Chee was one of the few Navajos with whom the government agents actually interacted, they saw his livestock operations as a model for other Navajos to emulate. They thought with just a little more education and instruction the rest of the Navajo sheepherders would, like Chee, make use of superior breeding stock to get better sheep, cull their herds to get rid of old and unproductive sheep, and change their herding practices. Chee had been fencing his land and using imported rams for decades. Most of his herds were the Karakul breed from Asia with black, brown, or gray backs and black legs rather than the curly white Rambalais. Because he had acquired enough wealth to do so, he had developed his own sources of water for his stock. The "Range Management Report" from the period states: "There is one well about ten miles west of Klag-e-toh which was drilled by E.C.W. [Emergency Conservation Work]. The 50,000 gallon storage tank and concrete troughs were put in by E.C.W., but no one but Chee Dodge can use them because he erected and owns the windmill that pumps the water."[3]

Chee also embraced modern husbandry techniques. Most other Navajos tended to keep older cows or sheep because they were large and handsome and to dispose of the younger ones, who would be more efficient breeders. They ran the ewes and rams together so breeding took place throughout the year. Lambs were frequently born in bad weather, which gave them a less than advantageous start and led them to be sickly and weak. The government officials thought that with more education the Navajos, like Chee, would adopt the new ways and come to see stock raising as a commercial activity designed to provide the largest possible cash income. But the vast number of Navajos did not share Chee's values when it came to using the new methods to maximize their income. They liked raising their stock just like their fathers and grandfathers had done. The traditional way of raising sheep was comfortable because it supported and interwove with the traditional way of life.

GOVERNMENT INTERVENTION

During the drought years of the early 1930s, the grazing situation on the reservation became worse, and government agricultural experts were sent to look over the area. Once they had figured in the average annual rainfall and the vegetation it supported, they calculated that the approximately 16 million acres accessible to the Navajos for grazing could support about 585,000 sheep units. For their purposes they figured that one horse was equal to five sheep and one cow was equal to four sheep. Goats and sheep were equivalent. This meant that four-fifths of the Navajo livestock was going to have to be eliminated.

When it rains, much of the Navajo Reservation drains into the

Colorado River, through tiny creeks flowing into narrow washes, which in turn converge into the wide, roiling, but temporary, rivers. The hard torrential rains of summer churned and carried the red dirt that had no grass to hold it, turning the rushing water reddish brown on its way to the Colorado. During those years the soil erosion was so bad that Secretary of the Interior Harold Ickes warned that if it was not checked, the reservoir behind Hoover Dam, which spanned the Colorado, would silt up in the next ten years.

In 1933 Hugh Bennett, head of the U.S. Soil Conservation Service, and John Collier, commissioner of Indian affairs under President Franklin Delano Roosevelt, presented the bad news on the extent of the erosion of their land to the Navajo Tribal Council in several meetings over the summer and fall. They gave some recommendations for ways to stop erosion, such as the construction of small dams and gully control structures, and pledged funds from the Federal Surplus Relief Administration to buy the excess sheep from their owners. By this time Annie's elder half brother, Tom, had graduated from St. Louis University School of Law and, after a short career as an attorney in Santa Fe, had been elected chairman of the Tribal Council. At the first meeting, Tom led the delegates in a lengthy questioning of Bennett. After a three-week recess to discuss the situation in their communities, the council voted to undertake the soil conservation program in principle and to begin sheep reduction at some later date.[4]

The following year, John Collier and agents of the Bureau of Indian Affairs went before the council again to urge them to speed up the stock reduction. During that meeting and subsequent meetings over the next few years, various schemes and inducements were presented—from buying the animals to offering wage work in exchange for the lost income when families had to reduce their herds. What the government was proposing would cause immense changes in the life of the Navajos, and the process should have been done slowly and thoughtfully.

Apparently Collier did not fully understand how deeply attached the Navajos were to their sheep. Although he had commissioned studies on other cultural topics, he did not seek an analysis of how the stock reduction would affect the Navajos. Perhaps the reason he pushed ahead was that the commissioner of Indian affairs serves at the pleasure of the president, and Collier did not know how much longer President Roosevelt would be in office. He wanted to complete the job while he was still in a position to do so. John Collier was sympathetic to the Indians and saw himself as working tirelessly on their behalf. Tom Dodge also supported him and during one meeting "gave Collier a very complimentary and eloquent introduction calling him the 'Plumed knight of the Indian cause.'" However, Tom Dodge was way out of the mainstream Navajo thinking on this issue, and the Navajos considered Collier then, and for decades afterward, as an evil force dedicated to destroying their way of life.[5]

DIFFERING VIEWS OF THE PROBLEM

Chee and Tom knew that the two sides simply saw reality differently. The government point of view was that severe erosion creates wastelands from what were once good fields for grazing and farming. Once the critical ratio of animals to plant cover is surpassed and the range has degraded, it is not sufficient merely to avoid increasing the herds; stock levels have to be reduced for the range to recover. Also, if herds are kept below the carrying capacity of the land, the sheep will be healthier and the lamb crop per head of sheep will be increased.[6]

Most Navajos did not accept the government explanation that the land was in bad shape because of too many sheep. They were accustomed to cycles of drought and figured as soon as the rains came again the grass would return. Traditional Navajos believed that the supernaturals gave sheep to the Navajos for their livelihood. When the flocks are increased, the gods see that the Indians care for their gift and send rain; but when the Indians give sheep away, the supernaturals fail to send rain.[7] Some believed that the reduction in grass was directly related to the government's poisoning of prairie dogs to reduce bubonic plague. The poison killed other burrowing rodents as well, and with the rodents gone, their tunnels collapsed, and the rain was not able to penetrate the soil as well.[8] Others thought the problems were related to the fact that they had been neglecting the old ceremonies, but a renewed cycle of ceremonies did not help.

Chee had been advocating for years that Navajo herdsmen raise fewer but better sheep. But he also knew that an immediate and large-scale reduction would cause grave economic and psychological problems for the Navajos, and he kept working for a compromise. Due to his limited education, Chee did not write well. He probably was not in school long enough to become proficient in spelling and punctuation. But that did not keep him from expressing himself. His analysis of the complex situation facing his tribe combined both a bone-deep understanding of the connection of the Navajos to their way of life with an intelligent comprehension of the reality facing them. Chee sent frequent letters to Washington officials through the assistance of the fathers at St. Michael's Mission, where he often took their offer of accommodations for the night. Through his letters, he appealed to anyone with any power to moderate the plans for reduction.

According to a story in *Navajo Biographies* based on an interview with his daughter Mary, "He arrived home late one afternoon, ready to settle into his big black easy chair and relax. Just as he stopped his car, the telephone rang inside the house." Chee sent Mary to answer it. It was the Navajo Agency superintendent, E. R. Fryer, who told Chee that grazing districts had been established and that a certain number of livestock would be allowed in each district. "The old leader sank into his chair, then rose and paced, finally stopping by the south window. He could look out and see a thousand of his cattle, fifteen hundred fat and wooly sheep, and hundreds of horses."

Chee had in the past lost hundreds of animals at a time to natural disasters. But there had always been the opportunity to rebuild his herd. This time the animals would be gone for good. He knew that even though his part of the reservation provided enough grass for his animals, he, too, would need to comply with the new regulations.

"Grief-stricken, Chee Dodge stayed in the living room sitting in his armchair, talking to himself, then brooding in long silences and refusing to eat any of the food Mary brought him." [9]

He agreed with the need for stock reduction, but the plans for achieving it seemed unnecessarily harsh. The first reduction in 1933 called for a straight 10 percent reduction of all flocks, with 75 percent to be ewes and 25 percent to be wethers (castrated males.) This did not take into account individual circumstances, so the large owners simply got rid of old and unproductive animals while those with small herds had to give up the ewes that were the basis of future production.[10]

ANNIE GETS INVOLVED

This devastating economic news needed to be explained to the Navajos, so meetings were called in every chapter house. Annie slipped into the Klagetoh chapter meeting one afternoon when a government agent was there discussing in English what the stock reduction would mean to the people of that area and how they would be expected to comply. Because those gathered there spoke only Navajo, someone was translating. From where she sat quietly in the back of the room, Annie was stunned at how inept the translation was. When she mentioned the incident later to her father, he exploded. "And you just sat there and listened? I sent you to school in Albuquerque to be educated so you could help your people and you just sat there," she recalled him saying.

"Boy, did I get the biggest scolding of my life," she added. It was a story she was to tell many times, when she talked to interviewers, addressed conventions, spoke to groups of school children, or told her own grandchildren about her life.[11] It seems to have been a turning point in her life—an indication from her adored father that she was ready to move from the background where she boiled coffee and made mutton stew at gatherings to being a participant in her own right.

In order to facilitate the painful process in which average Navajos were going to be stripped of a major part of their flocks —and indeed their economic and psychological security—Chee traveled the vast reservation constantly during this time, usually accompanied by Annie or one of his other children, meeting with Navajos individually, at chapter meetings, or at ceremonials. The spreading branches of a large tree would often constitute the only roof over these gatherings.

Annie would listen closely to what he said, sometimes marveling at her father's fluent oratory. And when the meeting was over she would question him on why he was trying to explain the purpose behind the stock reduction plans and why he wanted to convince the Navajos to go along with government decisions.

"Why did you say that?" she'd ask. "Most of them were opposing you."

"That's the way it is and it's going to be that whether they like it or not. I'm supposed to tell my people what to expect."

"Do you think the white man is right?" she'd ask.

"They're usually right," was his reply.[12]

CHEE'S RESPONSE TO THE STRESS

Standing at the fulcrum between the two factions took its toll on Chee. He had always had a taste for good Scotch and had imbibed at his home and with friends in Gallup and elsewhere. During the 1930s, Chee Dodge's already excessive drinking began to escalate. No doubt this resulted not only from the responsibilities of his position in this time of upheaval but also from his struggle to intercede between two cultures with vastly different world views. As one of the Franciscan fathers wrote, "Chee knew what the Government wanted him to do, and he tried to please, if possible. He knew what his tribe wanted him to do, and again he tried to please, if possible. Oftentimes this struggle for a balance between opposing factors caused Chee to do things that were considered by some the result of inconsistence and lack of oneness of purpose. But Chee was in the position of a man who is forced to ride two wild horses at one and the same time."[13]

Frank Mitchell in the book *Navajo Blessingway Singer* recalled how when visiting St. Michael's Mission one day, he learned that Chee had been out drinking in Gallup, going from house to house visiting his white friends and indulging in their hospitality. When he left the last place it was late and dark, and he stumbled off a bridge, falling into a wash with quicksand or thick mud in the bottom. He was soon stuck so he started hollering for help. A Mexican man living near the wash got out his lantern and, investigating the noise, found Chee and pulled him out. Chee by that time was a handsome man in his early seventies, with thick white hair. We do not know if the Mexican knew who his distinguished guest was, but at any rate he cleaned Chee up and gave him a bed for the night. Apparently it was raining upstream, because later that night water coursed at a considerable speed down the wash. Had Chee remained stuck, he would have drowned.

Frank Mitchell, with his friends Curly Hair and Son of the Late Little Blacksmith, decided to go by Chee's place and see if the rumor was true. They found him in a sweat lodge with some other friends, and he invited the three men to join him. According to Mitchell, Nanabah was not living with Chee at the time, but he had his cook fix dinner for his guests. After eating, the men talked late into the night with Chee relating, as he so often did, the stories of the Long Walk and the earlier days after the return. Eventually Mitchell and the others asked him if the story they had heard about him falling off the bridge was true, and he admitted that it was. He told them he was embarrassed and had not wanted it to be known, but they would not hear anything like that about him again.[14]

In fact, there were many incidents where too much drinking put Chee's life in peril, according to Alan Menapace, son of Chee's friend Rico Menapace. "He was in more car wrecks than any man I ever did see in my life and still live through them," Menapace said. "He'd come to town, and both he and the driver would get drunk. Chee would always sit in the back seat. One time they started home and nosed off a bridge, and the car went into a deep arroyo. Chee went through the windshield, and it scalped him. The hospital called Dad about midnight, and they said, 'We've got this big guy up here who's been in an accident and needs to be stitched up. But he keeps hollering "Rico, Rico," and he won't let us give him a shot or anything.' My dad knew who it was right away. So he got a bottle of whiskey and went over to the hospital. Chee had a cut on both sides of his forehead just like a big V, and his scalp was lying on the back of his head. So dad said, 'Let's have a drink, Chee,' and he'd have a drink and Chee would have a drink, and pretty soon Chee started singing in Navajo. Then my dad said, 'Ok, he's ready to start sewing up.' The whole time they were fixing him up, him and Dad was having shots of whisky." [15]

Fortunately for Chee he was wealthy enough to replace the cars he wrecked, though sometimes he had to leave part of his jewelry collection as collateral until he could raise enough cash for a new vehicle. Rico Menapace had set up his car dealership with help from Chee and sold Chee every car he ever bought. The Dodge family to this day continues to buy their vehicles from Rico's sons. When GMC started making a pickup, they showed pictures of it to Rico, who saw that it would be the perfect vehicle for the Navajos who have to haul wood and water. He went out to the reservation and visited everybody who had money. In a few days, he managed to sell twenty-eight pickups, one of them to Chee Dodge. The GMC representative was astounded. [16]

Chee also had more elegant cars. Dr. Clarence Salsbury, long-time superintendent and medical director of Sage Memorial Hospital at Ganado, wrote in his autobiography that Chee Dodge had some kind of fascination with wheels. "I drove a Buick car with six wire wheels, the two spares being placed in fender wells. Chee told Rico, the Buick agent in Gallup, that he wanted one just like mine. But when it came, it had only one spare tire, fastened at the rear. Chee refused to accept it. Somehow the dealer satisfied him with a makeshift arrangement, cutting two wells in the fenders to mount the spares." [17]

Although he was somewhat extravagant in his lifestyle and a shrewd dealer when it came to business matters and loans, Chee was also generous. When Dr. Salsbury realized that there was not a single X-ray machine in the entire 26,000-mile-square area he served, he began soliciting everyone he saw to give to the X-ray fund. Chee was one of the first donors, and when others heard about his gift, they too came up with donations. Later, when Chee took one of his grandsons to Ganado for a medical examination, he told Dr. Salsbury to order $500 worth of whatever equipment he needed and to send him the bill.

TOM DODGE CAUGHT BETWEEN CULTURES

Meanwhile, Annie's brother Tom was also being heavily affected by the continuing controversy as the issue of the need for stock reduction dragged on. He was caught between the federal government's insistence on action to preserve the range and the more laissez-faire approach of the Navajos, who believed that if the situation were left alone, the rains would eventually come again, or in some other way the situation would resolve itself. As an educated man, Tom understood the wisdom and inevitability in John Collier's mandates on stock reduction and was seen as a Collier supporter. At that time, the job of tribal chairman was not a full-time job so, in what was no doubt an economic move, in 1935 Tom accepted an appointment as an assistant superintendent of the Navajo Agency under the Bureau of Indian Affairs. That put him in the position of simultaneously representing two opposing camps: the BIA, which was pushing stock reduction, and the Tribal Council, which stood for the people who generally continued to resist getting rid of any of their livestock.

In May 1936, Tom resigned as tribal chairman. In a letter of explanation to John Collier, he wrote that to the Navajos "the entire program is so complicated and involved that no amount of explanation will begin to make them see any rhyme or reason in it. This utter confusion in their minds has had the effect of convincing them that the program was purposely made complicated and involved that they would not get wise to the plan to rob them of their resources and their livestock." He concluded by saying that since he had been too long identified with Collier's policies, there was no choice but to resign the chairmanship.[18] Although for many years Tom was the only Navajo with a law degree, and Annie and other prominent Navajos urged him to come back to help the tribe, he never returned for more than a brief visit. He spent the rest of his life working for the Bureau of Indian Affairs as the superintendent of other tribes.

In the year that Tom resigned, Chee was elected as a council delegate from the Crystal chapter. Having served for eighteen years as an unofficial leader, he now once again had a vote, and the family had continued official representation.

THE WAUNEKAS START A FAMILY

While Chee and Tom were heavily involved in tribal politics and Annie was also being drawn in, the daily work of running the Tanner Springs ranch continued to be a daily responsibility for Annie and George. It was during these years that the Waunekas were starting their family. Their first child, Georgia Ann, was born in 1931, and the next year James Henry was born but died as an infant. In 1934 Marvin was born, followed by Henry 1935, Irma in 1936, George Leonard in 1939, Timothy in 1942, and Franklin in 1945. Because of their remote home and the bad condition of the roads, some of the children were born at home without medical assistance. Some were difficult births, and Marvin, Henry, George, and Timothy had multiple disabilities, possibly cerebral palsy, perhaps because of trauma during the birthing process. The fact that the Waunekas were caring for their disabled children at home made additional work. The rhythm of life was dictated by the needs of the animals and the economics of sheep raising. Every spring the sheep were sheared and the wool sold. Later in the summer, the sheep had to be herded to the dipping station, where they were run through a solution to rid them of ticks and other pests.

Then it was time to get ready for winter. Bad roads that frequently got too much snow for a truck to maneuver made it wise to stock up on enough food to feed the family and the hired help for periods of several weeks when they might be cut off from even the nearest trading post. Into the underground storage cellar went twenty-five-pound bags of flour for bread, tortillas, and fry bread and hundred-pound sacks of potatoes and beans. In those days the beans were not as clean as those we buy in plastic bags today, so in the evenings Annie would bring out the beans she planned to cook for the next day and spread them on the table. Annie's daughter Irma remembers this as the time that the children would have a counting lesson as they helped pick out the rocks and other debris, getting the beans ready to cook. Once the beans were picked clean, they were washed and put in a pot on the back of the wood stove to slowly cook through the night.

Every fall the Waunekas slaughtered a colt less than one year old, cut the meat into strips, and put it to dry in the sun and turn into jerky. Later in the winter when the children had dry coughs, Annie cooked up the strips of horsemeat and fed it to them as a nutritious medicine.

She was adept at cooking other traditional Navajo delicacies as well. "My mother used to cook prairie dogs and make them taste so good," Irma recalled. "My father would catch four or five prairie dogs, and my mother cleaned then on the inside and took off most of their hair by singeing them over a fire. Then she stuffed them with plants and herbs and closed them with baling wire. When the fire in the ground had burned down, she'd lay the prairie dogs side by side over the coals, cover them, and let them bake. That was my favorite meal as a child." [19]

When it was time to slaughter a sheep, none of it went to waste. Irma remembers how, when the animal's throat was slit, her mother caught the blood in a basin. Later she mixed it with blue cornmeal, flour, and neck meat, sheep fat, onions, and potatoes, all chopped into tiny pieces. The mixture was put into the cleaned sheep stomach and boiled until it was solid. The intestines were cleaned by pouring boiling water through them. She made a special Navajo delicacy by wrapping pencil-thin intestines around larger fatty ones and baking them. And always, as she was working, she counseled her children, "If you just eat the muscle meat and throw away the rest of the sheep, you'll be the first to starve during a famine. Use every bit of the sheep, or you'll wish for the food you threw away." [20]

CHEE'S WIFE NANABAH DIES

In 1939 Nanabah died. Although she and Chee had lived apart several times, he had loved her deeply and was by all accounts grief stricken. When Annie got the news, she rushed to Sonsola Buttes. It was then that Chee finally told her that Nanabah was not her mother. At last, what she had suspected as a child was confirmed. Kee'hanabah, whom she had thought was her aunt, was her real mother, and Kee'hanabah's children were not her cousins, but her half brothers and sisters. Nanabah left her estate to be divided between her own children, Mary and Ben, while

Tom and Annie received tokens. Rico Menapace received a huge diamond ring.

Although the published biography of Chee Dodge mentions only his first wife and Nanabah and her sister, who were Chee's second and third wives, one of his two census cards at St. Michael's Mission lists eight wives and six children. Most of these women were related to each other, and the arrangements were not unusual according to Navajo standards.[21] It appears, however, that Nanabah was the female head of the household.

It cannot be denied, however, that even as an older man, Chee had an eye for attractive females. A woman from a prominent Navajo family was told by her mother how the mother had narrowly escaped becoming one of Chee's wives after Nanabah's death. At that time the mother was young, apparently in her mid to late teens. She entered the family hogan and found her mother straightening up—sweeping the floor, folding the blankets and carefully stacking them against the walls with the sheepskins, and piling up the dishes and pans in a orderly way. When the teenager asked her mother for an explanation for all the activity, her mother announced that a great man was coming to visit. Pressed for more information, she said that Chee Dodge had noticed the teenager and wanted her for a wife.

Having seen him and knowing that he was old and white-haired, the teenager ran from the hogan and kept running through the sagebrush for several miles until she came to her aunt's hogan, where she hid for several days, fearful of being married to a man old enough to be her grandfather. Today, decades later, the daughters of the teenager who attracted Chee's interest are extraordinarily handsome, and we might assume she, too, was very beautiful as a teenager. The issue of marriage to Chee Dodge was not pressed, and the teenager was left to grow up, finish school, and eventually marry someone else.

CHEE FACES STOCK REDUCTION

By 1940, the livestock on the reservation had been reduced to 620,000 head and by 1952 to 433,000. Chee dipped 3,570 sheep in 1937, but by 1944 his regular and special permits allowed a total of only 275.[22] The cattle herds at Tanner Springs had also seen a drastic reduction. When it came time for Chee to comply with the regulations and submit to the severe stock reduction, he offered to buy hay for the cattle so they would not be grazing on the already dry lands. His compromise was refused. Because he had the financial means, Chee was able to rent some off-reservation property and move a part of his stock there, but many animals remained on reservation lands. Government sharpshooters came to the Tanner Springs ranch and in one morning killed one thousand head of cattle while the family looked on in despair. When the shooting was finished and the cattle lay in heaps on the blood-soaked ground, Chee sent George Wauneka to round up friends and relatives to butcher the cattle and save what meat they could. But the task was enormous, and much of the meat spoiled. The rotting carcasses were dragged by the feet to the base of the mesa. Their bleached bones remained as testimony not only to what had happened at Chee's ranch but also to the reductions that had taken place throughout the reservation.[23]

Although Chee was deeply saddened by these events, he refused to be demoralized by them. One day Don Dodge, one of his grandsons, was sitting with him on a bluff near Tanner Springs. They were looking at the mesa to the southwest of the ranch and the mountains rising beyond it. "I don't want you to look just at that mesa or those mountains," Chee told the young man. "I want to you look to the mountains beyond those and the ones beyond those and to what lies even beyond." No doubt he gave his children, including Annie, similar instructions.[24]

CHEE REGAINS TRIBAL CHAIRMANSHIP

As the difficulties with stock reduction wore on and Navajo families faced reduced circumstances, Chee continued to do whatever he could for his fellow Navajos. In 1942 he was again elected tribal chairman. The ability of Chee to remain active in tribal politics despite his extraordinary wealth was unusual for the Navajos, who generally view persons of wealth with suspicion. Hard work leading to accumulation of material goods is valued, but those who make a good living are expected to share with their family. "Don't be too rich" is an implicit Navajo value. Navajos envy people of considerable means, but they also fear and resent them, figuring nobody can get really wealthy without overlooking their social obligations and doing other people in. The richer men were rarely elected to political posts. In fact, most delegates to the Tribal Council at this time came from the lower economic levels of the community. Affluence is also associated with witchcraft—the devious accumulation of wealth.[25] But in Chee's case, he was known to be a shrewd and hard-nosed businessman, one who expected his loans to be repaid, and there is no doubt that he was also generous, providing work for his relatives and donating money to hospitals and sheep to feed people at sings and other ceremonials. Actually, few Navajos could fathom how wealthy he really was. However, even a half century after his death, there are still a small handful of Navajos who maintain that despite all of his good qualities, Chee was a witch and had gotten his wealth through devious supernatural means.

During this term of office, Chee's health was not good, and at eighty-two years of age, he was increasingly aware that he wouldn't be around forever. He continued to train his children to carry on his work. Frequently when Chee and Annie would attend meetings together and a government official was present, he would request that Annie do the interpreting. But indulgence was not part of his makeup. If she made a mistake, he did not hesitate to correct her, sometimes witheringly, in front of the crowd.

ANNIE ELECTED TO GRAZING COMMITTEE

Eventually, Annie began going to meetings at the Klagetoh chapter house on her own or with George. She interpreted and stood up to the government officials when they overstepped their bounds. From a shy young woman who hid in the wagon at the Enemy Way ceremony and lurked in the back of the chapter house, she was becoming a confident leader. As she gained a reputation for persuasiveness and clear thinking, the members of her chapter recognized her skills and elected her to the Grazing Committee. Grazing Committee members were charged with mediating disputes over who had rights to what rangelands and overseeing sheep and cattle dipping, branding, and vaccinations. From there, she went on to become chapter secretary.

It was probably at this time, with much to do and vast distances to cover, that Annie acquired her lifelong habit of driving well in excess of posted speed limits. She told a friend that once during this time she had been caught speeding on Highway 66 and pulled over. She pretended to the sheriff's deputy that she didn't speak English, but she got a ticket anyway, although the officer noted the language problem on the citation. When she came before the judge in the border town later, the judge turned out to be someone who had known her and her father for years. He was amused that the young woman who was sought as a translator "didn't speak English."

During this time, Annie was away from home so much that George began spending time with his closest neighbor, Anna Chester, daughter of Arthur Chester, Chee's old friend. On May 7, 1941, Anna bore a child she and George named Eddie. We do not know what Annie's reaction was to this event. She had grown up in a household where her father had children by multiple wives, so it could not have been as much of a shock as it might have been in a culture where this was not so widely accepted. However, ten years later, she attempted to evict the Chesters from the stone house near the spring, saying she wanted to build a school there.[26] Arthur Chester's daughters appealed to the Tribal Council, saying their father had lived there for fifty years and had homesteaded the area. The Chester family remains there still, although there is contention between the heirs of both the Chesters and Waunekas.

An incident that occurred during this time indicates that Annie was well along in developing the dominant personality that would become her hallmark. Government officials were adamant about reducing the number of horses on the reservation, making people apply for grazing permits, and then sticking within the bounds of the number of animals allowed on their permits. It was 1945, when, as Annie related it, "A poor old Navajo woman with a grandchild had a palomino horse, a real nice one with a colt. I guess she was left out in getting a grazing permit for whatever reason. She brings this horse to the district super-visor and there I stood by the fence. She did everything she can to keep that one horse. She said 'Could I keep that one horse? It's all I have. I drag in wood with that horse. I go to the store with that horse.' She exhausted every effort, but the supervisor said, 'You have no business keeping that horse, old lady,' and he threw it into the pen for sale. That's when I got so mad. I used to be a good roper, so I went to the corral and roped that palomino and I got it out of the corral. And there was the district supervisor just writing away, asking, 'Whose horse is that?' I gave it back to the lady, and said, 'You take it home.' Just as she was starting to pull that horse out, the white man came and he was holding one end of the rope and I was holding the other end and that poor old lady was standing between us saying, 'Please let me have that horse.'

"I was closer to the horse than him, so all of a sudden I jerked this rope out of his hand and whipped the horse with it and the horse took off running. And I said, 'Okay, gentlemen, go get that horse.'"

While they fumed, Annie countered with, "Let her have the horse as long as she lives. She's not going to last too long." The old woman ended up living another thirty or so years, not dying until she was about 110. Later, Annie managed to get her a permit for twenty-five animals. "That was my first battle," she remem-bered.[27]

CHEE'S HEALTH WORSENS

Although Chee was tribal chairman again, he was slowing down. In those days the council met only quarterly. In 1944 he went to Los Angeles seeking a specialist in urology. The problem was probably prostate related, common for a man his age. Other-wise, he tended to his extensive business interests, spent the coldest winter months at the Arizona Hotel in Phoenix, visited friends in Gallup, and indulged his interest in fine silver and tur-quoise jewelry and diamonds. After World War II, a Jewish jew-eler in Gallup frequently traveled to Europe to buy diamonds from his impoverished relatives. Chee would always have first pick of whatever he brought back.

From time to time he used the diamonds as payment for debts. During World War II, the Lippincotts, the owners of the trading post at Wide Ruins where Chee and the Waunekas did considerable business, sold it to a man who was not able to maintain a good relationship with his Navajo customers. Traditionally, Navajos got the supplies they needed from the nearest trading post on credit and then paid off their bills twice a year when their wool was sold in the spring and their lambs were sold in the fall. With the big operation at Tanner Springs, the Waunekas needed large amounts of supplies and ran up big bills, although the Lippincotts had never worried about it, knowing they were always good for the money.

The new trader, however, began letting Annie and George know that he expected some payment, and soon. Apparently Annie discussed the situation with her father and one day strode in to the trading post and slammed her hand down on the counter in front of the trader. "This should take care of the bills," she said. On the counter was a diamond ring. It was so large, the trader was sure it was fake. On his next trip to Gallup, he took the ring to a jeweler for appraisal and was stunned to find that it was worth more than twice the Waunekas' bill.[28]

Despite being one of the oldest Navajos on the reservation, Chee continued to be one of the most modern in terms of ideas and plans for the future. His ideas always had a practical thrust. In a letter he wrote to the House Committee on Indian Affairs dated September 12, 1944, he stated, "All day schools should be eliminated and more boarding schools established. Eliminate any effort to teach Navajo language in the schools in that Navajos have to learn English to compete with other people in employment." He also called for more trade schools.[29] Despite his own taste for good whiskey he wrote, "I am convinced that liquor should not be sold on the Reservation."

In 1945 the Indian Council Fire gave its annual Indian Achievement Award to Chee Dodge. He was saving his strength for another lobbying trip to Washington, so his acceptance speech was read for him. He called for the Indians to have input into who was to be secretary of the interior, commissioner of Indian affairs, and the reservation superintendents. He called for more land, better stock, and more education for both adults and children. He asked for help and jobs for the young men and women coming back from the war. He concluded by asking for full citizenship with the right to vote, at that time denied to Indians in Arizona and New Mexico.[30]

In March of 1946, Chee and a few other influential Navajos were in Washington lobbying the House and Senate Committees on Indian Affairs for more schools to fulfill the promise of the Treaty of 1868 that there would be a teacher for every thirty students. The gist of their testimony was that only through increased educational opportunities would the Navajos be able to progress.

In that year, Chee ran again for tribal chairman. He had suffered a heart attack in July that led some electors to think he might not be up to the job. When the votes were counted, Sam Ahkeah, who had served under him as vice chairman, got the most votes, and Chee came in second, so Chee was to serve as vice chairman this time.

CHEE IS HOSPITALIZED

But Chee never took office. Around Thanksgiving he became ill with pneumonia, which apparently developed from a cold he contracted while campaigning in the cold, wintry weather.[31] On November 26, 1946, he entered Sage Memorial Hospital in Ganado, where he was cared for by his old friend Dr. Clarence Salsbury. Navajo Agency Superintendent Fryer visited Chee in the hospital and was surprised to see how pale his skin was where it had not been exposed to the weather for eighty-seven years. He came away convinced that Chee was the son of Captain Dodge.[32]

Dr. Salsbury visited Chee every morning to cheer him up, but one day the old chief insisted on knowing the truth about his condition. Salsbury then admitted to Chee that he was very sick.[33]

Chee had been baptized as a Catholic in 1932 during a previous illness. When he realized the end was near, he called for last rites, which were performed by the Reverend Francis Borgman. In a short biography of Chee, Borgman declared that Chee did not understand all the obligations of Catholicism, but he had wanted to enter the church because of his long-term relationship to the Franciscan Fathers. "I was always on your side," Chee told Father Borgman from his deathbed.

LIFE ENDS FOR "MR. INTERPRETER"

During Chee's hospitalization, Annie gave birth to her eighth living child, whom she named Lorencita. Despite her many responsibilities at Tanner Springs, she and Chee's other children and their spouses attended him faithfully, sitting by his bed day and night. One evening, Chee told them that he didn't have much time left. He looked solemnly at his two sons and two daughters and said, "Do not let my straight rope fall to the ground. If you discover it dropping, quickly one of you pick it up and hold it aloft and straight." Later that night he said he was going to pray and began to murmur some traditional Navajo prayers. Then he slipped into unconsciousness. At 6 A.M. on January 7, 1947, he died.[34]

By dawn, the news that the old chief was dead was spreading across the Navajo Reservation. The reaction of the Navajos to Chee Dodge's death was extraordinary. Navajos believe that no matter how good a person was in life, there is an evil component that, after death, can become a dangerous ghost and harm the living. Navajos also avoid much discussion of anyone who has died.[35] In Chee's case, however, the Navajo Tribal Council, meeting for their midwinter session just a few hours after Chee's death, approved a memorial resolution to their late chairman and adjourned the session for five weeks in respect.

Two days after Chee's death, the Franciscan Fathers at St. Michael's held a high requiem mass. Father Berard Haile, with whom Chee had worked long hours on translation and with whom he had shared many a meal and traded hundreds of stories, conducted the service, delivering the memorial sermon in the Navajo language. The bishop of Gallup also participated in the service, and priests from around the reservation came to sing or otherwise take part. Crowded into the little mission church with room for a hundred were more than three hundred people, most of them Navajos but also government officials, traders, and business associates.[36]

It was cold and foggy the morning Chee was buried, and the frost was thick on the sagebrush and pinyons. On the way to the funeral, Annie and her siblings were following in a car behind the hearse, which appeared to Annie to be covered with clouds. When the hearse finally turned off the highway and followed the long driveway that leads to the mission, the clouds rose and vanished. "I guess the Holy Spirit has finally taken him," Annie said.[37]

One hundred cars made a mile-long procession following the casket to a small veterans' cemetery established for Navajo war dead midway between Window Rock and Fort Defiance.

A resolution to the Navajo Tribal Council after Chee's death read: "When the Navajo Tribal Council meets next Tuesday at Window Rock, it will be for the first time since the death of our renowned and colorful leader, Chee Dodge. To many of our people, this council shall appear like a ship that has lost its captain; for at every previous meeting we have been encouraged with the confidence that in Chee we had a most capable representative, who not only knew and understood our problems, but also was about to present them with force and intelligence. . . . With his death we have lost our mightiest friend, the grandest old man of our tribe and its most illustrious member. His mind was our mind; his thoughts our thoughts; his words our words, his interests our interests; and even though he has been criticized for some of the things he said and did, the ultimate result was in practically every instance our benefit and gain."[38]

Two years later, on May 27, 1949, a gray granite monument supported by dark red concrete slabs and inscribed in Navajo and English was installed at his grave. After Chee's name and the dates of his birth and death, it reads simply: "The former Mister Interpreter here permanently lies in the Earth."[39]

II

On the Navajo Tribal Council

4

A Battle against Tuberculosis

CHEE'S PASSING left a leadership gap in both the tribe and his family. He was the center of his children's lives and the grand old man of the Navajos, respected by everyone except the Shiprock contingent, which continued to feel he had betrayed them during early negotiations for oil leases.

CHEE'S ESTATE IS DIVIDED

Dividing up his estate was not an easy job, as it included property, jewelry, valuable rugs, treasury notes, savings bonds, and outstanding loans. Estimates put its value between $200,000 and $300,000. Much of his jewelry and legal paperwork was in several large safes. As Chee lay dying, he tried to remember the combination to the safes and whisper it to his son Tom. But his memory failed, and Tom had to hire a safecracker to open the vaults. One account says that an appraiser was brought in to separate the jewelry and rugs and other goods into four large piles of equal value, and that each of Chee's children got to choose a portion. During a later discussion in the Tribal Council on opening a Navajo bank on the reservation, Annie revealed that the family had had to pay lawyers tens of thousands of dollars to straighten out some of the legalities and recover some of the invested funds, a situation she felt would not have pertained had the bank been controlled by the Navajos.[1]

Chee's daughter Mary and son-in-law Carl Peshlakai continued to operate part of the ranch at Sonsola, Ben took another section of it, and Annie and George remained at Tanner Springs. Tom had left the reservation and was working for the Bureau of Indian Affairs (BIA) at various reservations throughout the West.

One of the pieces of property Chee left was an abandoned

trading post near White Rock in southern Utah, halfway between Aneth and Mexican Hat. Annie's daughter Irma remembers that from time to time her parents would drive there to check on the buildings, but they always made sure to take water with them because Annie thought the water from the well there tasted oily. Eventually the family determined that the place was just a burden and sold it. Sure enough, the new owners discovered oil. When Irma protested, "Mother, we could have been rich!" Annie took it in her usual no-nonsense manner, saying "Well, what's done is done."[2]

A CHILD IS BORN

Annie was devastated by her father's death. He was such an overwhelming presence in her life that she had never considered life without him. Decision making regarding the running of the ranch was in their hands now, but otherwise life continued much as it had before for the Waunekas. Even after stock reduction, running Tanner Springs was a big job. By all accounts, although George worked hard, it was Annie who took over from her father as the boss of the outfit. The Waunekas also continued to add to their family. In 1950 Annie gave birth to her last child, a daughter named Sallie, who was mildly disabled.

The birth process began while George and Annie were still at the ranch, and all did not go smoothly. Sallie Lippincott Wagner, who with her husband ran the nearest trading post, writes about the event in her book *Wide Ruins: Memories from a Navajo Trading Post*. "Some of our more hair-raising trips were over the dirt road to the north. That was the route to the missionary hospital at Ganado and many were the Navajos whom we rushed there, badly injured, deathly sick or about to give birth. Annie Wauneka was one of the latter. Her husband, George, had come running into the store bug-eyed and pale. His wife had gone into labor but had trouble so he loaded her into a truck and, with a sublime faith in our abilities, brought her to us. But the baby arrived en route to the post and there they were out in front of the store, baby and all. However, Annie had retained the placenta and was in agony. The sand and dust were blowing. I took the baby inside and frantically phoned the Ganado Hospital for advice. I was told to put her in the back of our station wagon and get her to the hospital *quick!!* So while Bill put a mattress on the floor of the car and eased Annie onto it, I rushed around collecting sheets, blankets and clean clothes. I wrapped the baby up in such a bundle that from then on I had trouble remembering which end was which. We managed to get to the hospital all right—the doctor said just in time—but the new mother was delirious and once I thought that she was dying. George stayed to give his wife transfusions, but late that night he turned up at Wide Ruins half-starved and needing to be fed."[3] The baby was named for Sallie Lippincott. In a few days Annie and baby Sallie were back at the ranch.

RANCH LIFE

A varying number of employees and relatives helped out with the work of caring for all the children and the livestock. One of them was Ben Yazzie, who had begun working as a sheepherder for Chee at Sonsola Buttes and later transferred down to Tanner Springs. He lived with his family in two hogans in the southwest part of the ranch at the base of La Pinta Mesa. During some parts of the year, Ben Yazzie and his wife and children would take a wagon and camp out as he moved the sheep around to find fresh pasture. When the water holes dried up, he brought the sheep back to the headquarters so they could be watered at the spring. During the periods when the work increased, such as when the lambs were born or the sheep were dipped to control disease or the cattle were branded, other herders and ranch hands would be added to the payroll.

Ben's daughter Lydia Yazzie Whiterock was just a youngster in those years and remembered busy days with everyone sitting down to breakfast together in the Wauneka's house at what seemed to her at the time a huge table. The food was hearty: Cream of Wheat, fried potatoes, fry bread, homemade biscuits, and coffee. Navajos drink their coffee weak, and at that time it was considered an appropriate drink for children. Sometimes coffee was healthier for the children than plain water because at least it meant that the water had been boiled. Although the Waunekas had access to good water, many households had to rely on water brought in by a fifty-five-gallon drum from places where it had been exposed to numerous sources of contamination.

By that time Annie's half sister Ann Shirley from Sawmill was living with the family, looking after the children, and helping with the cooking and other household tasks. Toward noon, Ann Shirley would pack lunches for everyone, and the head herder's daughter, Lydia, would climb on her father's old paint horse and ride out to deliver them to the other herders working on the range with the sheep. All activities centered on the ranch headquarters, and except for Annie, those living there rarely left the place.

"I felt we were away from civilization," Lydia remembers, adding that she did not leave the ranch until she was four and a half or five years old. "One year, we had sheared the sheep, and this time I got to go along to the trader's down on Highway 66. My Grandpa Wauneka had a huge truck that we used to take bags and bags of wool to market. When we brought the wool in, we got a free Coke, in those little bottles like they used to have. I was so excited, I thought, 'Oh boy.' I remember I took a couple of swallows and immediately gave it back to my mom. It was too strong! When we got there, it was the first time I had seen white people. The trader had kids about our age. They were all running around there in the store with blond hair and light eyes. I just kept looking at them. When we were going home, I asked my parents whether that kid who was so white could see with his gray eyes." The pale eyes were such a contrast to all the dark eyes she had seen previously that the child appeared blind to her.[4]

While overseeing the ranching operations and the employees, Annie continued to work with the Klagetoh chapter as secretary, helping with the continuing problems with stock reduction and interpreting for Navajos who sought the help of the white doctors at the nearby hospital at Ganado. For four years she mulled over her father's dying wish, interpreting "Do not let my straight rope fall to the ground" as a desire to have his work for the Navajo People carried on. Tom was established in a career off the reservation; Mary was not interested in public life. That left her and Ben.

As the elections for Tribal Council approached, Annie began

talking openly about her possible candidacy, asking the opinion of the men and women in her district. The women—who had been able to vote since 1928, eight years after other American women had gained suffrage—were supportive, as were some of the men. The older, traditional Navajo men, particularly some of the medicine men, told her that she needed to stay home, do her chores, and take care of her children.

ANNIE RUNS FOR TRIBAL COUNCIL

But the die had been cast years before, and Annie decided to run, even though Lorencita was only four and Sallie was still just a toddler. Her opponents were two men, one of them a medicine man. Like any well-bred Navajo, she knew that the medicine man deserved respect. Annie did not speak against him while campaigning but just kept vowing that, if chosen, she would do her best. Of course, in this society everyone knew that she was Chee Dodge's daughter, and the memories of the late leader were still fresh.

Actually, the prospect of having a woman in a position of authority was not so unusual to Navajos. Traditionally, Navajo women owned their own flocks of sheep and controlled the home, the children, and the family's economics. The small groups that lived together and shared subsistence duties were organized around a head mother, whose opinions and desires were listened to and usually acted upon. Women were also actively involved in the decision-making process at the chapter level. Navajo author Ruth Roessel writes, "In many, if not in most chapters, it appears that men wait for the women to make motions or to determine the direction in which they feel the community should go before they enter the discussion."[5] The fact that the Tribal Council, with only one exception, had consisted of men was not something the Navajos had designed for themselves. When the first tribal councils were constituted, they were orchestrated by Washington bureaucrats—white men living in a society where their mothers, wives, and daughters were not allowed to vote.

Roessel writes that "in the early days of Navajo history, men expected and welcomed the participation of women in roles of leadership and decision-making."[6] However, that excluded the top rung of leadership. A Navajo myth tells of Woman Chief, who lived in the underworld and ruled so badly that her policies led to a complete break between men and women for four years. After a wise owl brought the men and women together, the men assumed the position of rulers.[7] Annie, however, was not running for Tribal Council chairman; she was seeking only the opportunity to be one of the council representatives.

The election was held March 5 and 6, 1951. For the first time on the reservation, formal secret ballots were used with photographs of the candidates beside their names. Those Navajos who could not read could vote by picture. Across the reservation, more than 75 percent of the eligible voters participated, some of them traveling sixty miles by driving a wagon over rugged roads or on horseback to reach the polling stations.[8] When the votes were counted, Annie had won a seat on the Tribal Council representing the chapters of Klagetoh and Wide Ruins. She was forty-one years old—healthy, politically astute, and more than ready to move into her new life.

Although it has been widely written that Annie was the first woman on the Tribal Council, in fact she was preceded by Lily J. Neil of Huerfano, New Mexico, who had served the previous four years and had been reelected. Neil was known as "talking woman" because she was not afraid to air her views, but she was badly injured in a car accident and resigned. When Annie was installed on March 20, 1951, fourteen days after the election, she was the lone woman. Two of her half brothers were installed with her: Ben Dodge, representing Crystal, and Justin Shirley, Kee'hanabah's son from Sawmill.

Annie was sworn into the Navajo Tribal Council in the Council Chambers built at the base of the Window Rock six miles south of Fort Defiance. The Window Rock is a towering sandstone formation with a hole, or window, through it. For as long as the Navajos have inhabited the area, the Window Rock has been an important shrine. Medicine men brought bottles to gather water for the Water Way ceremony, which was held to bring abundant rain. The council chambers are built in the shape of a large hogan, and around the interior walls runs a long mural depicting important events in history of the Navajo Tribe. Chee Dodge figures prominently in one of the sections. The chambers were built in 1936 when Indian Commissioner Collier decided that a new Navajo Central Agency was needed. Also constructed at that time were large low buildings to house the BIA offices. All the buildings are constructed of russet sandstone quarried in the vicinity.

AN ENERGETIC BEGINNING

In the years since Annie had lurked in the back of the chapter meeting, too shy to speak, she had learned to be forthright with her opinions. A review of the Tribal Council minutes over the years shows that new delegates usually do not take part in the discussions during their first months on the council. They watch their seasoned colleagues to see how to proceed. Not Annie. In her very first meeting as a council delegate, she stood up and, when recognized, launched into a relatively lengthy discussion of the Advisory Council, a smaller group that made recommendations to the larger body. She suggested a revision in the way the Advisory Council members were selected and slipped in the information that her predecessor had never brought back any information from the Advisory Council to the chapter. Her objections made the front page of the next day's *Gallup Independent,* but within the council her suggestions were neither acknowledged nor acted upon.[9]

Undaunted, the next day she was back on her feet, accusing the general superintendent of the reservation, a white BIA appointee, of approving resolutions without bothering to acquaint himself with the desires of the Navajo People. Later, she complained that the superintendent sat in the front of the council next to the chairman and continually whispered in his ear. She thought it made Chairman Sam Ahkeah look like a puppet, and it certainly did not appear as if the Tribal Council were exercising "self-government" if a white man was directing things. Soon after that, the superintendent no longer sat in front, although, of course, his real behind-the-scenes power was in no way diminished.

Like her fellow council members—and elected officials every-where—Annie was having to learn to work with the established bureaucracy, in this case the Bureau of Indian Affairs, which controlled the purse strings to the Navajos' money and had the final word on new programs. There is ample evidence that she found the presence of this "big brother" agency irritating.

In August, Annie was at a conference in Gallup speaking in her forthright way on the need for development—more and bigger schools, hospitals and sanatoriums, and water development in the form of deep wells and irrigation projects.

In her speech she addressed the need for more Navajo input in the direction of their own affairs, a theme she would return to often. She addressed young people training to be teachers, saying, "You must come back to your people after you finish your training . . . and try to make it a better land to live on. Of course you might have to fight to get a job and bump a white man off his desk, but we will help you do that. We need Navajos as teachers, social workers, doctors, nurses, clerks, stenographers, engineers, business mangers and even superintendents."

After railing against the purchase by the BIA of house trailers at $16,000 apiece to accommodate staff as well as the presence of the white staff in the first place, she concluded, "The Navajos must put forth all their efforts to rid Window Rock of incompetent and useless officials and get Navajos into as many jobs as possible. Otherwise we will be like monkeys in a cage for the rest of the Americans to look at." [10]

Over the next three decades that Annie would serve the tribe, she would have good and close relationships with a number of the white officials who worked for various government offices serving the Navajos, but she continued to be irked when money appropriated for Navajo needs ended up supporting bureaucrats instead. She wasn't so much anti-white as she was enthusiastically pro-Navajo.

ANNIE'S FIRST TRIP TO WASHINGTON

The following January, the Advisory Council was making plans to go to Washington DC to represent the tribe. At that time it was

not unusual for some of the council members to come to meetings slightly inebriated, feeling that a little alcohol loosened their
tongues and made them better orators. Then, as now, alcohol was
not sold on the reservation, and when some Navajos found themselves in a place where they could buy drinks freely, they tended
to overindulge. This, apparently was the concern when, during a
council session, one of the delegates suggested that Annie, being
the only woman on the council, go along to Washington "to make
it a habit to look after the Advisory Council." After a discussion
of whether the members of the council could be trusted not to
become intoxicated on the trip, and whether Annie needed to go
along, another member declared, "I say Mr. Wauneka is the man
to say whether she should go or not. We will have to talk to him
if we insist that she go and it is up to him to decide."[11]

Apparently the other council members didn't know how
things worked down at the Tanner Springs ranch. On February 8,
1952, Annie accompanied the Advisory Council members when
they boarded the Santa Fe Chief at 5:45 A.M. for the trip to Washington. As the years rolled by, her trips to Washington were so
frequent as to become nearly routine, but we can imagine how
exciting this first trip must have been for a woman who had rarely
been off the reservation and never outside of Arizona and New
Mexico.

WIDESPREAD TUBERCULOSIS INFECTION DISCOVERED
On the very day in February 1952 that the Navajo delegation was
visiting the White House, an unrelated event occurred that was
to have a profound effect on Annie's life. Newspapers reported
that a new drug to control tuberculosis—the most powerful drug
known—had been discovered in New York City.[12] Previously, a
group of young doctors from New York Hospital, which was affiliated with Cornell University, had gone to the Navajo Reservation to investigate an epidemic of infectious hepatitis that had
broken out in the BIA Boarding School at Tuba City on the northern fringe of the reservation. Working under the direction of
Dr. Walsh McDermott, chairman of the Department of Public
Health and Preventive Medicine at Cornell, the doctors treated

the three hundred sick children and soon had the outbreak under control. But what they found on the reservation, in addition, was widespread tuberculosis—nine or ten times the level of infection that existed in the general American population. As a result of this, a major effort was made to get more infected Navajos into hospitals. But doctors did not have much to offer except rest and healthy food. The body was supported, but lung tissues had to heal themselves. For some people this worked, but many died.

Now, with the new discovery, doctors could provide more than hope. Although the drug—isonicotinic acid hydrazide—was of proven worth, the full power of it was not yet known. The group of doctors from Cornell came back to the Navajo Reservation with a supply of the drug donated by the E. R. Squibb Company to treat the worst cases of tuberculosis among the Indians. Headed by Dr. McDermott, the team originally offered to help infected children in the small Tuba City hospital. Later, they began to administer it to patients at Fort Defiance Hospital.

Although the drug was provided at no charge and the doctors were donating their time, funds were needed for them to travel back and forth from their university. During the April council session, Annie made a motion, seconded by her half brother Justin Shirley, that the tribe put up $10,000 to be used exclusively to transport these doctors between New York and the reservation.[13] The measure was passed, and the council asked that the doctors report back to them on how their work was progressing.

In August another doctor was addressing the Tribal Council, reporting that all of the TB beds at the Fort Defiance hospital had been filled and that Congress had appropriated about $350,000 to pay for the use of about 400 beds in other parts of the Southwest for Navajos with tuberculosis. Many of the delegates rose to protest that the money should be used to build more hospitals on the reservation. Furthermore, they contended, Indians were not welcome in many communities. How would the Navajos be treated if they had to leave the reservation? The doctor tried to reassure the delegates, and then Annie arose to speak. She said that they should all feel grateful for the funds and that it was up to all of them to tell their constituents that they could go to the hospital for treatment. She added that after the sick people had the information, it was up to them whether to seek treatment.[14] As previously discussed, this is a typical Navajo sentiment, the Diné being generally noncoercive when it comes to others' behavior. In a paper on practicing social work among the Navajos, Jimm Good Tracks, a social worker and school guidance counselor, wrote: "Any kind of intervention is contrary to the Indian's strict adherence to the principle of self-determination. The less assimilated and acculturated the individual, the more important this principle is to him. . . . In native Indian society, no interference or meddling of any kind is allowed or tolerated, even when it is to keep the other person from doing something foolish or dangerous." Later he states, "The Indian child is taught that complete noninterference in interaction with all people is the norm, and that he should react with amazement, irritation, mistrust, and anxiety to even the slightest indication of manipulation or coercion."[15]

It was probably this belief that one had no right to tell someone else what to do that was guiding Annie that day when she was suggesting giving the tubercular Navajos the facts on treatment and hospitalization and then letting them decide for themselves whether to seek the white doctors' help. However, as the years passed, she came to change her opinion on this situation profoundly.

The subject of the need for more hospitals was to come up again and again in Tribal Council discussions. Although the government officials did not deny the need for more beds, they tried to explain to the council that building a new hospital meant not only funds for the hospital itself, but would require adding infrastructure such as water, sewers, electricity, and telephones to areas not served by these utilities. It would also necessitate building proper housing for the doctors and nurses—all of them white and from outside the area—as well as training of auxiliary staff. Getting enough doctors to come to the remote reservation was a struggle, and for years the BIA Division of Public Health and later the U.S. Public Health Service relied on doctors who volunteered for duty as a way of discharging their expected public service and avoiding the draft.

A WORKING MOTHER FACES PRESSURE

Annie joined wholeheartedly in all of these discussions both in the council and committee meetings and in private meetings with public health officials. Her energy and intellect grew with the challenges. But on the home front, life was getting complicated. Because of the bad roads and the great distances some of the delegates had to travel between their homes and Window Rock, the tribe provided a group of small rooms and apartments where the council delegates could spend the night during sessions. Although Annie made use of these quarters occasionally, during this period she was usually driving back and forth between Tanner Springs and Window Rock every day the council was in session, a round trip of about 150 miles. Sometimes George went with her, but he was not as fond of the endless political wrangling as Annie was, and on the days he accompanied her, he usually left the discussion after a while and sat in the pickup or chatted with other Navajos outside. More often, he, along with Ann Shirley and the Yazzies, watched over the house, the children, and the stock.

At this time Annie also began what was a career-long attempt to stay in touch with those who had elected her, so she drove to isolated hogans and attended meetings and ceremonials where people gathered and talked about their concerns. In those days Tribal Council members on official business wore a badge, hence Annie gained the nickname "Woman with a Badge."

Fortunately the Waunekas made enough money off their ranching operation to support the family. Frequently family funds subsidized Annie's work. In 1952 council members were paid $25 a day salary and per diem plus 10 cents a mile for the days the council was in session. Sometimes the Tribal Council would conclude its monthly business in a week; other times it would take much longer to hash out difficult issues, such as the annual budget. Members were also annually allotted fifteen meeting days with constituents at $9 a day, which added a total of $135 to the salary every year.[16] Annie far exceeded this number meeting with her constituents. Lydia Whiterock remembers wondering if this woman who had previously been such a constant presence in their lives had established another home somewhere since she was gone so much. She was left to wonder even more when her father said one day that Mrs. Wauneka was going to be gone for two weeks. This was probably for the first trip to Washington DC.

The pressures on Annie were in many ways no different than those faced by any working mother, especially those with a long commute. She was helped by the presence of her half sister Ann Shirley and her husband's willingness to be both mother and father to the children for periods of time long before that role had any sanction in either the white or Navajo culture. Like fathers in most cultures, Navajo fathers are openly affectionate with their children, play with them, and take an interest in their lives. So with George's involvement and Ann Shirley's help, the household continued to function more or less normally. Before long, however, Ann Shirley came to feel that the household where she'd helped out so long was too tumultuous for her. The endless discussions of politics were too great a contrast to the peaceful life she had led and wanted to continue to lead, and so she left.[17]

We don't know whether Ann Shirley's departure was the determining factor or if it was just one of a number of complications, but Annie eventually decided that all the children who were able to attend school should be put in St. Michael's boarding school just outside of Window Rock, where the nuns could watch over them. This included the Yazzie children, since they were part of the household. Lydia was only four, quite young to be away from home. On the day that Annie took all of the children to be enrolled in the school with the big sandstone block buildings, Lydia was terrified of the nuns in their black habits and white wimples and thought they were monsters. Years later Lydia asked her mother why she'd put her in school at such a young age. Her mother told her that "Mrs." (Annie) had said it was time for her to be in school, and apparently Lydia's mother didn't feel that she had any choice in the matter. Lydia's father, Ben Yazzie, being uneducated, always deferred to Annie and relied on her to make good decisions for his family. When shearing time came, Annie took part of the wool from Ben Yazzie's flocks as reimbursement for the tuition she had paid to St. Michael's on behalf of her herder. Later on the Yazzie children transferred to schools where the board and tuition were free.[18]

ANNIE IS HANDED THE TB PROBLEM

Meanwhile, in the council and committee meetings, talk of tuberculosis continued. In January 1953, the Cornell medical team made a report to the Navajo Tribal Council. They gave information about the forms of tuberculosis and said that the new drug was working well on the Navajo patients who were receiving it. However, despite access to the latest treatment methods, vast numbers of Navajos with tuberculosis were not being seen by doctors, and the disease was spreading. The speech had been carefully worked out with a team member who was an anthropologist and linguist, so that the concepts would be understandable to the medically unsophisticated council members, but they would not feel like they were being talked down to. Chairman Sam Ahkeah and the other delegates got the message and knew some response to the crisis was necessary.

What happened next in a council meeting in June 1953 has been retold dozens of times by Annie herself and by others recounting her story.

"Doctors reported that the tuberculosis was killing Navajos like flies," Annie said. "This man [a council delegate], he got up and looked around and said, 'Where's the lady?' He said, 'You women can take care of the sick far better than we men can. So let's appoint her and get her to work.' I'd heard about the tuberculosis, but there was nothing I knew about tuberculosis. They didn't even give me a chance to say yes or no. Made a motion, second, voted and I was in. I had my work cut out."[19]

The first step, however, was to go home and tell George that she was the chair of the new Health and Welfare section of the Community Services Committee and in this position had to help deal with the tuberculosis problem. For once, George was not supportive. He was sure that she was going to infect the family.

"You stay off of that," he told her. "Here we are living healthy and you're going to bring home this disease."[20]

But she thought about the old people coughing through the days and nights, spitting blood in their dark hogans. There was also the inalterable image of the many weeks she had spent as a child nursing other students during the flu epidemic. She had been able to do nothing for them and had watched helplessly as they suffered and died. Such traumatic childhood experiences burn into the human memory bank and affect decisions in profound ways. Annie had not been able to help much back in 1918, but maybe now she could do something to save Navajo lives. As the council member who nominated Annie to head the Health and Welfare section indicated, Navajo women, like mothers the world over, watched over the health of their families. In many cases this meant gathering and dispensing herbal medicines. Older women sometimes became medicine women, although the percentage of those who learned the complicated ceremonials that allowed them to be singers was low compared to the men who did so. Annie would not become a medicine woman in the traditional way, but there was a place in her society for what she was to do.

Annie's decision to accept the challenge of chairing what soon became the Health and Welfare Committee, committing all of her formidable will and energy to tackling the tuberculosis problem, was the major event that defined the next thirty years of her life, eventually thrusting her to the national platform of Indian health care concerns.

In July 1953, Dr. Kurt Deuschle, a BIA doctor at Fort Defiance Hospital who was working on the Cornell University project, came to give the Tribal Council an update on the progress of the fight against the disease. Annie listened closely as he began with an explanation: "Tuberculosis, as you know it, most commonly affects a person's lung, but it can also affect his brain and bone, his bowels and his kidneys. We know that this condition is caused by a living, growing organism, which cannot be seen by the naked eye. It is necessary to take an instrument, called a microscope, and examine the sputum or spit of a person having tuberculosis and through one of those he sees the tubercle—which appears as a small, red worm—and it is this organism which causes tuberculosis. I think it is very important to point out that the way tuberculosis is spread is through the cough of a person who has tuberculosis of the lung. When he coughs he sprays out these germs, these little red worms. The healthy person that breathes the air in which this spray is found, is subject to tuberculosis. As many as ten others can get tuberculosis from that one person."

After he explained the importance of a patient entering a sanatorium for bed rest and treatment with the new medicine, Dr. Deuschle got to the central point of his speech—the failure of patients to stay in the hospital until they were cured. Of the 300 Navajo patients who had been sent to off-reservation hospitals during the previous ten months, 63 had left after writing letters to their relatives asking to be picked up and taken home. This behavior could, perhaps, be understood from the patients sent to hospitals off the reservation who found themselves far away from their families and their culture. But those who stayed nearer to home were behaving the same way. Of the approximately 100 TB patients at the Fort Defiance Hospital, 33 had left.

"This is a very sad picture," Dr. Deuschle advised the delegates. "First it hurts the person who has left the sanatorium. That means that he will get sick again and either die or be readmitted to another sanatorium. In addition to this, that person again has the opportunity to infect and spread the disease to his own family, to his relatives and friends. Another unfortunate thing that happens is that the drugs which are very powerful and very, very effective, lose their effectiveness against these germs if the treatment is stopped. People who return later and go into the sanatorium may find that those drugs are no longer as strong as when they entered the sanatorium so the first opportunity of treatment carried out to completion is the most important thing to get people well."

He also advised them that the waste in money for these patients who left before being cured was probably about a quarter of a million dollars annually. Although the U.S. government was paying the bills out of allocated funds, there was no assurance that the funds would be replenished when they were all spent.

Having told of his frustrations, he then turned to the Tribal Council, asking the question that had these doctors stymied: "Why do people leave before treatment is completed and what do we do about it?" Later on, during questioning, he said he did not favor regulations mandating that patients remain until discharged, which, in effect, would turn the hospitals into prisons. He preferred education instead so that patients would understand why they needed to remain until their course of treatment was concluded.[21]

Annie was not content to ponder and philosophize. Wanting to see the situation for herself, she asked if Dr. Deuschle could arrange for her to accompany a nurse to visit the patients. The doctor, as well as some of the other delegates, agreed that this would be a good idea.

THE NAVAJO VIEW OF ILLNESS

The problem of why the patients were fleeing the hospital went to the very heart of the Navajo culture. A brief look at the tribal beliefs surrounding sickness gives an idea of the profound disparity that existed between those views and modern medicine. It was a wonder that any Navajos stayed in the hospitals at all.

Navajos classify diseases by cause rather than by symptom, maintaining that all trouble and illness are a result of a state of disharmony with the surrounding world, other people, and the supernatural environment. When all things in the universe are in tune, people have good health. But countless events can upset this harmony to cause sickness: a person can have a bad dream, break a taboo, or come into contact with such contaminating forces as spirits of the dead, non-Navajos, or Navajo witches. A whole range of animals, including snakes, bears, coyotes, and porcupines, can bring illness. Touching a tree struck by lightning or gathering and cooking with the wood from such a tree was thought to be a cause of tuberculosis.

Many Navajos also do not make a distinction between religion and medicine, considering them aspects of the same entity.

The patients, once they feel ill, do not act on their own but instead consult with their immediate family. The family calls in a diagnostician, who by various techniques—a common method is by hand trembling—discovers the cause of the illness. It could be the result of an evil thought years before or a chance encounter with an unclean animal. After the diagnostician has indicated the root of the illness and suggests what "sing" or ceremony should be performed, someone in the family looks for a medicine man who knows the required ceremony. All the relatives cooperate to come up with the money to pay the medicine man his fee, sometimes many hundreds of dollars.

Most Navajos put great trust in the punctilious ritualistic performance of the medicine man as he follows a complicated ceremony—from one to nine days long—and continually assures the patient that all is well. The ceremony might include massages, heat treatments, and the ingestion of medicinal herbs and emetics to promote vomiting for internal cleansing. The singer usually insists that whatever talking the attendees do among themselves concern subjects of health and strength, of times people were treated by "sings" and got well, of good crops and fat animals. The people at the ceremonial include nearly all the patient's relatives and friends. He or she knows that all these people have gathered for the express purpose of focusing their attention on the patient, bringing their influence and expectation to bear on the illness.[22]

That stands in contrast to what went on in the hospital. The patient was taken out of the bosom of the family, even sent to another state. Not only was the hospital filled with strangers, but the patients became strangers to themselves and each other as their familiar clothing was put away and they had to wear hospital gowns or pajamas and eat unfamiliar foods. Most were unaccustomed to sleeping in a bed or living by the clock. The meals were no doubt nutritious and deemed appropriate by the hospital dietitian, but they were certainly unrelated to their usual mutton and fry bread. Navajos are very modest and do not undress even in front of their spouses. Undressing for a physical was highly embarrassing. They did not understand what a thermometer was for or why a nurse would want to take their pulse. The doctors didn't stay with them continually, as the medicine man did, but came and went at long intervals. When the doctors did come, they were always asking them how they felt, pressing and poking them. The Navajo hand trembler or diagnostician did not need to ask; he or she told the patient what was wrong.[23]

Furthermore, every Navajo knew that many people died in hospitals, leaving these cold, large, white rooms filled with ghost spirits that would probably make you really ill even if you had entered healthy. Because Navajos tended to wait until their relatives were deathly ill before bringing them into the hospital, and because the few reservation hospitals were ill equipped and poorly staffed, the chances for getting out alive were not good. Robert Trennert writes, in his study of Indian health care, "Records kept by the Navajo Medical Center in Ft. Defiance showed that between January 1, 1939 and November 1, 1940, a total of 343 tuberculosis patients were hospitalized, 230 of whom died."[24]

When Navajos did decide to seek modern medical care, they were more attracted to the mission hospitals, which were usually better staffed and supplied than the crude government hospitals.[25] From time to time a doctor would be posted to the reservation who had a particular empathy for Navajos and insight into their way of life. One of these, Dr. Clarence Salsbury, who had cared for Chee Dodge until the end, was a missionary rather than a government doctor. He practiced in a private hospital in Ganado supported by the Presbyterians. Although he had trouble convincing some of the Navajos in the area that they should come to the hospital when necessary, he eventually became so trusted that even medicine men came in for help and sent their families.

Dr. Salsbury, however, did not have the facilities to provide the long-term treatment needed by the many Navajos suffering from tuberculosis, so they had to go to government hospitals where the medical staffs were well meaning but unwilling to modify standard medical practice to accommodate cultural differences.

ANNIE VISITS TB PATIENTS

All of these anomalies separating Navajo and Western views of medicine Annie knew so deeply in her consciousness that she probably wouldn't have even been able to articulate them when she first began her assignment. What she didn't know about was tuberculosis and how to explain it to her people.

She went to Dr. Deuschle, telling him that he would have to educate her about the disease because she did not want to be "runnin' out there and tellin' those people something I don't know." So for three months she went to the Fort Defiance hospital and studied tuberculosis and sanitation. This woman with the eleventh-grade education read books Dr. Deuschle gave her, talked to patients, and looked at sputum under the microscope and X-rays on the light box.

"I wanted to see with my own eyes what kind of bugs the doctors were talking about. I had to know there actually were germs," she said. "To explain to other Navajos about tuberculosis, I had to find out all about it—what it could do to a human being, where it came from."[26] Every time she saw Chairman Ahkeah he asked if she had gone to visit the patients yet. He and the other council members were anxious for her to get going with the education program, but she reminded him that the disease had been around for a long time, and she would go only when she knew what she was talking about.

Finally Annie felt she was ready. She got in her pickup and started driving to the hospitals. First she went to a hospital in Colorado Springs with more than four hundred Navajo TB patients. When the Woman with the Badge would walk in and start addressing the sick Navajos in their own language, they initially thought she was there to take them home. Instead they soon discovered her message was quite different—they would have to stay in the hospital, maybe six more months, maybe two more years, depending on how sick they were.

First, she would explain what she had learned about tuberculosis, that it was a disease that covered the whole world. "The Navajos thought that they were the only ones who were discovered to have it," she recalled. "That was a sad story. So when I told them that this was a white man's disease, a colored man's disease, this is everywhere, they were relieved. They were relieved."[27] Since there were no words in their language to explain either the disease or the concept of germs, she invented a phrase for the tubercles, calling them in Navajo "bugs that eat the body." At some point in her visit at each hospital, she would have all the Navajo patients come down to the hospital laboratory with her to see their X-rays and their sputum under the microscope, while the doctors pointed out the infected sections of their lungs and the strange organisms that were too small to see with their eyes alone.

Although she understood their depression, she tried to be encouraging. "At home sometimes, you just eat bread and coffee, but here you get three big meals a day. The doctors give you wonderful new drugs. You sleep a lot and pretty soon you can go home cured." [28]

Annie knew that Navajos are very close to their families and their livestock. They worry about their sheep when they are away for only a few days. She carried a bulky tape recorder with her and let each patient make a recording to send home to his or her family. Back on the reservation, she saw that the mothers and fathers and husbands or wives got to listen to the tape of their loved one's voice and were able to make a recording to send back, reassuring the patient that all was well with the family and with the sheep and the horses and urging them to stay in the hospital until they were well.

After her trip to Colorado Springs she went to Tucson to visit the patients at Barfield Sanatorium, to New Mexico to visit Valmora and Fort Stanton, both near Albuquerque. Annie stayed about a week at each hospital, making the tapes and visiting with the patients while reassuring them that remaining in the hospital was best for them and their families.

Since Annie was frequently away from the reservation, she was often called upon to speak for her people. Apparently her years of work with her father had taught her to weigh her words carefully. When she was in Los Angeles visiting a sanatorium, several television reporters heard she was there and wanted to interview her about starvation on the Navajo Reservation. She must have sensed an attempt at sensationalism because she declined the invitation, explaining that she felt that any publicity would not bring out the full truth.

Now, having spent more time learning about tuberculosis and its devastating effects on both the individuals and their families, she changed her mind from her first public comment on the issue—that people should be told about the availability of hospital care and allowed to decide for themselves—to being a strong advocate of patients entering the hospital and staying there until they were cured.

OTHER COUNCIL ISSUES

Although tuberculosis was a major problem for the Navajos and their government, it was not the only situation that needed attention in this huge area that was similar in development and resources to a Third World country. During this period the reservation was even more depressed economically due to a string of years in which the weather was unfavorable for stock raising. Furthermore, many Navajo servicemen had arrived home from World War II to a difficult situation—they'd lost their grazing permits during the stock reduction and were unable to find wage work. In the winter of 1948–49 a series of severe blizzards and unprecedented snowfalls accompanied by bitter cold resulted in the loss of nearly half the year's lamb crop and about a quarter of the cattle. This was followed by several years of drought, which further reduced the flocks.

Then in October of 1953, a disease called bluetongue, originally from Africa, began afflicting Navajo sheep, mainly in district seventeen—Annie's district. The disease could be treated with penicillin, and Annie traveled with the veterinarians throughout the district, explaining to the people about the disease and treatment. However, even though the lambs were cured, the health regulations said they could not be sold until thirty days after their lesions had healed. This left many herders temporarily and seriously short of cash. They had been buying groceries on credit from the traders for months or possibly a whole year, and now their bills were due. Some of the traders were willing to buy the lambs, but at a much reduced price since they would have to hold them—and hire somebody to take care of them—until they could be sold. The people Annie was representing were her neighbors and her friends, and she knew they were living close to the margin. She worked with some other council members to pass a resolution for the tribe to put up $24,000 to buy the lambs at the standard market price and hold them until they could be legally sold on the open market.[29]

BACK ON THE ROAD

Once the council session was over, Annie was back to the business of helping to spread the word about modern tuberculosis treatment. Late that summer, Dr. Walsh McDermott, director of the Navajo tuberculosis project, had reported to the Tribal Council that the cutting-edge drug treatment Navajos were receiving in four hospitals—Tuba City, Fort Defiance, Sage Memorial at Ganado, and Winslow—seemed to be working. Half of the patients had shown considerable improvement, one quarter had shown some improvement, and a quarter had not shown any improvement but at least had not gotten worse. He also explained the problem of drug resistance that occurred when people began treatment and then stopped before they were completely cured, and he indicated that if a patient's infection became drug resistant, the germs that this patient would pass on to others would also be drug resistant. He warned that the drugs needed to be used cautiously and also told them that other drugs being tested at New York Hospital might counter the drug resistance problem and would be made available as soon as they were proven safe. He also explained that even when the drug was used successfully, if a great deal of lung tissue had been damaged before the cure, the dead tissue needed to be cut out.

He thanked the council members for their help and encouraged them by saying, "you are ensuring that when patients are brought to the hospital with tuberculosis they get the most up-to-date treatment it is possible to give at any place."[30]

Under questioning, Dr. McDermott estimated that there were between 1,200 and 1,500 active cases of TB among the 75,000 Navajos. Except for the few hundred in the hospitals, these people were spread out over a reservation the size of West Virginia. They were without treatment because they either refused to go to the hospital or had left before they were cured. They were not only jeopardizing their own chances for a cure, but as long as they continued to live in close quarters with other family members, they were spreading the disease.

With renewed resolution, Annie set out to find these people who were so reluctant to take advantage of the white doctors' medicine. She knew it would take a combination of tact, humor, compromise, and doggedness to convince her fellow Navajos that they should seek treatment, but she probably could not have predicted how long or hard she would have to work.

Sometimes she traveled alone. Heading off into the remote corners of the reservation took courage, although there is little indication that she gave much thought to her personal inconvenience or the discomfort and dangers she might encounter. A vehicle breakdown could mean a walk of many, many miles. Even today there are few paved roads to serve the vast reservation. A 1947 government report estimated that there were fewer than one hundred miles of all-weather roads and two thousand miles of dirt roads and tracks. The situation had not improved by the 1950s. The condition of the roads meant that it cost three times more to operate a vehicle on the reservation than it did elsewhere.[31] Frequently Annie found herself heading to a remote hogan on tracks through the sagebrush that existed simply because the household's wagon or pickup had driven that way often enough to crush the grass and bushes. The hard, infrequent rains give these roads the texture of a washboard, and traversing them even slowly can be a bone-jarring experience for the driver and destructive to every part of a modern vehicle. These lonely tracks were never visited by a grader, and Annie spent many hours digging herself out when she got stuck in the mud or sand on roads that were little more than paths.

When night fell, she slept wherever she was. Navajos have a tradition of hospitality, and she found everyone generous even if all they had to share was tea and fry bread. Because of her privileged upbringing, she had slept on beds most of her life, but she did not hesitate to lie down for the night on a few sheepskins next to the fire in a remote hogan. Since she was frequently in the home of an active TB case, she did inspect the source of the water used in the house and insisted that her own water and the cup that she used be boiled. In caring for her own health she was modeling proper sanitation for her hosts, though one wonders if the Navajo families considered her modern or merely odd.

Sometimes she had company on these trips, traveling with another member of the Health and Welfare Committee, a public health nurse, and a driver. Howard McKinley, another Tribal Council representative, was secretary of the Health and Welfare Committee and worked closely with Annie. "There was one young woman out by Crownpoint that they never could find," he remembers. "Every time she would see us coming she would scale up a high cliff and watch us go to her hogan. My approach was to find what clan they belonged to. There was one woman who didn't want to go into the hospital. Nobody could get her in there. I found out that she was in my clan. I went right up to her hogan, met her, and said, 'Mom, I dreamed about you last night. I dreamed that you went to the hospital and got well in a short time.' Since I addressed her in a traditional way, she was more receptive. After we talked a little more she said, 'I'm ready. Let's go.' "[32]

A FEW PATIENTS ARE CURED

During this time Walter Cronkite featured Annie and her work on a program in a television series called *Twentieth Century,* and the nation got to see Annie in action, visiting an elderly woman she had known for years, one of a group termed "recalcitrant patients." Two little girls were playing in the background. Their parents assured Annie that they had been taken in for X-rays, but she conceded to the unseen interviewer that she was not going to take the parents' word for it but was going to check the records at the hospital.

After chatting with the elderly woman for a while, Annie explained: "This lady says that she doesn't need to go to the hospital to cure her tuberculosis. She wants to use this herb over there.

Okay, let's see this herb. This is the medicine she is using for tuberculosis at the moment. (She looks at it in the jar). It is very, very bitter. She says this is for TB, so we have a new discovery here. She says, 'This will cure my tuberculosis.' I say, 'Good old grandma, let's say it will, so take it first and then take your pills.' So she's happy. She says, 'I'll eat my pills along with this bitter liquid.' You kind of have to work with them." [33]

By spring of 1954, Dr. Deuschle was back at the Navajo Tribal Council reporting that fewer and fewer Navajo patients each month were leaving against advice, and that even some of those who had left before being cured were requesting readmission. A dozen patients had been sent back to the reservation cured. Annie's work was taking effect.

But there were still more than a thousand active tuberculosis cases on the reservation, and with each cough, each wad of phlegm expelled on the floor, another young mother, another toddler, another weak old grandfather was exposed to the disease. And when these Navajos did get sick, their first call was to the medicine man. These wise old men—part doctor, part psychiatrist, part herbalist—could cure many Navajo illnesses. Yet even their strongest herbs were no match for tuberculosis. As long as the sick people put their faith in the medicine men and delayed more appropriate treatment, they got sicker and weaker and spread the disease to other members of their household.

Convincing both the medicine men and their patients of this without causing offense or arousing hostility presented a serious challenge. As long as the medicine men were continuing to accept what were clearly tuberculosis cases and treating them with herbs and ceremonials, Annie and her committee and the health officials were constantly in the position of bucking traditional culture. Annie needed to find a way to make the medicine men partners in the modern health care system so that they could continue to treat the problems they could cure while referring their tubercular patients to the white doctors without losing prestige. Until she had the medicine men on board, the struggle against tuberculosis could not advance.

5
The Tuberculosis Campaign Intensifies

EVEN AS LATE AS THE MID-1950S only a small percentage of Navajos had much formal education beyond elementary school. What they knew of the world they had learned from their parents and grandparents. They might know some English, but they spoke mostly Navajo and did most of their business at remote trading posts, rarely venturing into even the few tiny crossroads settlements that passed for towns. Medicine men had tremendous popular support, and anything to do with white people or the Euro-American culture was highly suspect. This is the situation Annie Wauneka faced as she struggled to bridge the gap between what she knew modern medicine could offer her people and their willingness to accept it.

Because of their reluctance to seek help from white doctors, many adults and children died unnecessarily. One who was plucked from the brink of death was Albert Hale, who became an attorney and was president of the Navajo Tribe from 1995 through spring of 1998. He may owe his life to Annie Wauneka's persistent attempts at health education. He grew up in Klagetoh, and Annie had clan ties to his family. She would visit his parents occasionally, and as she did everywhere, she gave her advice on health in general and tuberculosis in particular. When Hale got TB as a child of eight, his parents at first did not seek help from the white doctors.

"My family was very traditional," he recalls. "They did not believe in modern medicine. I remember ceremonies being prepared for me and that last one where my fever was just over the edge. I was lying there in my mother's arms, and my mother's tears were coming down, and the medicine men were doing their thing. They painted my body black. Then I guess my mother just couldn't take it anymore, and they managed to get a vehicle and hauled me over to Sage Memorial Hospital. I was still all black. At the hospital I was tied down so I couldn't move and I had all these IVs coming in. I was in the hospital for several months, and Annie came to see me."[1]

MEDICINE MEN AND TUBERCULOSIS

Finally Annie and the BIA doctors managed to arrange some meetings with a few of the medicine men. In the fall of 1953 and the following spring, Annie and the doctors on the tuberculosis team brought together groups of about a dozen medicine men from various areas. In an intense education program, with Annie acting as translator, the medicine men received the same information that Annie herself had studied when she became head of the Health and Welfare Committee. With increased understanding between the two sides, compromises were made. In an effort to give patients the benefit of both schools of medicine, it was agreed that those patients who were not acutely ill with tuberculosis or some other ailment could delay their trip to the hospital for a short time to allow them to schedule a sing—a traditional ceremony—before they checked in.

Although the meetings were a productive start on cooperation between the two vastly divergent medical systems, we can be sure that the government BIA doctors viewed many of the Native treatments skeptically, and the medicine men had a hard time accepting some of the scientific data. In one Tribal Council session, Manuelito Begay, a council member as well as a medicine man, told how the doctors and medicine men had met and exchanged information on their medical treatments. Begay, who had been a medicine man for forty-five years, said that since the meeting, he had been recognized as a colleague by the white doctors and was treated with more respect when he brought a sick child to the hospital or came to visit someone. However, he made the point that he did not believe the white doctors' theory on the cause of tuberculosis.

"They tell me it is inflicted by a person coughing in your face," he said. "Right away I disagree with it. A person should not be that weak to be susceptible to a man's cough. We know how a man gets to be afflicted with tuberculosis. One is the ceremony about the Wind Chant. If something goes wrong with that, it is tuberculosis and, if lightning strikes you, tuberculosis is the result."[2]

His speech must have left Annie and the medical people in attendance in despair, but many more Navajos believed his version than Dr. Deuschle's story that when your sick grandma coughed on you, little red worms much too small to be seen entered you and began eating your lungs.

Annie liked to tell the story about an argument she had had with a revered medicine man over his sick granddaughter named Elizabeth, who had run away from the sanatorium at Fort Stanton. Annie had accompanied a public health nurse to a cattle sale near the trading post at Rock Point looking for this young woman. She found the sick woman near the corral and had begun talking to her when the grandfather approached and accused Annie of making his granddaughter sick. He asked her who was paying her to take all the Navajos away to die. When she told him that the Navajo Tribe was paying her a salary as a tribal official, he was not mollified. Sensing an entertaining scene, other Navajos at the sale soon surrounded the three of them, ready to support the medicine man, roaring and clapping every time he challenged her.

The medicine man told Annie he knew how to treat tuberculosis. She decided to jolly him along. "Wonderful," she said, "I've been looking for a Navajo who knows how to cure tuberculosis all these years. Where have you been hiding? I wish you would have come a long time ago. How do you treat tuberculosis?"

He explained that he mixed the pitch from the pinyon pine tree with grease and sagebrush and boiled it in a bucket with water and had the patient bathe in it, then take a sweat bath. He also had the patient swallow warm pinyon pitch.

Then Annie told him about the white man's treatment. "They get good food, good beds, clean linen, clean this an' clean that. Let 'em sleep an' rest. How about you?"

"They don't have to do that."

"Are you ready to go up against the competition?" she asked.

"Yes," he replied.

"Fine," she said. "I'm with you today. I'm going to get rid of this nurse. I'm tired of her. I have to interpret for her. I have to chew her words."

She then told him that he should get all of his medicine for curing tuberculosis ready and in ten days she would come back and take him to Fort Defiance where the white doctors would have their needles full of medicine and their knives ready to cut people. She would interpret for him. "Let's beat those old darn doctors. I'm tired of them," she said.

Just when he must have been congratulating himself on having defended himself and his profession admirably, Annie began telling him what he would have to do to fulfill a government contract to treat TB. He would have to erect a couple dozen sweathouses and collect great big bottles of sterile pinyon gum. He would have to sterilize his equipment and bring a woman in to cook for the patients—as well as provide something more nutritious than the slapjacks and coffee he suggested.

The crowd was definitely on his side until two old ladies came out of the group and asked to speak. "You, Spiderwife Medicine Man," they said. "You're nothin' but an alcoholic. We see you drunk most of the time. What are you going to do about that?"

After a short discussion of how he had better not get drunk and let her down, Annie wrote down the date she would return to pick up him and his paraphernalia to go to Fort Defiance. Then she turned to leave. He was surrounded by people congratulating him for standing up to the council representative and the nurse. Annie told the nurse that, because of the commotion, they might as well leave and try to get Elizabeth, the young woman they had come for, another time.

As they were talking, the medicine man came over to them. He must have reconsidered all that would have been required of him. "I want to tell you I cannot treat tuberculosis. I'm sorry I committed myself," he said. So Annie asked him to call everybody back and make the announcement. When they had wandered back, he said, "I've decided I'm not going to treat tuberculosis." But that was not enough for Annie. She reminded him that he had told her he didn't *know how*. She questioned him further, asking him if any other medicine men of his acquaintance knew how to treat TB, and he replied, "No." At that point Annie asked him to tell his granddaughter she should go back to the hospital.

Annie concluded her story, "So the next day Elizabeth was with us, back to the hospital, an' she's still alive today. When I see her she always comes up an' says, 'I remember you.' I says, 'I do too.'"[3]

Since Annie related this story years after it happened, the actual event may have differed in some small details, but it does give a good idea of what she and the health officials were facing when they were pitting the importance of the new treatment for tuberculosis against the traditional herbal medicine and curing ceremonies. We can also see that by this time she was beginning to rely on creative methods of spreading the word and feeling strong enough in her opinions to confront a medicine man in public.

MORE HELP TO SPREAD THE WORD

It was not just the medicine man who needed to be convinced of the worth of the new treatments—it was the Navajo People as well. Annie and the members of the Health and Welfare Committee could not do it themselves. Spreading the word of modern tuberculosis treatment over the canyons and mesas to the remotest sheep camp would require engaging the help of more opinion makers. The Advisory Council, a select group of Navajo Tribal Council representatives, spent five hours at Fort Defiance Hospital looking at X-rays, learning about drugs, and asking penetrating questions about the treatment of tuberculosis.

Since so many Navajos did not know how to read, or preferred not to even if they knew how, Annie worked with health officials to use the modern technology of the day: film. She enlisted students, friends, and relatives to "star" in movies on tuberculosis and childhood diarrhea. The dialogue and narration were, of course, in Navajo. Navajos love movies, so this became an effective method of spreading the message of prevention. One of the doctors said that the film was "as important a tool for treating TB as the drugs."[4]

By this time, because of her activism and willingness to speak out, Annie was becoming recognized as an important player in the battle against tuberculosis among the Navajos. In April 1954, she attended a conference of health professionals working with Navajo tubercular cases, and in May the health service doctor arranged for her to attend a national meeting on tuberculosis with representatives from all forty-eight states. Then in June she was off to the University of New Mexico for a conference on social welfare.

All the reports discussed at these meetings indicated that nearly as important as the new drugs in treatment of sick Navajos were visits from members of the Health and Welfare Committee or people from their area, good interpretation, and help in the exchange of letters between hospital and home. This treatment for homesickness is so basic and cross-cultural that it seems strange it was not begun earlier, and it lends some credence to the Navajo complaint that patients in off-reservation hospitals were not being treated with a full measure of compassion.[5]

Even family visits, however, were the occasion for a clash of the Navajo and mainstream cultures. When a Navajo family arrived at the hospital, they expected that everyone, including the children, be allowed to visit the patient. Standard practice in hospitals at that time dictated that youngsters not be allowed in hospital rooms because they frequently have colds or other viruses that can be spread to the patients. But the Navajos did not understand that, and depending on the doctors or nurses running the show, compromises were often made so that only obviously sick people were prohibited from visiting. Sometimes medicine men were brought in to bless the operating room. Some white doctors kept the medicine men and their feathers and paraphernalia out altogether; others allowed the blessing to take place before the room was cleaned and prepped for the surgery. In one case, lightning struck a tree on the grounds of a hospital in Southern Arizona where some Navajo patients were being treated. Two of the patients fled, and those who remained were terrorized. A medicine man was called in, and his cleansing chants were carried throughout the hospital on the speaker system.[6] Annie frequently acted as a go-between in situations such as this.

A few years later, Annie was to get a personal taste of the role that cultural disorientation can play during hospitalization. She had gone on a summer trip to Alaska to visit Juneau, Sitka, and Anchorage to investigate health care services for Alaskan Indians and Inuit. She never did make it to visit the Inuit, however. While in Alaska, she was taken ill and ended up in the hospital in Anchorage with a group of the local Native Americans. It is ironic that during this episode, she herself experienced the culture shock she had spent so many years trying to cushion for Navajos who found themselves in off-reservation medical facilities. She didn't understand the language the other patients were speaking and feared that they were talking about her. Because the sun never really sets that far north during the summer and it's always light, she refused to stay in bed and was up wandering around the hospital all night. The nurses were concerned and urged her to go back to bed and get the rest she needed. Part of the dietary regimen at the hospital was a daily dose of fish oil, but that was just too strange for Annie, and she refused to try it. After two days, she had recovered sufficiently and was happy to be out and headed home.[7]

GEORGE RUNS AGAINST ANNIE

By the fall of 1954 it was time for Annie to face her second election. She was just hitting her stride, and there was no question that she would run again. However, this time the residents of the Wide Ruins and Klagetoh chapters convinced the popular and amiable George Wauneka to run against his wife. Annie tried to get him to drop out, but for reasons of his own—perhaps as a lark—he stayed in the race. He really had no interest in politics and did not campaign for the office. But the fact was, he was well liked in the area, and he was a man.

As Annie was conducting her own campaign, she also lent moral support to Irene Stewart, who had served as chapter secretary and was running for the council in the Chinle chapter. It would be a relief if there were another woman on the council, she said. Stewart has written that Annie encouraged her when she felt that the electioneering was beyond her. "We'll join up and really work. There is plenty to do," Annie told her. "We will go places together, so work hard."[8]

When the day of the election came, Annie was concerned that George actually might win, but when the votes were counted, he had only 18 to her more than 300.[9] Irene Stewart was beaten by one of her male opponents, though she continued to work in her chapter, serving on the school board and as president of the PTA. Annie returned to the council as the lone woman.

Paul Jones was elected chairman of the council. Having worked extensively as a medical interpreter, he was to be a staunch supporter of the drive to persuade TB patients to accept modern treatment. Early in his term he announced that although he was a medicine man, he knew which diseases he could cure and which medical problems needed to be referred to the white doctors, such as appendicitis and gall stones. He reminded the delegates that the methods of the Native doctors and the white doctors differed greatly. For example, medicine men made lots of noise with rattles, and white doctors simply talked to their patients. He urged all the council members to help and advise their constituents, to prepare them so that they would understand the difference in the treatment they would receive at the modern hospitals.[10]

MORE HEALTH AND WELFARE COMMITTEE WORK

With the inauguration of the new council came discussion of which delegates Chairman Paul Jones was going to appoint to the various committees. The committee appointments were not going to be made immediately, but the business of several of the committees, particularly the Health and Welfare Committee, needed to be continued. A major tuberculosis conference in Gallup was coming up in a few weeks, plus the U.S. Public Health Service was coming to the reservation to take over Indian health care from the BIA. New clinics were being planned, and committee members were needed to interact with the new programs.

Two of the four members of the previous Health and Welfare Committee had not won reelection, so some new appointments, even if temporary, were needed. Apparently in back-channel discussions some of the delegates were saying that one person—obviously Annie—was getting too much attention and too many off-reservation trips related to her work on the Health and Welfare Committee. She had crossed the line of the Navajo cultural norm by being too visible and standing out too far from her colleagues. In the April 1955 session, one of the delegates mentioned "one certain person is taking all of the gravy" and urged the chairman to appoint some more members to the Health and Welfare Committee.

This irritated Annie immensely. Although it was true that she had done some traveling, she had paid for some of it out of her own pocket. Any travel money she had requested didn't begin to cover the wear and tear on her pickup nor the time she spent away from home. Immediately, she stood to defend herself, saying that she had asked one of the other members of the Health and Welfare Committee to attend a meeting in Crownpoint. "He said he was not interested in health. He said, 'I am interested in rodeo.' I asked him to attend some of the health meetings elsewhere if we were called upon to do so and he said 'I really cannot understand it,' so that was the end of it." She concluded, "You have to be interested in this health deal and throw yourselves into it to satisfy the doctors and the patients which I can assure you is a difficult thing to do, but I hope if the committee is going to be designated, they will get into the deal and see if they are doing a job. I do not expect to get on that committee again. Thank you." [11]

In fact, Annie did attend the meeting in Gallup and was reappointed to the Health and Welfare Committee as well as to the powerful Budget and Finance Committee. A report on the proceedings of the Working Conference on Services for Hospitalized Navajo Tuberculosis Patients indicated that the theme of the conference was "An Improved Patient Program through Better Communication." The interest of the Tribal Council in the Navajo TB patients, heralded by Annie, had finally been noted by the health professionals at the hospitals caring for the patients. The conference opened with a buffet dinner that "represented the first occasion in the history of Gallup when the speakers' table at a public dinner was occupied entirely by Navajo Indians." Talks were given by Navajo Tribal Council Vice Chairman Scott Preston, by Howard Gorman, a leading council member, by medicine man Manuelito Begay, and by Annie. Preston spoke of the Navajos' wish to cooperate with the white doctors and urged the white medical professionals to "respect the integrity and seriousness of purpose of the native medicine man." [12]

"As I see it, all the diseases which hurt the Navajo people may be divided into three kinds," Scott Preston said. "There are those diseases that we medicine men have given up on. We know that you white doctors have better cures than we do. One of the diseases of that sort is tuberculosis. Then there is sickness which comes from getting too close to where lightning struck. Right now there are probably some patients in this hospital who are sick from that illness and you doctors have no way of even finding out what is wrong with them—but we medicine men can, and we are able to cure such cases. A third type of illness is snakebite. You can cure that, and we Navajo also have our own medicines for that." [13] Mr. Preston was given a standing ovation at the end of his remarks.

It was an important articulation of the message Annie had been spreading, given even more importance coming from someone who was both an important leader and a medicine man himself. And at least some of the government doctors were open to what Scott Preston had to say. After the speech, a pediatrician from the Tuba City Hospital asked if it would be appropriate to build a hogan near the hospital so that sick babies would not have to endure a difficult trip home for a ceremony. Preston suggested that the doctors consult the local medicine men.

THE PUBLIC HEALTH SERVICE ARRIVES

The arrival of the U.S. Public Health Service (PHS) signaled a major improvement in the health delivery system for the Navajos. As a result of intense lobbying efforts in which Annie participated, the responsibility for Indian health services was transferred from the BIA Health Department within the Department of the Interior to the PHS within the Department of Health, Education and Welfare. The PHS provided services on the reservation through its Indian Health Service (IHS) arm. The health system no longer had to compete with the other aspects of Indian affairs and other bureaus in the Interior Department for adequate financing and personnel.

Shortly after the IHS took over in 1955, the Cornell doctors told the directors that they wanted to expand their tuberculosis project by setting up a clinic for a pilot study on how modern medicine could be presented in an acceptable form across cultural and linguistic barriers without compromising essential medical standards. Part of the project would be a study of home drug treatment in early cases of tuberculosis. The Tribal Council had already agreed to the project, and the IHS concurred. Once the Cornell team received the go-ahead, they had to find the right community—it had to be a typical Navajo community, neither too modern nor too primitive. Annie worked with the doctors to determine the best place, ruling out Klagetoh, which was on a preliminary list, because she knew that if her home district were chosen, it would appear that she had influenced the decision. Eventually the group selected the Many Farms and Rough Rock district. It had good roads because it was only fourteen miles north of Chinle, the gateway to Canyon de Chelly, a heavily visited national monument. Annie had good political relations with Selth Begay, the council delegate from that area, who had one year of college and was open to modern ideas.

On September 16, 1955, Annie accompanied the doctors to Many Farms, where Selth Begay had called a meeting in the local irrigation office to announce the establishment of the clinic. As chair of the Health and Welfare Committee, Annie gave the introduction, telling the crowd of the benefits of the new clinic, which would include an X-ray machine. "Then TB can be detected early," she said. "Home treatment will be given to patients by some of the finest doctors in the country. These medicines are going to be tested out here under the very worst conditions. . . . We members of the Tribal Council have discussed this clinic; we have considered all sides of the question and we have concluded that this is one of the best things being done for our people. So we are asking you for your cooperation."

She then told the assembled Navajos that the clinic would treat all kinds of sickness—from head colds to pneumonia and early cases of tuberculosis. She concluded her speech with welcome words on the reservation, where employment was always scarce: "As many jobs as possible will be given to Navajos."[14]

One of the positions for which Navajos were recruited was that of "health visitors" who went out on the reservation to help the public health nurses by covering more territory. Annie and Paul Jones advised the doctors not to choose people for this job who were too young. They said that the visitors should be fully mature and have children of their own to understand the problems of parents with sick children. They should also have a few gray hairs to be respected by the elders.[15]

Annie continued to go to tuberculosis-related meetings, learning and sharing with others what the Navajos had learned about getting the Diné to treatment. In October 1955, Dr. James Shaw, the new head of the Navajo office of the IHS, appeared before the council to report the progress he and his staff had made in bringing improved health care to the Navajo Reservation. The capacity of the practical nursing schools training Navajo young women had been doubled, young men were being trained as sanitation technicians, money to build eighty homes for health professionals was being made available, $750,000 was appropriated for a new hospital at Shiprock in the northern part of the reservation, and $250,000 was earmarked for a complete study of Indian health needs. He also mentioned that a two-hundred-bed hospital—large by reservation standards—would be built to serve as a medical center housing specialists and high-tech equipment.

Dr. Shaw concluded with the information that a recent study had shown that the majority of Navajo illnesses were serious infections, all of which were preventable. "We should be working mutually to keep people well rather than expending so much energy to cure them once they are ill," he concluded.[16]

As she had accepted the challenge to help keep tuberculosis

patients in the hospital, Annie took up the cause of disease prevention. She had already cooperated in the making of the film on sanitation and prevention measures; now the Woman with the Badge got back on the road—sometimes alone, sometimes with the IHS nurses.

TEACHING DISEASE PREVENTION

Annie went to traders and grocers and asked for their old boxes and lard tins. In those days, many of the fruit and vegetable boxes were made of wood, and Annie piled these in the back of her pickup. She also took soap and large cans with lids. When she got to a hogan where the dishes and food staples were stored on the floor, she would bring in some of the boxes and cans, stack them up, and show the women how to put the flour and sugar into the cans and how to store the food and dishes in ways that would keep them cleaner. She taught them how to wash dishes in clean water and then cover the dishes with a cloth. She inspected their water barrels and water buckets to see that they were as sanitary as possible.

"They didn't even realize how to keep things clean," she later recounted. "Some of the children just had terrific impetigo; they didn't know how to clean these sores. Lice, what have you, no privvies!" She worked with the public health nurses to get the children treated for lice and with the sanitation technicians to teach the people she visited about building outhouses a reasonable distance from the hogan.[17]

Annie was surprised to learn that such basic and necessary subjects as home sanitation and personal hygiene were not being taught in the schools, and at a council meeting she gave a long speech advocating the beginning of some kind of program for the children, with hopes that the students would take the message home. She worked with the Arizona and New Mexico Departments of Education to develop a program. When she learned that non-Indian tuberculosis patients were receiving health education in the off-reservation hospitals, she began talking to the Navajo patients and the nurses and received their agreement that training in tuberculosis prevention would be beneficial for the Navajos as well.

Annie also took her message to public gatherings. At the ceremonials, she would investigate the source of the drinking water. "If they were haulin' it from a pond I said, Throw that out. Get it from a windmill or some pump. Cause you're feeding human beings. You're not feeding dogs. So I made them bring better water for these big community affairs." When she went to a sing where a medicine man was performing a healing ceremony, she would go into the kitchen and suggest to the organizers that they take the medicine man outside and feed him. While he was occupied, she'd quietly clean up his paraphernalia with hot water and soap. Usually he did not even notice.[18]

A great number of the Navajos were receiving surplus commodity foods. Some of the items, such as flour and cornmeal, were familiar, but the canned minced ham, cheese, and powdered milk were new to many of the recipients. Annie set up some programs to teach the women to use these nutritious, but strange, foods. She told them that the powdered milk was intended for the children and not for the baby goats to whom many families had been giving it.

During this time, Annie began a weekly radio program broadcast from station KGAK in Gallup on health topics. The program was sponsored by Pet Milk. Most Navajo families had a radio then, and every Sunday morning Annie would pick a seasonal topic on some aspect of health—from baby care to waste disposal—and bring information to the Navajos in their own language on preventing disease and living a healthier life. In the winter she would talk about pneumonia and other dangers of the cold, and in the summer she would discuss flies, diarrhea, and food spoilage. Of course, she also urged mothers to give their children milk—and for families with no electricity for refrigeration and no access to fresh milk, canned milk was ideal. Through her program, she gained another nickname and became affectionately called "The Milk Lady."

After bringing up discussion of the new polio vaccine in council and convincing the other delegates that it was in general use throughout the rest of the country and not harmful, she began urging parents on her broadcasts to have their children inoculated. During rodeo season she would advise the people running the concessions to cover the food and serve it with proper utensils, to use paper cups and plates, and to wash the other dishes. "Then I'd get out there, inspect, and see that they were doing it right." Preparing and serving the food her way took more energy and expense, and she frequently met with resistance. "Some of them didn't like it," she admitted.[19]

MONEY FOR BETTER HOUSING

The living conditions of most Navajos made it extremely difficult for people to maintain even minimal sanitary conditions. Hogans, made of logs and chinked with mud, were in many ways practical homes, their thick walls offering warmth in winter and coolness in summer. But frequently they were crowded and had dirt floors. The doctors could cure infections and tuberculosis, but people living with dirt floors and open doors and windows were facing continual reinfection. With the corrals close to the hogans, flies were a health problem during the summertime. It was obvious that people needed to upgrade their homes, adding at the very least wooden floors, glass and screens in the open windows, and screen doors. Annie told a writer, "Housing is so critical on the reservation we don't have housewives, we have shack wives."[20] But among these people cash for such things was short—most of them simply could not afford the materials that would make their hogans healthier places to reside.

So Annie and her committee members went to the Navajo Tribal Council and asked for funds to provide floors and windows. The conservative council members could not see the relevance of her request and voted it down. She was incensed that they would mouth support for improved health care while sitting in the council chambers but fail to follow through to provide help for their destitute constituents.[21]

Annie was out there in the dark, smoky hogans and saw the flies, which had come from the manure in the corrals, crawling on the food and around the mouths and eyes of the children. The

Navajos needed the wooden floors and windows, and she would see that the people got them. It was into her pickup again and out to the chapter houses, where she began talking to the people, telling them what the housing improvements would do for them. If the other council members wouldn't see things her way on the basis of logic, she would find another way to convince them. Over the next three months she went to people she knew, relatives and friends of those currently in sanatoriums. If they did not want their loved ones to come back home only to get sick again, they should pressure their Tribal Council delegate to vote for the funding. It was their money after all—money that came to all of them from leases for the oil and gas. She found out which council members had relatives who were either currently ill or had been cured, and she went to them. Did they want their mother or brother to have to go away again? The other council members could not resist the grassroots movement, and when they next met, they appropriated $300,000 to launch a program for better housing and sanitation. The federal government kicked in some money, too.

"I threatened them," Annie explained with her exuberant laugh that boomed out when she was amused or delighted and that shook her whole body. "It worked!"[22] It was not much money, considering the need, but after that a slow improvement began to be seen on the reservation.

Despite the fact that Annie went after this funding, no one should construe that she was overly free with tribal funds. In fact, she was frequently the one to put the brakes on discussions of what she saw as unreasonable spending. During an October 1956 discussion of giving a total of $1 million in aid to destitute Navajos, Annie listened to several hours of testimony, then stood up and recited the total figures for welfare payments to Navajos from the states of Arizona, New Mexico, and Utah. She warned her colleagues to seriously consider how the additional money might affect payments that their constituents were already receiving.[23]

WORKING IN THE NAVAJO WAY

On her trips throughout the reservation, Annie never forgot that she was a Navajo. She exhibited traditional Navajo courtesy even if she was bringing new-fangled ideas. She wasn't coming as an outsider, like the white public health nurses. Whereas a white visitor might be uncomfortable in a hogan, seeing only that it was cramped and dark, Annie entered it feeling perfectly at home. The sheep milling in the corral, the smell of their dung, and the pungent fragrance of roast mutton ribs were not just familiar — they were part of her.

Generally one does not enter a Navajo compound, leap out of the car or truck, and knock on the door. It is considered polite to park away from the hogan and wait in the vehicle. Usually the family dogs rush out and surround the car, making enough ruckus to let those at home know there is a visitor. Someone from the household then appears, and the visitor can get out of the vehicle. Navajos do not vigorously shake hands but hold the other's hand briefly in their own. After that, the visit can begin.

Entering a hogan, especially that of an elderly person, Annie first asked about the people's relatives and reported on the welfare of her own. Then they would talk about ordinary concerns — money matters, rain or drought, and the grazing prospects for the sheep. The white culture's method of getting down to business after only a cursory "Good morning" or "Good afternoon" is considered rude and abrupt. Only after the traditional pleasantries, which might consume a considerable amount of time, would Annie turn the talk to health and tuberculosis.[24]

Despite her adherence to custom in the way she approached the household, simply giving the kind of advice she was dispensing was unusual behavior for a Navajo. On the other hand, the Navajo moral code holds that helping others when aid seems to be needed is one's obligation. Annie's help — information on health and sanitation — came bundled with a request that the household members improve the cleanliness of the hogan and get anyone with suspicious symptoms in for an X-ray. Polite Navajo manners dictated that anyone making a request leave an out for the other party to graciously decline the request.[25] Given this Navajo mind set, one can only imagine what an isolated Navajo woman might think when someone of Annie Wauneka's stature arrived at her hogan carrying piles of boxes and suggestions for rearranging her cooking area. Her advice verged on the edge of bossiness, but she apparently knew how far she could go. She was respected, and it seems she knew just how to treat each person she visited. Because of this, she was extraordinarily effective.

Her cajoling was not confined to the remote parts of the reservation. In February of 1957, she and the other Health and Welfare Committee members arranged to have the mobile X-ray unit parked outside the council chambers, and she exhorted all her fellow council members and the office and support staff to get an X-ray during the lunch break. She wanted them to become familiar with the mobile unit before it went out to the chapters later in the summer, but she also suspected several of the council members of having untreated tuberculosis and was anxious to get them under doctor's care.

Even with her prodigious energy and enthusiasm for her task, Annie and the other committee members were becoming overwhelmed with the enormity of the task in front of them. Annie requested on behalf of the Health and Welfare Committee that the council assign the duties to two separate committees, which it did. At that time the council also established an Office of Community Services for the administration and management of tribal programs for education, welfare, law and order, relocation, and health and provided a budget of $7,900 for six months. With her increasing national and regional conference participation, Annie was thrilled to finally have access to secretarial and administrative help and not have to borrow these services from other offices. "It has been difficult going from office to office looking for paper and pencil and trying to get reports written," she said after the vote.[26]

TAKING THE PROBLEMS TO WASHINGTON

Because of Annie's growing reputation for speaking out and commanding attention when she did, Chairman Jones asked her to accompany him to Washington DC in 1958 to give testimony before a Senate subcommittee on appropriations for labor, health, education, and welfare. Although by treaty Congress must fund Indian services, it votes on the level of appropriations each year.

Before Annie left for the East, she made good use of the Public Health Service advisers and the Community Services Committee to help her prepare a speech that was full of statistics. She told the senators that the most recent figures showed that more than twice as many Navajo babies died before reaching the age of one year than did babies in the general American population. Four times as many Navajos died from influenza and pneumonia, twice as many from accidents, and thirteen times as many from dysentery, gastritis, enteritis, and diarrhea. Her goal was to obtain more money for staffing and housing an increased medical staff.

She told of going to both government and private doctors for suggestions on how many doctors were needed on the reservation. "The general consensus of opinion was that we should have one doctor for every 1,000 Navajos," she reported. "With our population of 30,000 Navajos, our present ratio is one for every 3,000 Navajos. The ratio of our dentists is one for every 8,000 Navajos, while in the general population it is one per 1,900," she said. No eye specialists nor ear, nose, and throat specialists were employed on the reservation, she stated, and no elective surgery was being done in any of the IHS hospitals due to a lack of nursing staff. In addition, she told the subcommittee:

A majority of my people live many miles from hospitals and health clinics. Besides traveling great distances, many of our sick people are required to sit and wait long hours in waiting rooms before their turn is reached to see a doctor. There have been instances where some patients have been asked to come back the following day due to the inability of the medical staff to examine and treat such large groups.

As a result, Navajos become disgusted and discouraged, which makes them reluctant to ever return to the hospital until their sickness has reached the point where doctors are unable to help them. They either become chronic cases or die.

She concluded her presentation forcefully by calling the attention of subcommittee members to a bureaucratic regulation that made no sense when applied to the Navajo situation. "It is my understanding that the future year's allotment of money is based on the previous year's patient workload," she told the senators. "How do you expect patient workloads to increase when there isn't enough staff to take care of the present load? Very little, if any, progress can be made on this basis, and our people will continue to suffer needlessly." In the end she asked the committee to appropriate $45 million for the Public Health Service to serve American Indians.[27]

THE PROBLEM OF RECALCITRANT PATIENTS

Back home on the reservation and in the country, the new drugs were beginning to conquer tuberculosis. The doctors in the clinic at Many Farms were continuing their work on treating a segment of the population near the clinic on an outpatient basis. However, because the compliance of the general American population was greater than that of the Navajos, the rate of TB on the reservation was still five or six times the rate of disease off the reservation. Although 340 Navajo adults and children were under hospital care, many Navajo tuberculosis patients still left the hospital against medical advice. When these people were contacted, they would offer various excuses for leaving. Some parents would say they wanted to have a ceremony for their child before sending the little one back to the hospital. But the promised date for return would come and go, and still the infected person remained at home. Even the toughest persuasion did not work in some cases. Public health workers and the Health Committee were in despair. Tuberculosis would never be conquered on the Navajo Reservation if the more than 235 active cases continued to infect their family and friends.

Annie had begun her fight against tuberculosis thinking that her people could be convinced to seek modern treatment for the disease if they were given the right information and if treatment conditions were improved. But now, she was frustrated. She had spent weeks on end driving to remote hogans. She had given speeches at chapter houses and ceremonial gatherings. After seven years of trying every approach she could think of to convince these recalcitrant cases to accept treatment, she had to concede that firmer measures were needed.

Arizona, New Mexico, and Utah state laws provided for involuntary confinement of active TB cases, but on the Indian reservations this authority was given to the surgeon general of the Public Health Service under the direction of the secretary of health, education and welfare. For this authority to be activated, the Navajo Tribe would have to request it. Annie Wauneka and the IHS doctors knew well the Navajo reluctance to coerce others to do something, and they deplored the idea of sick people being hauled into court. But they could go no further in eradicating the disease without some way to deal with the hard core of recalcitrant patients. The IHS staff prepared a resolution, and Annie joined them in presenting it to the council. They anticipated a fight from the other council members, and they got it.

A CALL FOR INVOLUNTARY COMMITMENT

Several Indian Health Service doctors joined Annie in the Tribal Council chambers. After an opening statement by one of the public health officials, Annie stood to defend the need for involuntary commitment of infectious persons to hospitals. Even if everyone agreed, the Navajo Tribal Council could not put the measure into action by itself. All it could do was make a resolution requesting the IHS to seek permission from the secretary of the interior to sanction involuntary commitment. But she needed to convince her fellow delegates to make that request.

She began to enumerate the areas where the AMAs (people who had left the hospital "against medical advice") lived—fourteen people in Torreon, eighty-five at Bluewater Lake, and more at Borrego Pass. At each mention she looked toward the council member representing that area, subtly trying to make it his responsibility as well as hers to bring them in. She told of going to Crownpoint to a hogan looking for a particular woman whom she did not know. When the woman came to the door and saw Annie, she denied being that individual. "She has gone," she told Annie. When Annie related the story there was laughter of recognition from the other delegates. Later she said that there was a council member who was a TB carrier and a member's wife who needed to be X-rayed. Despite the fact that the infected delegate and the woman's husband were lawmakers themselves, Annie said, they were always arguing with the public health officials.

When the open discussion started, one delegate after the other stood to say his piece. Most of them felt conflicted, wanting to honor the old ways, not wishing to give the white doctors the power to send their neighbors off the reservation to lonely months or years in sterile hospitals, yet aware that people with untreated tuberculosis could infect many others. Hour after hour, Annie and the public health officials listened and occasionally reacted.

Part way through the day and a half of discussion, one of the doctors responded with elegant sarcasm. "If any of you consider that your religious teachings prompt you to defend the right of your fellow Navajos to contaminate and ultimately kill the other members of your tribe by degrees, you ought not to support this regulation. But if you feel the Navajos who are not affected should be protected against this disease, you should support the resolution," he said. One wonders how the message ended up after it had been translated into Navajo.

Annie knew that she had to lead the delegates to the correct vote, yet she could not be seen as having forgotten her Navajo values. "We respect the medicine man," she said in one of her many speeches during the session. "We would like to have a medicine man come before us and say that he can cure tuberculosis. . . . I can say that we are eager to see them so we don't have to send them [TB patients] off the reservation. I asked Scott Preston [tribal vice-chairman] if he can cure tuberculosis and he says he can't do it."

This call for a medicine man appears to be pure theatrics. After all the medical conferences devoted to tuberculosis that Annie had attended by this time, she no doubt realized that curing the disease was far beyond the scope of any medicine man.

After hours of discussion over two days, she was obviously frustrated and stood to speak once again. "If you just tell us to leave the Navajos alone, the TB people, let them drift away, we are willing to do that. We will save money, because the council members do appropriate quite a sum of money for committees such as health." She then told a story of going with a public health nurse to try to find a runaway patient and spending two days running all over the Chinle area trying to find the person. She reminded them that she and other Health Committee members were paid for the time they spent on tribal business from money appropriated to the Health Committee plus mileage. This money was wasted if they did not accomplish their goals.

"Another thing," she added, "we have gone to Washington asking for more money for Indians. If they find out we are not active and not interested in the TB program, they are going to . . . cut the budget. So whatever you do, gentlemen, it is up to you and if you don't pass this resolution, we don't have to do that running around. That is all I have to say."

Vice Chairman Preston, the medicine man who had admitted he couldn't cure TB, concluded the discussion with an emotional disclosure: "I have a grandchild, a woman, who I tried to convince to go to a hospital. She objected. Finally I convinced her and she said she would go in four days. Before the four days were up, she had a hemorrhage and died. While I made every effort to have her go to the hospital within the last hours, it was too late."

Then it was time for the vote. The count was 59 delegates for and 6 against giving the Public Health Service permission to ask the secretary of the interior for a regulation on involuntary confinement.[28]

It was not until November 1961, nearly three years later, that the regulation was finally in place. At last the Health Committee had the necessary authority to insist that people with contagious diseases—not just tuberculosis—go in for treatment. Patients were allowed a hearing before a tribal court if they wished to protest their commitment.

Annie was becoming one of the most powerful members of the Tribal Council, and she was spending more and more time watching out for the health of the Navajos. But she was soon to learn that her power and influence were not enough to protect her own family.

6

Alcoholism and Peyote

IN THE SPRING OF 1959 it was again election time. Annie, who was now forty-nine, did her usual campaigning and was returned to office, as were Paul Jones as chairman and Scott Preston as vice chairman. Jones appointed Annie to the powerful Budget and Finance Committee, and she began educating herself on the various topics with her usual vigor.

A MEMBER OF THE OLD GUARD

Annie was beginning her ninth year as a delegate. As her time on the council increased with repeated reelections, she became one of a group of more traditional Navajos known as the Old Guard. She had a near encyclopedic memory of previous actions of the council, especially of budgetary issues. If an appropriation had been made for something or discussed in committee, she remembered it or knew where to find the information immediately.

Her knowledge did not come without work. When she needed more information on a subject, she would go to the government officials in charge of that area and request background papers. Or she would ask them to make an appointment for her with an expert in Phoenix or Albuquerque. At night, she would read stacks of reports so she would be prepared to discuss each issue intelligently. As new council members replaced others, the newcomers were usually unsophisticated in parliamentary procedure, and Annie was frequently standing up to straighten out matters when too many motions were on the floor or were not seconded, or when a long list of provisions in a resolution made it unwieldy.

In a typical instance, during protracted budget hearings by the full council stretching over two sessions of twelve days in June and nine days in July of 1959, she stood to speak forty-six times on twenty-six different topics, including the leasing of tribal lands, the appointment of judges, the procurement of quality bulls to improve Navajo cattle herds, Boy Scouts, veterans' assistance, and the budget for the tribal fair.

By this time, her manner was becoming even more forthright and her remarks from the floor more incisive. "I demand a complete and full report on this particular enterprise before we take any action," she said in one meeting in a typical display of outrage at what she perceived as incompetence or subterfuge. At that time the Navajo Tribal Council needed the approval of the secretary of the interior through the BIA to spend their own funds being held in trust. When the BIA area director held up on a technicality the release of Navajo money to cover the budget that had been adopted, Annie took him to task. "We know all Bureau employees, when you start to question them on important matters, start to beat around the bush. I think you just want to kill time. . . . We are not getting direct answers here." She went on to excoriate the area director, asking why he had not been present during important budget discussions, and refused to accept his diplomatic answer that he had been called to Washington. By the end of the discussion she was so incensed that she was requesting the chairman to dispatch a direct telegram to the secretary of the interior, asking that the area director, the assistant area director, and another of their associates be fired immediately. "These three individuals are out here with no intention of promoting the Navajo affairs," she protested. "They are here to downgrade the integrity of the tribe. That is my feeling." [1]

Although the level of her remarks might not seem out of place in a state legislature or the U.S. House of Representatives, their tone was very unusual for the soft-spoken Navajos who, although willing to debate issues endlessly, tend to be more diplomatic and indirect.

NAVAJO MEDICAL DICTIONARY

While Annie was taking on broader duties in the council, she continued to devote a great deal of time to medical issues. In May 1959, Annie and the IHS doctors announced that work on an English-Navajo dictionary of medical terms had finally been completed. Annie had worked with the doctors over several years to put together the volume, sometimes having to invent new words for the unfamiliar practices of the white doctors. The need for this was profound. As one of the doctors in need of this information wrote: "it is not possible for the interpreter to parallel English lexicon in translation, as is possible in translating from closely related European languages, such as French and Spanish. Rather, the interpreter must choose terms which are only roughly equivalent. . . . The interpreter must translate concepts, not words . . . the quality of interpretation is not determined as much by whether or not there is a word in Navajo for a given idea or thing, as by the degree to which the interpreter understands the subject matter."[2]

Often a trained medical translator was not available when needed, and white doctors had to rely on any bilingual Navajo who was around—sometimes an office clerk or even a janitor—to interpret. One doctor drafted an untrained hospital employee for a quick translation and found that the translator had told the patient he needed an appendectomy when the doctor had ordered a routine X-ray. Another IHS doctor was trying to explain possible surgery to a Navajo patient with a thyroid tumor. The patient ran from the office terror stricken. The interpreter had told the sick man that the doctor intended to cut his throat! Although the job of translation could never be considered easy, the medical dictionary was an enormous help to doctors, translators, and, of course, patients. Another publishing achievement was an article in the *American Journal of Nursing,* under Annie's byline, in which she told the story of how she educated herself and other Navajos about tuberculosis and encouraged them to seek treatment.[3] Around this time she was also named to the U.S. surgeon general's Committee on Indian Health Care and that required traveling to out-of-state meetings.

A FAMILY TRAGEDY

On June 1, 1959, Annie's half brother Ben, who had also been a council delegate representing the Crystal chapter, was found

Chee Dodge, left center, and a friend relax outside
his cabin at the Tanner Springs ranch. On the left,
Annie Dodge Wauneka enters the cabin. (Courtesy
of the Irma Bluehouse Collection.)

Above: Henry Chee Dodge when he worked as a scout and interpreter at Fort Defiance. Taken around 1885. (Photo by Ben Wittick. Courtesy of the Museum of New Mexico, Neg. No. 15950.)

Top right: Chee Dodge built a large home on his ranch at Sonsola Buttes near Crystal, Arizona. (Photo by Milton "Jack" Snow. Courtesy of the Navajo Nation Museum, Window Rock, Arizona, Catalog No. NAV-176.)

Bottom right: Chee Dodge's offspring gathered for a portrait: (from left) Annie Wauneka, Tom Dodge, Mary Peshlakai, and Ben Dodge. (Courtesy of the Irma Bluehouse Collection.)

Top left: Annie Wauneka (second from right) joined
two public health nurses to visit the hogan of John and
Elsie Teller in Fort Defiance, Arizona, on July 8, 1960.
(Photo by Eugene Price. Courtesy of the Navajo Nation
Museum, Window Rock, Arizona, Catalog No. L-762.)

Bottom right: Annie Dodge and George Wauneka were
married in a traditional Navajo wedding ceremony
at the Tanner Spring Ranch in October 1929. (Photo by
Milton "Jack" Snow. Courtesy of the Navajo Nation
Museum, Window Rock, Arizona, Catalog No. NH1-18.)

Above: Annie Wauneka received the Medal of Freedom
from President Lyndon B. Johnson on December 6,
1963. On the far right is Under Secretary of State George
Ball. Annie Wauneka was chosen for the honor by
President John F. Kennedy, who was assassinated before
the ceremony was held. (Photo by Cecil Stoughton.
Courtesy of the LBJ Library, CA-41-26-WH63.)

Top left: Annie Wauneka joined Robert Redford for
an ecology conference held in Canyon de Chelly in
Chinle, Arizona, on June 21, 1984. (Photo by Kenji
Kawano. Courtesy of the photographer.)

Bottom left: Annie Wauneka studied for three
months with the Bureau of Indian Affairs doctors,
learning about tuberculosis, before she began
educating her fellow Navajos about the disease.
(Courtesy of the Irma Bluehouse Collection.)

Above: Annie Wauneka received an honorary
doctorate from the University of New Mexico in June
1973. (Courtesy of the Irma Bluehouse Collection.)

Top left: In Annie Wauneka's frequent travels to Washington DC she always wore her traditional Navajo style of dress, making her stand out on the street and in the halls of Congress. (Courtesy of the Irma Bluehouse Collection.)

Bottom left: While Annie Wauneka was the consummate politician, she also excelled in the skills expected of the typical Navajo woman. Here she enters a fry bread contest at a summer fair. (Courtesy of the Irma Bluehouse Collection.)

Above: Gesturing with the pointed finger is unusual for a Navajo but was typical for Annie Wauneka. Here she speaks at the Utah Oil Mining Conference in Mexican Hat, New Mexico, in 1958. (Courtesy of the Navajo Nation Museum, Window Rock, Arizona, Catalog No. NNM.)

An official portrait of Annie Wauneka early in her years as a tribal delegate. (Courtesy of the Irma Bluehouse Collection.)

dead near the railroad tracks in Gallup. He had been beaten around the face and head. Ben was generally a pleasant fellow who ranched and raised his family on land he had inherited from his father, but he did have a problem with alcohol. Ben had been in jail for nine days on a charge of drunkenness and had just been released. He apparently began drinking again immediately upon his release, fell in with the wrong people, and ended up in a fight.[4]

According to one friend's recollection, Ben had begun drinking with his father when Chee was still alive. Annie's sister Mary also tended to drink heavily, although her drinking was less public. Ben's death, as well as memories of her father's exploits while under the influence of too much alcohol, were to give Annie another—and even more challenging—target for her energies.

THE NEW ALCOHOLISM COMMITTEE

Within a few months of Ben's death, the Navajo Tribal Council decided that the problem of alcoholism among the Navajos was of great enough concern to warrant its own committee, and Annie was made the chair.

Annie knew as little about alcoholism as she had about tuberculosis when she began her Health and Welfare Committee work, and although she accepted the committee appointment with enthusiasm, it took her some time to begin to learn the scope of the problem.

During 1962, Annie concentrated on her new job of heading the Alcoholism Committee. There was a monumental task ahead of her. More than 80 percent of on-reservation arrests were for alcohol-related offenses. As usual, she began by doing research. She was a frequent visitor in both the IHS and BIA offices, asking for background material. The bureaucrats respected her and knew she was serious about her job, so they hunted up documents and made appointments for her. For months she talked and read and asked questions. She must have thought of all the people she knew whose lives had been affected by overconsumption of alcohol—her father's embarrassing incidents and his car wrecks, her brother Ben's tragic death, and her sister Mary's problems with alcohol.

On April 26, 1962, when Annie stood to report to the council, she admitted that the alcohol situation still had her baffled. "It is a vast type of problem, and it is a difficult one. It takes more than just a few minutes discussion. We could easily stay far into the night. Instead of pointing to other groups, other agencies, it is our problem.

"This is a very serious thing and it is no laughing matter. Appearances of people who are afflicted might be comical, but the end result is so serious that we need to do something about it." She reminded the delegates that they had worked together to control many of the diseases that had plagued the Diné, and they needed to get to work on alcoholism.[5]

In early December, Annie was back in the council with a more complete report from the Alcoholism Committee put together with the help of a consultant the committee had hired. The report gave no easy answers, no simple solution. This time there was no just-discovered miracle drug to stop the epidemic. The report estimated that 70 percent of the adult population drank, as did 80 percent of youngsters aged seventeen to twenty. Of the 114 people interviewed, 74 drank alcohol before breakfast, which was the deciding element separating the social drinkers from those considered alcoholics. Most bought packaged wine in Gallup and drank it under the stars at the edge of town. Other times it was purchased from bootleggers at rodeos and ceremonials. Navajos seldom drink alone. Instead, men squat in a circle and pass one bottle around.

This report concluded that the cause of drinking by Navajos was despair over the irreconcilable aspects of their lives. The men wanted to support their families, but two-thirds of them were unemployed and did not want to leave the reservation to find work. They had an average of only four years of schooling, not enough to hold a skilled job. The report concluded that alcoholism "causes poverty, death, disease, disintegration of family and loss of productivity. It should be very alarming to the tribal leaders and administrators."

Annie's remarks added to the information in the report. When the respondents were asked why they had to go on drinking, they didn't seem to have the answers. "It is just that they cannot over-come this habit," she said. "Once they partake of alcoholic bev-erages, they just lose themselves. . . . So many of these people need help and they admit that. They seem to think that matters are hopeless and it is very encouraging to people when some-one takes an interest in carrying out a rehabilitation program for them. We often think that these people are hopeless and they don't care. But in these interviews, it was found that this is not so. They themselves want to be rehabilitated." Later, she added that most of the Navajos were drinking fortified wine, the cheapest and most damaging type of alcohol.[6]

ORIGINS OF NAVAJO DRINKING
The fact that the roots of Navajo alcoholism are complex has been borne out by other researchers. Stephen Kunitz and Jerrold E. Levy studied Navajo drinking behavior for years and concluded in their book *Drinking Careers* that it had its origin in early white American drinking behavior. Early patterns of binge drinking de-clined in the mid-nineteenth century in the eastern United States but spread to the frontier areas. Binge drinking, where drinkers consume alcohol until they pass out, was characteristic of the be-havior of trappers, miners, soldiers, and cowboys who spent long periods away from town and then indulged heavily when they had the opportunity. These individuals encouraged this style of drinking among the Western Indians.

Shortly after the Navajos returned to their reservation fol-lowing captivity in Fort Sumner, the railroads came into their area and brought liquor. According to Kunitz and Levy, "The rail-way construction camps and station towns spawned innumer-able saloons that sold whiskey openly to Indians."[7]

Later, when the area became more civilized, alcohol sales needed to be somewhat undercover. Until August 1953, federal law made it illegal to sell intoxicants to Indians. New Mexico repealed its law in September 1953, but Arizona maintained its law until late in 1955. The Navajo tribe, however, prohibited—and continues to prohibit—alcohol sales on the reservation, although every neighborhood has its bootleggers, and everybody knows who they are.

Since some of the earliest Navajo drinkers were two of the highest-ranking chiefs—Manuelito and Ganado Mucho—other Navajos equated drinking and drunkenness with high status. It was, of course, Manuelito's chronic overindulgence that led the Indian agent to depose him and replace him with the young Chee Dodge in 1884.[8]

Older Navajos in the western portion of the reservation told of alcohol coming to their area as early as 1890. "Riders dispatched by wealthy Navajos brought liquor to the reservation from various sources: ranches north of Flagstaff and south of Winslow, Arizona, and a still run by Mormons north of Lee's Ferry. All of them remarked on the high price of whiskey, usually a yearling calf for a gallon of whiskey. At these prices only the rich could afford to drink, a circumstance that we believe had an important influence on Navajo attitudes toward drinking."[9]

There is some evidence that Chee Dodge may possibly have been one of these bootleggers in his early years, and that this is one of the ways he managed to accumulate his large herds of cattle.[10]

REASONS FOR INCREASED DRINKING

By the 1930s, drinking on the reservation was steadily increasing. New Deal work projects gave more Navajos an income, a reflection of an overall move from a barter to a cash economy, and better roads and more vehicles brought off-reservation liquor sources closer. By the middle of the decade, the majority of the arrests made by the Navajo police were for drunkenness or possession of alcohol.[11]

Besides the reasons for excessive drinking detailed in the Alcoholism Committee report, sometimes Navajos drank simply because alcohol facilitated conviviality in social settings and was the proper thing to do for people who could afford it.

In *Drinking Careers* we read: "A number of men said that alcohol made them better speakers at public gatherings and that many Navajo politicians would drink before addressing large audiences. An important quality for a Navajo leader was that he be able to speak well and persuasively. The Navajo word for leader, naat'aanii, means speaker or exhorter, and the initiation ceremony for a leader involved the anointment of his lips with pollen from the plants of the four sacred mountains to enable him to make 'powerful' speeches." [12]

Clearly, Annie, her committee, the Tribal Council, and the Indian Health Service were facing a complex problem with social, cultural, and medical ramifications. Annie always emphasized that she herself did not drink. "I always walk the chalk line," she would say, referring to the line police officers would drawn on the pavement when they stopped drivers suspected of being drunk. Anyone too inebriated to drive would not be able to balance and walk along the line.

Annie did have her addiction, however: caffeine. Navajos generally are heavy coffee drinkers, and Annie was forever sitting down with friends in their homes or at the Window Rock Inn to chat over a cup of coffee. Former council member Howard McKinley, who served with her for years on the Health Committee, told of a trip they had taken together to the medical school at Loma Linda University, a Seventh Day Adventist institution in California. When they went to the cafeteria for breakfast, they discovered that the religion bans the drinking of coffee. By the middle of the morning Annie had such a caffeine withdrawal headache that she and Howard borrowed a car and went off campus to find a coffee shop so she could get her morning "fix." [13]

OTHER TRIBAL BUSINESS

As important as alcoholism was, it was not the only major matter affecting the tribe. Late in 1963, Annie was off to Washington to testify before a Senate appropriations committee for an increased budget for the Public Health Service. She and the IHS officials with whom she worked in Window Rock had been distressed to realize that not only were they not getting an increase in funds the following year, but they would actually face a reduction in services. She knew she had to do what she could to alert the senators to the health needs of the Navajos and other American Indian groups. She had planned to fly by chartered plane from Window Rock to Albuquerque to pick up a scheduled flight east, but a major snowstorm grounded the small plane. Canceling her presentation was not an option for her. As a stock herder, she was used to working through bad weather conditions, to hunting down the last sheep that needed to be in the corral, to digging her truck out of a snowbank if necessary. Determined to present the speech the IHS staff had helped her to prepare, off she went through the blizzard by car to Gallup, where she boarded a train for Washington.

When she finally stood before the Senate committee, she called to the attention of the members that the net increase for the 1964 Indian division of the Public Health Service budget was to be only $1 million for health programs for the entire country, an amount she deemed far too low considering that the Navajo tribe itself was increasing at the rate of 3 to 5 percent annually, with six babies born for every death. She was armed with statistics showing that there would be a reduction in services at all the Navajo Reservation hospitals. She also talked about the need for more public health nurses, medical social workers, dentists, sanitation engineers, and field health stations.[14]

PEYOTE BECOMES AN ISSUE

In the 1963 tribal election, Raymond Nakai won the post of chairman. Annie, of course, was reelected and was finally joined by another woman, Mabel Hesuse. Nakai, an announcer for a Navajo-language radio program in Flagstaff, had run in two previous elections. Although he hadn't won, he did gain name recognition. Nakai presented an interesting platform. Playing on the continuing bad feelings over the stock reduction, he indicated he would not enforce the grazing regulations so that subsistence sheepherders could increase the size of their flocks. He promised to fire Norman Littell, who had been the tribal lawyer since 1947, claiming that Littell had too much influence. And, in great contrast to Chairman Jones, he courted the votes of those Navajos who advocated the freedom to consume peyote, a hallucinogenic plant.

At that time there was a small but growing interest in the Native American Church, which advocated chewing the peyote plant to achieve visions. Peyote—a small hairy cactus containing eight psychoactive alkaloids including mescaline—was being touted as a traditional religion, although peyote had not been used historically by the Navajos. The religion was introduced into the area in 1931 but was outlawed by the Navajo Tribal Council in 1940. Originally it combined elements of Christianity with parts of Native American ceremonies from the Kiowa and Comanche Tribes of the southern Great Plains, but the local version added some Navajo ritual as well.

According to Stephen Kunitz, the use of peyote fit in well with traditional Navajo practice. One reason for its popularity was that with declining income in the face of stock reduction, Navajo families found it difficult to pay for the traditional healing ceremonies that involved feeding a large number of guests for five to nine nights. "The peyote ceremony lasts only one night and is, consequently, more economical than most Navajo ceremonies," Kunitz writes. "Its ritual is simple, standardized and not difficult to learn for either the lay participant or the religious leader. As it introduced no new beliefs about the cause of disease and denies none of the central Navajo beliefs, it is easy to use as a substitute for traditional ceremonies."[15]

Kunitz also credits the long apprenticeship necessary to become a traditional medicine man with making the peyote ritual more attractive. While young men with wage jobs didn't have the time to either learn or conduct the traditional ceremonies, they could learn and perform the single-night peyote ceremony, thereby gaining status in the community.

Annie's strong opposition to peyote was well known. She equated the mind-altering effects of peyote with the drunkenness achieved from drinking alcohol. She was also a Catholic who attended mass regularly, and the priests were definitely anti-peyote. Furthermore, she saw it as an incursion of non-Navajo influences on the reservation. In a particularly rancorous Tribal Council session, two visitors gave pro and con reports on peyote and whether its use on the reservation should be sanctioned.

After the reports, the council discussed the issue for a day and a half until straight-laced Annie thought she had had enough. When recognized by the chair she said, "It appears that this is a very disgusting subject. However we did not start it ourselves. The People have urged the council to bring it up. But the laws of Arizona, Texas and New Mexico prohibit it. All that would have to be changed for the council to even consider it. Let's go on to more important business." The council did move on to other matters then, but it was only the first of many times that peyote practice would draw Annie into the controversy.[16]

Although Raymond Nakai was not formally a member of the Native American Church, he was not against the use of peyote and had many supporters among those who advocated its use.[17] Peyote use was prohibited on the reservation, but Nakai said he would call off harassment of the Native American Church members and work for legalization of peyote use for religious purposes.

Nakai's softness on the peyote issue pitted Annie against him from the start and was the beginning of years of acrimony on the council between him and his supporters and the Old Guard with regard to a number of matters in addition to the peyote situation. Annie was also a longtime friend of Norman Littell, the tribe's general counsel. Although Annie was now known nationally in the field of Indian health care, Nakai did not appoint her to the Health Committee, nor was she returned to the Budget and Finance Committee.

DROUGHT RELIEF PROGRAMS

The provision of water, the ever-defining issue in the arid Southwest, took up many council hours during the early 1960s. A prolonged drought had gripped the reservation for nearly ten years. Work had begun on rural water systems on the reservation as a result of a federal law passed in 1958. The measure provided money for water tanks, sinks, faucets, and pipes on the nation's Indian reservations. Each tribe was required to participate by furnishing labor, transportation, and other materials. The need for these facilities was desperate. Deaths on the Navajo Reservation from gastrointestinal diseases were twenty times what they were in the general population, largely attributable to polluted water. Annie and the public health nurses could tell the people to be careful of their water sources, to wash the dishes in plenty of water, and to bathe the children regularly, but sometimes the only water source at all for miles and miles was a scummy pond also used to water the sheep and other livestock. When every drop had to be hauled in fifty-five-gallon drums in a wagon or somebody had to ask a neighbor or relative to drive their pickup to the water source, people had to use the water that was available and not use it lavishly.

Funds for improved water systems were vitally important to the tribe. The reservation was much too vast and the location of the households too spread out to bring a spigot to every hogan, so the improvements were concentrated in areas where several households were clustered together. Annie worked with the IHS representatives to see that the facilities were correctly located and that the people they were to serve knew how to use them.

In 1963, Federal money was again available to the Navajos to construct deep and shallow wells and some sewer systems. The council was split on whether to accept the money and participate in the program, particularly when Annie cautioned that when the water systems were completed, they would be turned over to the tribe to operate and maintain. How would they plan for the expense of the operation and eventual replacement of the system? This was a gift from the federal government that included a liability.

Her concerns were answered by Dr. Charles McCammon, the current head of the local IHS office, who told the council that the recipients could be charged for water and sewer services to create a fund for operation and upkeep. That this was news to Annie and to many of the delegates indicates how unaccustomed most of them were to the common details of urban life, even something as basic as utility bills. With this assurance, the council voted to proceed with the new water systems.[18]

The fact that the water systems were sorely needed was underscored by the fact that soon the drought had worsened to the point that the council approved the expenditure of $200,000 to buy water tanks and to pay truckers to haul water to the areas hardest hit with dried up shallow wells and water holes that held only red mud or dust.

The drought also reduced the natural forage for the sheep and other livestock. The council members had numerous times voted funds for emergency grain purchases for distribution to sheep herders whose animals were starving for lack of good range. The problem was compounded by the fact that many people were running sheep without permits, thus exceeding the carrying capacity of the rangelands. In the spring of 1962, the council had finally voted to take measures to bring into balance the number of animals on the reservation and the available grazing land within the next three years. Remembering the anguish everyone faced during the previous major stock reduction, Annie was anticipating resistance from her constituents. But this time it was remarkably smooth. Six months later a report given in the council meeting indicated that a sale of cattle, horses, and unproductive ewes had reduced the number of livestock on the reservation by 7,844 sheep units (a cow is equal to four sheep units; a horse is equal to five sheep units.)

Thirty years had not erased the lingering bitterness over the stock reduction overseen by John Collier, but much had happened in the intervening decades. The council members were better educated and more willing to trust the scientific information that was documenting the overgrazing, and with more roads and cars and trucks available on the far-flung reservation, more information was available on how families were faring.

RECOGNITION FOR ACHIEVEMENT

Word of Annie Wauneka's work on tuberculosis care and her other projects began to spread beyond the reservation. In the fall of 1959 Annie's work was recognized nationally when she was awarded the Indian Council Fire Achievement Award by the Indian Council Fire, an organization of Indians of many tribes. It was the same award that had been given to Chee Dodge in 1944, and this was the first time it had gone to a parent and child. The award was given at a ceremony in Chicago, and because it was such an honor, George went along with Annie on the train. By now, Annie was a seasoned traveler, having made numerous trips to Washington and other areas of the country for meetings. But George had remained the homebody. Once he got to Chicago, he found he did not enjoy traveling as much as his wife did. The tall buildings held no interest for him. The road into his ranch might see a pickup or two a day. In Chicago, that many cars passed by in a second. He was homesick for the wide sky and quiet peace of Tanner Springs, and he was worried about the ranch, his sons, and the sheep. He didn't like to fly, so in Chicago Annie put him on a train for home and concluded the trip by herself.[19]

In 1959 she was the first Indian to receive the Josephine B. Hughes Memorial Award, and that same year she was named Arizona Woman of the Year by the Arizona Press Women's Club in recognition of her community service. Also in 1959 she received an award for her work in public health from the Arizona Public Health Association. All of these awards were most surprising for the time. Non-Indians rarely recognized the work of anyone outside the dominant white culture since reservations were considered not part of ordinary American culture, but more like worlds unto themselves. The reasons for this were a mixture of cultural preference, lack of education, and outright racism. Most Indians stayed on or close to their reservations, and there was little opportunity for interaction with the white culture. Except for the unusual few, such as Annie, Indians lived separate lives, well out of the mainstream of American life.

In Annie's earlier terms on the Tribal Council, the work was part-time, but now Annie was working almost every day for tribal interests, leaving George to look after those of their children who were still dependent and to manage day-to-day affairs at Tanner Springs. Georgia Ann and Irma were in their mid-twenties and out on their own. Franklin and Lorencita were in their mid-teens and of growing independence, and Sallie was nine. The disabled boys still needed care, which George provided with help from various relatives.

Just how unusual Annie's position was is illustrated by the

collapse of a program in her own jurisdiction of Wide Ruins. As Annie reported in council, the Mennonite missionaries in Wide Ruins had begun teaching a number of classes in the area and attracted eager adult pupils, many of them women. But after three weeks the program was discontinued because the pupils had ceased to attend. The women pupils had returned to their hogans at the end of the day to find angry husbands. No firewood had been gathered, no groceries had been procured, the horses were left unattended, and dinner was not ready. "Nothing had been done all day but using paper and pencil" was the husbands' attitude. What a contrast to easy-going George Wauneka, who cooked and cleaned for his disabled sons and was happy to oversee all aspects of the ranch while Annie interacted with the wider world.

A TELEGRAM FROM WASHINGTON

Then on July 1, 1963, a telegram arrived for Annie from Washington that would thrust her forever from the back roads of the Navajo Reservation to the front of the American stage. The telegram was from the White House and said: "I am happy to inform you of my intention to award you the Presidential Medal of Freedom. This is the highest civil honor conferred by the President of the United States for service in peacetime. By Executive Order signed earlier this year, the criteria for the award were expanded so as to include especially meritorious contributions to the security of national interests of the United States, world peace, cultural or other significant public or private endeavor. . . . The presentation of the medal to the thirty-one recipients for this year will take place in September. With warm best wishes and congratulations, John F. Kennedy."[20]

Attached to the personal announcement was a list of the other recipients, an eclectic and stellar mix that included cellist Pablo Casals, AFL-CIO president George Meany, former Supreme Court justice Felix Frankfurter, author E. B. White, and artist Andrew Wyeth. Marian Anderson, the noted singer, and Genevieve Caulfield, teacher of the blind in Southeast Asia, were the only other women nominated.

The next day Annie responded to the president: "I have just received your telegram advising that I have been selected as a recipient of the Presidential Medal of Honor. It is with deep humility and gratefulness that this great honor has come to me. It has always been your duty to serve our great country and my people and I am deeply appreciative of the recognition you have bestowed on me. May the Almighty bless you and bestow upon you wisdom and courage and strength during these times when our country greatly needs your leadership. Your humble servant, Mrs. Annie D. Wauneka."[21]

The scheduled presentation was just two months away. Annie began her preparations.

7

Awards and Acrimony

THERE IS NO INDICATION why President Kennedy selected Annie from among hundreds of equally illustrious potential honorees suggested by his advisers. It might have been an attempt to heal relations with the Navajos, which had been uneasy. Attorney General Robert Kennedy, the president's brother, had published a popular article attacking Indian land claims against the federal government generally and singling out the Navajo Land Claim cause for specific ridicule.[1]

WAITING FOR INFORMATION

By September 4, Annie had still not heard the final date for the awards and needed to make travel plans. She telegraphed the White House, expressing again her deep appreciation for the nomination and concluding, "I await further instructions as to when and where the awards will be presented."

A White House special assistant wrote back that the date of the president's award ceremony was being postponed by one month. He promised to let her know the details in a few days but advised that it would probably occur about November 1. October 29 arrived, and she still had no further information. This was nerve wracking to someone so far away from the action in Washington. Telephones on the reservation were few and didn't always work. Had the message gotten lost? Would the ceremony take place without her? She again telegraphed, asking, "in order that I may arrange my itinerary which will allow me to travel to Washington, if that is necessary, I would appreciate being advised as to the date that the awards will be made."

But the ceremony had to be delayed again. This time it was set for December 6. Meanwhile, Annie set about gathering gifts to take along. She had a pair of Navajo moccasins made for the president with thick white soles and a suede vamp that came up around the ankle. A much smaller pair, almost duplicates, were made for the little boy the nation called John-John. The press sensed a good story in Annie Wauneka and her work on the reservation. *Life* magazine sent a photographer, who took pictures of her visiting the sick in the hospitals and shopping in a trading post to purchase the presents she would take to Washington.

Then on November 22, just two weeks before the ceremony, Annie and the Navajo Nation joined the rest of America and the world in shock and mourning. President Kennedy had been shot in Dallas.

John F. Kennedy had been popular with Navajos, and the tribe joined the nation in grief. After a week of mourning and a nation-binding funeral, it was time for Americans and their government to get back to work. President Lyndon Johnson had the Medal of Freedom recipients notified that the ceremony scheduled for December 6, 1963, would take place as planned.

Annie had a week to get herself to Washington. Her preparations included another shopping trip during which she purchased a silver and beaded bolo tie for the new president and a silver pin for Lady Bird Johnson. The moccasins she had planned to present to President Kennedy were left behind, although she did take along the gifts intended for John Jr. and Caroline. Because of its link to the tragedy, *Life* magazine decided not to run the feature it had planned highlighting her work.[2]

On her way to Washington for the presentation, Annie stopped by to see her brother Tom in Pawhuska, Oklahoma, where he was the superintendent of the Osage Indian Agency. The local paper sent a reporter to interview her and ran a long story about the Navajo woman who was going to Washington to receive the nation's highest award. The reporter wrote that "she had a outward appearance of calm, but exploded with verbal enthusiasm with eyes that dance and an infectious laugh." The story ran with a photograph of Annie and Tom in front of a portrait of their father.[3]

THE MEDAL OF FREEDOM CEREMONY

Although no one in her family accompanied her, once in Washington Annie met up with Maurice McCabe, who had served as executive secretary for the Navajo Tribal Council for twelve years, and Mrs. McCabe. McCabe was representing the tribe and was also a clan relative. In the growing antagonism between Nakai and his camp and the Old Guard of which Annie was a part, McCabe, one of Annie's confidants, had his own private war against Nakai, who had promised during the campaign to neutralize McCabe's power and was cutting him out of the action.

On the morning of December 6, 1963, Annie awoke in a Washington DC hotel room. She dressed in her usual sturdy oxfords and a purple velvet blouse and colorful tiered skirt of dark blue print silk made for her by her daughter Georgia Ann. She then added four matching silver concho pins to the front of her blouse, put on some bracelets and rings of silver and turquoise, and did up her hair in her typical two-lobed bun wrapped with white yarn. Lastly she slipped around her neck a heavy silver and turquoise squash blossom necklace that had belonged to her father. Though Chee had been gone for twelve years, it was a way of taking him with her. The little daughter who had been so often overlooked, who was relegated to herding sheep while her half-siblings attended private schools, was now about to receive the Medal of Freedom, the highest civilian honor in the land, for following in her father's footsteps and serving her people.

The ceremony, which began shortly after noon, was held in the state dining room of the White House. At the front of the room was a marble fireplace, its mantel and side columns draped in black. Lady Bird Johnson was on hand to greet the honorees as they arrived, and she and Annie, both Westerners, chatted briefly while others were arriving. The audience included the Supreme Court justices, members of the cabinet, and friends and relatives of the honorees. Jacqueline Kennedy, who was still in mourning, attended the ceremony seated behind a screen.

After opening remarks by Under Secretary of State George W. Ball, President Johnson came forward, saying, "Over the past two weeks, our nation has known moments of the utmost sorrow, of anguish and shame. This day, however, is a moment of great pride. In the shattering sequence of events that began 14 days ago, we encountered in its full horror man's capacity for hatred and destruction. There is little we do not now know of evil, but it is time to turn once more to the pursuits of honor and excellence and of achievement that have always marked the true direction of the American people."[4]

Then, as the recipients were announced individually with a very short recounting of their achievements, each stepped to the front of the room and was awarded the handsome medal attached to a red, white, and blue ribbon. Angier Biddle Duke, chief of protocol, assisted in the presentation. The Medal of Freedom—a white star encircled by six golden eagles—had been redesigned by President and Mrs. Kennedy. Each honoree also received a citation. Annie's read: "Vigorous crusader for betterment of the health of her people, Mrs. Wauneka has selflessly worked to help them conquer tuberculosis, dysentery and trachoma. She succeeded in these efforts by winning the confidence of her people, and then by interpreting to them the miracles of modern medical science."[5]

LUNCHING WITH THE CHIEF JUSTICE

Afterward, the recipients were further honored at a reception and luncheon in the State Department dining room. Newspaper reports say that a small crowd gathered around Annie to congratulate her and ask about her outfit and jewelry. When it was time to eat, Annie was seated at a table with Chief Justice Earl Warren. Then, it was on to a reception given by Secretary of the Interior Stewart Udall in his office. Annie and Secretary Udall had been friendly since he had been elected to Congress in the 1950s representing a district embracing much of the Navajo Reservation. Udall had grown up in the little Mormon town of St. John's near the reservation and as a child had heard about Chee Dodge, the famous Navajo leader. He had followed Annie's work on tuberculosis. When the White House had sent a circular around to government departments announcing President Kennedy's intention to give the award and requesting suggestions, Udall had submitted Annie's name. She had also been recommended by officials in the Department of Health, Education and Welfare who knew of her work on the reservation.

Secretary Udall's reception was well attended by members of Congress, Indian Commissioner Philleo Nash and his staff, and representatives from the Department of Health, Education and Welfare and the Public Health Service. Undoubtedly some of these people had never before spoken to an American Indian and viewed Annie as something of a curiosity. Even Pulitzer Prize-winning author Thornton Wilder, another of the Medal of Freedom recipients, showed up. In introducing Annie to his guests, Udall said, "Annie has been a kind of one-woman Peace Corps in Navajo land." Then he turned to her, saying, "It is my feeling that in honoring you today we did honor not only to you yourself, your family and friends, but also to all the Indian people of the nation—they have been honored along with you." Annie, gracious as ever, but with her usual loquaciousness somewhat subdued by the August company, responded by saying that she would cherish the medal and the honor as long as she lived. Apparently she was relaxed enough to enjoy herself at the event, because a reporter commented that she was smiling and at ease.[6]

BACK TO WINDOW ROCK

But ceremonies must come to an end, and by the weekend Annie and the McCabes were headed back to the reservation, where the contentiousness in the council was growing. The council did stop for a short time on December 9 to listen to Annie tell them about her experience. She conveyed her mixed feelings of sadness at the tragedy surrounding President Kennedy's absence from the ceremony and her own excitement. Then she graciously added, "It is with you Councilmen and the previous Councilmen with their efforts behind me, working with them continuously, helping me in every way they can, that is how I was promoted to get this particular medal. I appreciate this very much and everyone of you is entitled to this award. I think we all got it together, but I was singled out to get it for you."[7]

She also mentioned the Navajo People and her own constituents in Klagetoh and Wide Ruins, thereby bringing everyone under the umbrella of honor. This was another instance of Annie's ability to function across cultures. While she did not hesitate to stand out or speak out when she was working for one of her causes either on the reservation or in Washington, she knew that the Navajo way was to not cause attention to oneself, to strive not to stand out from one's associates. By indicating that the honor was shared—by those who had helped on committees and others who had voted with her and for her—she was drawing a blanket of Navajo respectability around the experience.

Although Annie continued her interest and work on health care issues, particularly alcoholism, this period marked a gradual drift in her career toward more involvement with tribal political issues. She had served on the council for thirteen years and was comfortable with the Navajo political process. She had traveled to a number of conferences throughout the country, had been to Washington many times on lobbying trips, and had capped it with the Medal of Freedom ceremony. She had learned to talk to national-level officials, had found them responsive to her interests, and was not shy about approaching them when matters of Navajo politics began to intermingle with national-level concerns. This was the beginning of a drift in her career from grassroots organizer to power broker.

NORMAN LITTELL'S SITUATION

Annie showed her political acumen and willingness to wade into legislatively muddy waters when, in the early months of 1964, dissension swirled through the Navajo Tribal Council on a number of matters that pitted delegate against delegate. Annie was in the middle of all of it. One of the major issues was the employment of Norman Littell, an attorney who had been hired to represent the Navajos in 1947 when Chee was alive. The two were friends, and apparently Chee trusted him. Annie, following and building on her father's alliance, became a staunch ally, standing up for Littell even when some of his financial dealings with the tribe were questionable.

To understand the enormous brouhaha that ensued, with

Annie as a major player, it is necessary to look back a few years and briefly recount Littell's interaction with the tribe and the history behind the cases on which he worked. Every five years when Littell's contract was up for renewal, he went before the council and asked for a raise. In 1957, Annie led the discussion on whether to grant the raise, leavening it with humor by saying that in the old days the leaders would have picked out one of the most worthy young women and given her as a wife, but since that was no longer appropriate, they would have to compensate Littell with money. The delegates agreed to do so with a vote of 66 to 1. Another time, Annie spoke up for Littell in a meeting saying, "I look upon these attorneys as men with a flashlight. I think they throw light upon and uncover hidden facts which overcome various oppositions . . . in a sense a guiding light for the Navajo people. These people have brought immeasurable progress to the Navajo people."[8]

During his long tenure, Littell was involved in many tribal affairs, including restructuring the regulations on traders. In the 1950s he won several significant cases, one of which secured for the tribe the right to enforce its ban against the use of peyote. As early as December 1958, Raymond Nakai, then a radio announcer in Flagstaff, had been waging a campaign against Littell on his radio program with damaging, possibly libelous statements. Littell complained to the radio station owner, and the attacks stopped.

THE INDIAN CLAIMS ACT

But the main reason that the Navajos had to have a lawyer was to represent them in land claims cases. In August of 1946, Congress had approved the Indian Claims Act and set up the Claims Commission. Quite simply, the Native American tribes maintained that they had owned all of North America before the arrival of the Europeans, and because the land had been taken from them, they deserved to be paid for their territory. Congress agreed and ruled that Indian tribes could sue the federal government for various losses, including aboriginal land.

Littell had also worked on the incredibly complicated case

involving division of the Executive Order Reservation land that had been used in common with the Hopi since 1882. It will be remembered that when the Navajos had returned to their traditional home after release from Bosque Redondo, they were given only a portion of their original homelands as their reservation. As their population expanded, they began moving to the west outside reservation boundaries into areas they had formerly occupied. Then in 1882 President Chester Arthur had signed an executive order creating a 2,472,095-acre reservation "for the use and occupancy of the Moqui (Hopi) and other Indians as the Secretary of the Interior may see fit to settle thereon." Given the state of education and communication among the Indians during that time, it seems certain that few if any of the Hopi and Navajo families living on the "new" reservation were aware of the order.

When Indian Commissioner John Collier instituted the stock reduction program in 1937, the entire area on which the Navajo and Hopi lived was divided into eighteen grazing districts. Grazing district six, wholly within the 1882 Executive Order Reservation, was set aside for the exclusive use of the Hopi. The rest of the 1882 area was divided into districts where only Navajos were to be given grazing permits, recognizing Navajo settlement of the area as a fact. The one hundred Navajo families living within district six, where only Hopis were to stay, had to relocate.[9]

Although many Navajo and Hopi families lived peacefully side by side, there remained plenty of antagonism. Some of it dated back many generations; some was exactly what would be expected when different cultural groups are competing for scarce natural resources. However, by the mid-1950s, the contention would grow beyond grazing areas and water sources. It appeared there was much more at stake than grass, sagebrush, and a few springs and watering holes. Geophysical surveys for oil and uranium companies indicated that a vast storehouse of natural resources might lie beneath the disputed area. The tribe that controlled the land might realize millions of dollars. In 1956 the Hopi Tribe filed a brief with the Department of the Interior, claiming exclusive rights to all minerals in the 1882 Executive Order Reservation. Norman Littell reported this to the Navajo Tribal Council, warning them that this was a serious situation and that they would have to take a defensive position.

THE BEGINNING OF *HEALING V. JONES*

Eventually, in 1958, the Navajos and Hopis were authorized by congressional legislation to enter into a federal lawsuit to determine their respective rights to the nearly 2.5 million acres. The suit, called *Healing v. Jones* after the men who at that time were chairmen of the Hopi and Navajo Tribes, was heard for a month in 1960 in Prescott, Arizona, with the Hopis claiming that the entire 1882 Executive Order area should belong to them.[10] Norman Littell was most interested in protecting the mineral rights and the subsequent economic advantage for his clients, whereas the Navajos themselves were more concerned about maintaining control of the land as a place for both people and sheep to live.

Among the witnesses were Annie's son-in-law, Ed Plummer, head of the Navajo Tribe's Land Investigation Department. Ed, who was married to Georgia Ann, was the son of Old Guard council member Ned Plummer. Annie appeared as the only witness on the final day of testimony, describing the religious and emotional ties of Navajos to their place of birth.[11]

After two years of consideration, the court ruled that except for the exclusively Hopi district six, the Navajo and Hopi Tribes had "joint and equal rights" to the land. With Navajos settled all over the area as well as the possibility of high-stakes mining opportunities to who-knows-what under various locations, neither the Navajo nor Hopi Tribe was about to give up claim to one square inch. So, in practical terms, this decision settled nothing. Mainly it set the stage for more controversy.

Although the *Healing v. Jones* decision was generally regarded as a defeat for the Navajos since it did not give them sole ownership to that vast area with its potential resources, it did establish for the first time the tribe's legal rights to the disputed land. At least that is the interpretation Littell put forth when discussing the decision with his Navajo clients. It certainly was to his benefit to do so. Norman Littell, in a move apparently not announced to the Tribal Council but approved by the BIA and former chair-

man Paul Jones, had amended his contract so that the *Healing v.
Jones* matter was considered a claims case in which Littell himself was entitled to 10 percent of the value of the land he "recovered, saved or obtained" for the tribe. The government had
suggested this method of payment for the claims cases because
many tribes were without funds and would not have been able
to hire an attorney without this option. However, Littell, as the
lawyer for a tribe with some financial resources, was already getting a salary to cover his time. When the terms of his contract
were made public, there was considerable grumbling among the
council delegates.

NAKAI'S WAR AGAINST LITTELL

One of Raymond Nakai's election promises was to get rid of Littell although the attorney had four years to go on his contract.
Since Nakai had campaigned against the upholding of the peyote
ban, and since Littell had fought on behalf of the Navajo Tribal
Council for the right to that ban, it was clear that the two would
not work together amicably. So once Nakai took office as chairman early in 1963, he began work on his promise, visiting Washington with some attorneys of his own choosing and consulting
with Secretary of the Interior Udall on his complaints against
Littell.

Following a pattern begun when the first Navajo agent was
sent by the federal government to the reservation, duly elected
Navajo adults had to go to the secretary of the interior for permission to fire an employee. In the forty years since Washington
officials had set up a central Navajo government, many Navajos
had become educated in white-run schools and were fully competent to handle their own affairs, but the paternal attitude still
persisted. Chairman Nakai's primary issue was not the rights of
the Native American Church members to use peyote, but whether
Littell had a right to 10 percent of the value of lands recovered in
the *Healing v. Jones* decision—which would be an enormous sum.

In November of 1963, just before the Medal of Freedom ceremony, Udall had determined that *Healing v. Jones* was not a claims
case and issued an order to cancel Littell's contract, accusing him

of dishonest and gross misconduct in dealing with the Navajo Tribe. Udall's solicitor ordered tribal records seized, and a truckload of filing cabinets from some council offices were taken to Nakai's garage. Executive Secretary Maurice McCabe's files were also taken, including personal materials such as his income tax returns. When McCabe accompanied Annie to the Medal of Freedom ceremonies, his interactions with Udall at the events surrounding the festivities must have been frosty indeed.

Despite the fact that Annie and Udall had been friendly, as soon as she got back from Washington, she and some of the rest of the Old Guard went into action to defend Littell's position with the tribe and to prevent Nakai from carrying out programs they deemed detrimental. Littell got a temporary injunction against Udall to stop him from interfering with Littell's job as general counsel for the tribe.

WAR OVER THE TRIBAL BUDGET

After the first of the year, with everyone still stirred up over the Littell issue, it was time for the Navajo council members to start work on the 1964 annual budget. The Old Guard and their sympathizers, with Annie at the helm, confronted Nakai's camp on every item, and the arguments were fierce. The debate went on and on for three and a half months. Because the delegates were receiving pay and per diem expenses for every day they kept up the wrangling, and translators and other staff were also on the payroll, it cost $3,000 a day to keep the council in session. It was typical of Annie to participate frequently in the council discussions, but during this period she was especially vocal, questioning closely the need for many expenditures. One of the problems was that she was chafing at not being in her accustomed seats on the Budget and Finance Committee and the Advisory Council. Although some council members were content to merely sit in the general sessions and vote when called upon to do so, she was used to knowing the business of the tribe in detail. She also remained irritated at Raymond Nakai for his vendetta against Norman Littell and his poor treatment of her friend Maurice McCabe. It is interesting to note that the one committee budget that was approved with little discussion and no dissent was that of the Health Committee.

Eventually, the contest between the Nakai and Littell camps became personal. In August, a council member stood to praise Chairman Nakai and his work and to lay the blame for the dissension on the terms of Littell's contract. "Yes, there are some of you who are praised for receiving things as Freedom Medals, but all you want to do is hang on to this Littell," he stormed. "We don't want Littell, we want him out!" Mabel Hesuse also accused Annie of initiating the divisions. "We were about to unite until Annie Wauneka was given the floor," she said one day during a particularly rancorous council session. "Now there is disorder. She is being praised for receiving an award somewhere, a Medal of Peace and Freedom. We would like to respect her, to hear something good from her, but every time she is given the floor her speech is not of sound judgment."[12]

Annie had been more outspoken on the issue than was acceptable in Navajo culture. Instead of working quietly for consensus, she had continually and openly lobbied on the behalf of Norman Littell, a white man, against the Navajo chairman and other council members. Hesuse's speech against her was an indication that the fact that she had been awarded the Medal of Freedom still rankled in some quarters.

Despite the fact that some of the delegates were irritated with her, when the Advisory Council, now called the Advisory Committee, was reorganized and expanded, Annie was one of those elected to the post. She won her spot by only two votes, but it meant she was back on the inside, privy to details of tribal administration, and was able to take a more active part in the decisions.

Annie continued to be relentless in her disapproval of Raymond Nakai, even denouncing him over the radio. By now, news of the problems in the Navajo Tribal Council had spread to the far reaches of the reservation, and a delegation of Navajos came from several districts to address the council. Every speaker laid the cause of the problem on Norman Littell. One woman, however, brought up the possibility of witchcraft being involved in stirring up the trouble. Among the Navajos, that was a serious charge indeed. She did not mention Annie directly, but since she was responding to Annie's denouncement of Nakai over the radio, the implication was that she might be involved. She also accused the council members of wasting money with the long council sessions and day after day of wrangling—money that belonged to all the Navajos.[13]

A LETTER TO PRESIDENT JOHNSON

On December 31, 1964, Annie took the opportunity to take her battle on behalf of Norman Littell directly to President Johnson when she responded to an invitation to attend his inauguration. Aware that letters dealing with Indian matters were routinely routed directly to the secretary of the interior, against whom who she was lobbying, she sent the letter to the LBJ Ranch in Texas, rather than to Washington in a bid to gain the attention of the president himself. After opening with her acceptance of the invitation to the inaugural, she continued in ten single-spaced pages to detail what she and her contingent saw as abuses by the secretary of the interior. She mentioned irregularities in the budgeting process and missing funds in the hundreds of thousands of dollars since Nakai took over the chairmanship, accused the Interior Department of rushing through oil and gas leases, decried the "character assassination" being committed against Norman Littell, and in general bitterly denounced the interference of the secretary in Navajo tribal business. The letter states, "We, the largest tribe of Indians in this country, have conducted our affairs for over seventeen years, imperfectly no doubt, but with growing competence. Are we and other Indian tribes now to be forgotten in your fine stand for justice and civil liberties, and are we to remain subject to Udall's internal colonial policy of domination and exploitation unknown to you, while abroad in other countries the United State advocates and support democratic processes and insists on freedom from colonialism? This ugly page in Indian history has been written. Udall cannot unwrite it." After several paragraphs laying the crisis in Navajo politics at the feet of Secretary Udall and Indian Commissioner Philleo Nash she continued, "As a Freedom Award winner (with gratitude to you for this high honor), I agree with Sergeant York that freedom is not something you fight for once and win; it is something we must keep on fighting for."

Perhaps in an effort to lighten the tone of her letter, if not the message, she concluded, "I have seen newspaper reports before the election that Udall had joined the District of Columbia Bar, not, as he said 'for lack of confidence as to the outcome of the election, but as an insurance policy against a rainy day.' We appeal to you as the Great White Father, for rain. With warmest Seasons Greetings in which I know that the Navajo people would join me, I add this prayer: Let it rain, Mr. President, let it rain!"[14]

The last section was typical of Annie's humor, but although she was an articulate and powerful spokesperson for the Navajo, and although she surely believed passionately in the ideas set forth, the letter does not sound like it was written by her alone. It was possibly a group effort, and no doubt Littell himself had a role in its composition.

Now not only was Annie defending a white tribal employee against other Navajos, but she had also taken an essentially tribal issue to the federal government for intervention. Annie's strong and continuing support for Norman Littell is somewhat mystifying. She was ordinarily clear thinking and able to discern any attempt by non-Navajos to take advantage of her people in any way. Perhaps her backing of Norman Littell was influenced by her continuing emotional ties to her father's memory and her efforts to make herself worthy according to Chee's standards by carrying out his policies and supporting his allegiances.

To the White House, Annie was just another disgruntled local politician, and she was attacking a powerful member of the president's cabinet. But because Annie was a Medal of Freedom recipient, her charges were deemed important enough to be looked into. Lee C. White, associate special counsel to the president, routed the letter to Udall's office for comment, and on February 10, 1965, about six weeks later, one of Udall's assistants sent back to the president's office a five-page explanation which began, "Since early in 1963 when Raymond C. Nakai was elected chairman of the Navajo Tribal Council in a bitterly contested election . . . the Navajo tribal government has been in a state of almost continuous turmoil," and went on to explain or rebut all of Annie's allegations.[15] Like everything else in Navajo politics that year, it was fast dissolving into a bitter "he said, she said" dispute, but it appears that many of Annie's allegations were the result of the lack of information flow between the two camps and the heightened atmosphere of suspicion, so that even ordinary occurrences took on the flavor of the nefarious.

JUDGE SIRICA HEARS LITTELL MATTER

Simultaneously, Annie and Maurice McCabe were in Washington testifying in Federal District Court in front of Judge John C. Sirica in support of Littell as Littell tried to get a permanent injunction against Udall's interference with his performance as tribal attorney. Annie firmly expressed her belief that Littell was able and honest and had rendered good service to the Navajos. Testifying against Littell were Nakai and six other Navajos, including Mabel Hesuse. The case seemed to rest on Littell's salary and whether he could consider the *Healing v. Jones* dispute a claims case for which he was entitled to additional compensation. Judge Sirica was expected to take several months to make his decision.[16]

When Annie returned to the reservation, awaiting her was a letter from solicitor Lee White saying that since litigation was pending on the Littell versus Udall matter, he was not at liberty to write a detailed response to her long letter, adding, "The charges you have made against officials of this Administration are too serious to be acted upon without substantial proof. A preliminary investigation suggests that you may have been misinformed as to the conduct, as well as the purpose and motives, of those officials. Certainly that is our hope."[17] And almost certainly that was indeed the case. The letter was only two paragraphs long, and Annie was no doubt frustrated at its brevity. She had no way of knowing that Lee White had requested and received a thorough explanation that probably took Udall's associates many days of work to put together.

Annie's battle made news across the reservation, and many people disagreed with her position. She acknowledged this herself in a council meeting by saying that the Sunday morning radio program for Navajos was supposed to be for tribal announcements, not politics. "Last Sunday a Mrs. Bedona from Tuba City got on and denounced me asking that I never come to the Council again. I was the troublemaker and I was this and I was that," she quoted. However, she indicated that she had no intention of backing down.[18]

By May, Judge Sirica issued a permanent injunction against Secretary Udall that prohibited him from firing Norman Littell. In his opinion, Judge Sirica wrote about Annie's appearance on behalf of Littell, saying, "The wisdom, honesty, sincerity and judgment manifested by her while she was testifying in the contempt proceeding and also in this action . . . has greatly impressed the Court. . . . She testified that the Council members are 'able and capable to handling the Tribal affairs.' . . . I think she is a woman of character. I think she is a truthful individual, and this argument made by the Government that her expenses were paid does not hold a grain of salt with the Court because how else would she get here? You certainly would not expect her to pay her own fare. There is nothing improper with counsel paying her expenses. But she did come, which is more than Mr. Nakai."[19]

On June 10, Annie fired off a letter to Lee White referring to their earlier exchange of letters and decrying his suggestion that she "may have been misinformed," citing Sirica's opinion. She concluded with: "The President has made it clear that he will not tolerate corruption in his government. What, then, does he intend to do about Udall?" When White sent the letter to Udall for a reply he scribbled, "She's a wild woman. I see no purpose in a reply!" White did reply to Annie, however, stating blandly, "We are aware of the very deep emotions that are involved in this troublesome matter and will continue to follow it closely.[20]

ANOTHER HEALTH CRISIS

All of this sustained contention and the constant tension and meetings had finally caught up with Annie, however, and she was exhausted. Her doctor ordered her to take a thirty-day rest.

By August, political infighting had to be put aside temporarily as a real health crisis loomed that needed Annie's attention. Dr. George Bock told the Tribal Council that the Indian Health Service had confirmed five cases of bubonic plague on the reservation originating from prairie dog fleas. Annie knew that she could arouse interest in such a problem by lending her prestige to the campaign and thus could help to bring it under control, so she drove her truck from chapter house to chapter house, spreading the word on the importance of avoiding these familiar rodents. Prairie dogs live in underground villages, and Navajo children love to watch their comical actions. Both children and dogs try to catch them, but they are very fast, scurrying to dive to safety down one hole, only to poke their heads up again after running through a tunnel. When a child or dog was able to catch a prairie dog and bring it back to the hogan, it was, in the overwhelming number of cases, a sick animal.

Fortunately, by 1965 the health care situation on the Navajo Reservation had improved tremendously in the decade since Annie had begun to wage war on tuberculosis. With the IHS now in charge, public health nurses, many of them Navajo, could be enlisted to help spread the word on the prairie dog problem. The field staff was always happy to have Annie's help, however, since her voice carried weight in health matters.

The next summer Dr. Bock returned to the council, reporting that the prairie dogs were still a health menace. Within the last three years, ten cases of plague had erupted on the Navajo Reservation, and widespread deaths of prairie dogs had been reported in the Window Rock and Shiprock areas, indicating an infected population. Dr. Bock warned the delegates that when plague swept over Europe and later China, it had killed a large number of people in both areas. Annie had been doing research on the situation and was able to tell the council that the best international experts did not recommend vaccination because immunity required four successive injections and lasted only a few months.

Years later, Dr. Bock would remember Annie's visits to his office. "She would come in and tell me she was looking for the facts on whatever topic was on the table then," he recalled. He'd explain what he could to her and give her books or articles to read. "Then she would take these bits of information and go back to the people and share it with them so they would understand what the problem was," he added.[21]

After giving their report, both Annie and Dr. Bock urged the other delegates to take the message to their home chapters and also to warn their constituents that if they felt ill they should not to go to the upcoming Gallup Inter-tribal Fair, where thousands of Native Americans congregated from throughout the West, nor to any of the local fairs.

During this period Annie also took time to attend the Third National Conference on Indian Health in Washington. Part of the discussion centered on mental illness among Indians. Annie brought up the subject of alcoholism, still the number one problem on the Navajo Reservation, and the growing incidence of peyote use and the Native American Church, which she continued to fiercely oppose. When the conversation turned to trachoma, which was curable but continued to be a big problem on the reservation, once again Annie took a major role in the discussion, saying, "They used the same wash basin day out and day in and the same face towels. They have to be taught that if a person who is infected with trachoma comes in and washes his face in the basin, then the next person picks it up. The basic problem is in the homes, to understand that you have to have sufficient water to keep clean. The Navajos have to haul water and you know what that means." Then she turned to the doctors there to ask for advice. "How should we go about it to aid this prevention through health education?" she asked. When one of the doctors suggested the public health nurses, Annie answered that she thought the Navajos themselves should take responsibility. "If we are going to learn as Indians, we are going to have to do it through our own Indian youth. What are they being born for, after all?"[22]

She frequently made an effort to support those Navajos who were working to further issues she considered important. When visiting hospitals she'd call together all the Navajo employees and tell them to take their jobs seriously and to represent the tribe well. She also gave them the opportunity to vent their frustrations.

ANNIE'S FIRST CLASH WITH PETER MACDONALD

Throughout the fall of 1965 and into 1966, the Littell versus Udall and Old Guard versus Nakai disputes continued to simmer in the background, affecting practically every situation that arose involving the Navajos and the federal government.

These were the peak years of Lyndon Johnson's War on Poverty, before the Vietnam War seemed to overshadow everything in Washington. In the spring of 1965, the Advisory Committee had established an Office of Navajo Economic Opportunity to oversee the $9 million the tribe had received from Washington. They named as its executive director an attractive young Navajo engineer named Peter MacDonald, who had returned to work for the tribe after a promising career with Hughes Aircraft in California. For some reason, perhaps because he was brought in by Raymond Nakai, Annie took a dislike to him. She might also have resented him because he had lived away from the reservation for many years, and she saw him bringing in unnecessary modern influences. In his autobiography, *The Last Warrior*, MacDonald writes that one afternoon after he had been working for the Navajo Nation for about eight months, Annie came up to him during a council recess, pointed her finger at him and said, "Young man, you go back to Los Angeles. We don't need you. We don't need you at all. You go back to Los Angeles." MacDonald writes in his defense:

I was not trying to bring new ideas that would disrupt the people. I was trying to restore pride in being a Navajo. I was giving up success in the white world to help my people.

But I felt that all this woman could see was someone who was assisting Raymond Nakai, part of the new guard. She would rather focus on politics than on the mutual concerns that would benefit her, her children, and her grandchildren.

I also resented her condescending manner. She was limited in her experience, yet she rigidly focused on the fact that I was not a part of her group, choosing to mistrust my intentions rather than to see me as an ally. . . . I will never forget that experience, and the image of her angry face and accusing finger are indelibly etched in my mind. . . . Annie Wauneka struck me as an antagonist rather than someone with a plan for the future of the people she claimed to love. And while she ultimately did much good from her council position, she also was, in my mind, viciously divisive and needlessly hurtful throughout the years to follow.[23]

As it turns out, MacDonald later had his own problems with being divisive. After serving four times as tribal chairman, he ended up in prison on charges of fraud, bribery, conspiracy, and ethics violations, but that occurred in the 1990s, long after he first returned to the Navajo Reservation.

Lecturing with her pointed finger for emphasis, particularly when she was excited or very serious, was an Annie Wauneka trademark. This was unusual behavior for Navajos, who generally avoid pointing with their hands or fingers. If they need to indicate something they will do so by nodding their head in the necessary direction or point with pursed lips. As an elderly traditional Navajo explained: "To point . . . is to deride or hold up to scorn. Even to point at a material object with the finger is to assume a posture of violence, whether intended or not. We use the face or the body or merely the lips, for the hands are deceptive things without brains and are hired things without souls."[24] If someone as acculturated as Peter MacDonald had trouble with her pointed finger, we can assume there were others more traditional who were also offended; however, it seems not to have blunted her effectiveness nor the overall affection of most of the Navajo People toward Annie.

LITTELL LOSES HIS CASE

In September one of the problems causing the divisiveness in the council took a step toward resolution. The U.S. Court of Appeal reversed Judge Sirica's ruling and defended Interior Secretary Udall's "broad authority vested by Congress to oversee Indian Affairs." In other words, the court said Udall was within his rights to step into the Navajos' affairs and dismiss their attorney, Norman Littell. Annie did not take the loss gracefully. She issued a statement saying that the ruling "if followed through all the way would put us back to the days of Fort Sumner where the Secretary and the Indian Agent told us what to do and we had no voice in the matter."[25] Although Littell attempted to take his fight to the Supreme Court, the justices refused to hear the case, and within six months, he was gone from the reservation. He maintained, however, that he was still due money from the claims cases. In 1980, after a long fight in and out of the federal courts in which Littell sought a $2.8 million settlement, he finally agreed to accept $795,000.

Back in the fall of 1966, however, having battled on behalf of Norman Littell for the last four years, Annie now faced a battle of her own. She had another election coming up, and she had suffered from much negative publicity.

8

Overseeing Baby Contests
and Student Protests

DESPITE THE FACT THAT ANNIE and the rest of the Old Guard
campaigned heavily against Tribal Council Chairman Raymond
Nakai, other factors were in his favor. Many of the Navajo elec-
torate supported the easing of the enforcement of regulations
against peyote. Largely because Nakai won by large margins in
precincts where the Native American Church was strong, he was
given another term. Some of the Old Guard lost their seats, but
Annie Wauneka retained her slot. The new council was more supportive of Nakai and granted him the power to appoint members
of the Advisory Committee. Oddly enough, despite their years of
very public disagreements, he returned Annie to that important
body. When the Supreme Court refused to hear the Udall versus
Littell matter and Norman Littell resigned his position, the rancor in the Tribal Council lessened even more with that target of
contention gone.

AT HOME IN KLAGETOH
About this time the BIA was deciding to close down the boarding school in Klagetoh because there was an insufficient supply
of water. At Annie's request, the BIA turned the buildings over
to the community. After some discussion and over a period of
months, the houses were given to a group of families with children who needed to catch the bus to attend school in Ganado.
When it came to deciding who would live in the principal's house,
the residents of Klagetoh told Annie they wanted her to live there.
"This is a leader's house," they said. "We need you here with us,
not in Window Rock."

So Annie and her daughter Sallie moved into the large orange
sandstone block house, while George and the boys stayed at Tan-

ner Springs. Annie kept the house simple and never used the electric lights in the daytime, even in dark hallways. Although she had nice furniture and many large and colorful Navajo rugs, she was aware that if she acquired too many conveniences or luxuries she'd be setting herself up for criticism. "Lots of people come in here, and they look around, and they don't see any expensive things around here. I guess they're happy," she told a reporter.[1]

By that time, Sallie was in a wheelchair, and it was easier for her to get around in the more modern house. Sallie was slightly retarded, probably due to her difficult birth, although she functioned well. When Annie had to be away overnight, a relative who lived nearby looked after Sallie. As Annie became more prominent nationally, articles appeared about her and her work in magazines and newspapers around the country. They usually listed her as having five or six children, rather than nine. She did not often bring up the sons George was caring for at the ranch. Although beliefs about retarded and disabled people have changed considerably as Navajos have received more education, traditionally it was thought that handicapped children were the result of the mother having broken a major taboo—such as killing a relative, being a witch, or having sexual relations with someone too closely related. Since the Waunekas knew none of these were the case, and they apparently preferred not to deal with questions and accusations, they just kept quiet about some of their children.

On the rare occasion that Annie discussed her disabled boys with friends, she said that even as they grew older they would always be like children, and rather than spending her life caring for them, she had to work for all Navajo children. Caring for several disabled family members in a home with no modern conveniences must have presented numerous challenges for George. There were clearly limitations on what he could provide. At times various professionals suggested that the boys would do better in an institution, but George was adamant that they belonged at home under his care. Annie visited frequently, taking in supplies and fresh food regularly and consulting on ranch business. There was no phone line out to Tanner Springs, so all interaction had to be done face to face.

Most Navajo men know how to cook simple meals, and George was no exception. Sometimes there were other family members or hired helpers around to cook, but when this was not the case, he would cook for himself and the boys. His grandson Milton Jr. recalls, "The thing that I remember of my grandfather's devotion to my uncles was him walking carrying a kettle in one arm, maybe two or three loaves of bread under his arm and a pot of coffee. He was happy and glowed and patted their heads and poured each one coffee and gave each one equal shares of food and they were all laughing and happy. My grandfather gave me a feeling of the sacredness of life by his relationship with my uncles."[2]

THE BIG SNOW

Throughout 1967 Annie and the rest of the council worked on routine matters neglected during the years of wrangling. As the year wound down, everyone agreed that it had been a period of calm where life had gotten back to normal in the political area. But the year wasn't over yet. When snow began to fall on the morning of December 13, 1967, neither Annie nor anyone else was concerned. On the dry grasslands of the reservation, winter precipitation is welcome and necessary. Even the lower rangelands like the Wauneka's ranch at Tanner Springs get a significant portion of their annual moisture through snow. Without it, there would be little spring grass. However, the snow kept coming and coming. One storm followed another for eight days. People were snowed in all over the reservation, some with medical problems or no food. More than half a million sheep, goats, and cattle were either frozen or stranded without feed.

Life came to a standstill on the reservation. All the roads were closed with the exception of a single highway connecting Window Rock to Gallup and the outside world. The U.S. Army, Navy, and Air Force sent helicopters to transport food, fuel, and hay to stranded Navajos and to fly doctors to places where they were needed. Radio broadcasts told stranded Navajos how to signal their needs.

When the snow finally stopped, Annie used her influence to see to it that Highway 191 connecting Ganado, Klagetoh, and

Wide Ruins to I-40 (the old Highway 66) was one of the first roads cleared so that anyone who could make it to the paved road could make it out. It also made it possible for her to commute from Klagetoh to Window Rock, where she could help in getting out supplies. Rescue efforts were just getting underway when the temperature dropped to −25 degrees, making conditions even worse for those still snowed in. Flying became risky for the rescuers.

Eventually the military helicopters, most of them flown by pilots just back from steamy Vietnam and unused to the problems caused by freezing weather, made more than a thousand trips and dropped 300 tons of hay and 225 tons of food. Luckily George and the boys had plenty of food due to the Waunekas' practice of laying in big supplies of beans and potatoes in the fall. But for those Navajo less forward looking or unable to afford to buy ahead, volunteers stuffed big burlap feedsacks with cornmeal, rolled oats, rice, canned meat, peanut butter, and raisins for the drops. Doctors looked after cases of mumps and sniffles in the hogans and ordered the airlift of 115 people to hospitals, mostly for frostbite or obstetric attention. Annie was a blur of activity, helping with the provisions and the scheduling. Quick action meant that only six people died and livestock losses were only 5 percent.

Both *Time* and *Life* magazines sent reporters and photographers. *Time* wrote about one elderly Navajo, Sidney Yazzie, who walked ten miles through drifts to the White Water trading post and stuffed his burlap sack with groceries. When the trader asked why he had not ridden his horse, Yazzie replied simply, "The horse didn't want to go."[3]

BOARDING SCHOOL OR DAY SCHOOL?

The spring following the big snows, a bumper crop of grass was coming up. Annie began spending more of her time and attention on the bumper crops of little Navajo children who not only required health care but also needed to be prepared for life in a world that was wholly different from what any Navajo had experienced before and, what's more, was at odds with many traditional Navajo values and beliefs.

One of Annie's first speeches after having been elected back in 1951 was a round-table discussion where she lobbied for more boarding schools. Leaning on her own experience at boarding schools, she urged that all Navajo children be educated in state-accredited boarding schools on the reservation, close enough to home so that parents could see their children frequently. "The day schools were a failure from the start," she said.

Scattered families and hogans many miles apart makes it hard for the children to attend classes. To attend a day school is very hard for the child. He learns how to keep clean, is told to learn the white man's language during the day. But he returns home to his hogan, he finds no conveniences, his parents are still clinging to the old way of living, and the child is caught between the Indian way and the white way.

Boarding schools are best for the Navajo children because they attend school nine months of the year. They learn fast, can keep clean, have a sufficient diet, good sleeping quarters and a good recreation. When every child of school age is actually in school, we will know we have begun to solve our problems. Once we have education, the other problems will be taken care of. Lack of education has caused many of our young men and women as well as the old people to pass their time drinking, bootlegging, and using peyote.[4]

In the spring of 1968, Robert Kennedy, then a senator from New York, was traveling around the country, visiting Indian reservations and conducting investigations for a special subcommittee on Indian education. In early April, he held hearings in Flagstaff, and although Annie was not on the program, she attended anyhow.

Noting that 65 percent of Indian children dropped out of school, Kennedy opened the meeting by saying, "We have not done all we could to encourage the Indian child to improve his education and become the lawyers, doctors, engineers and teachers they are capable of becoming." Kennedy found out that Annie was in the audience and called her forward, asking, "Could you just make a short statement as one of the most respected members of the Navajo tribe and one of our most respected citizens in the United States? Could you just make a short statement about the problems of the Indian education?"

Annie was never at a loss for words in situations about which she felt passionately, and she was more than happy to comply. She told Kennedy and the assemblage that she thought it was time for the Navajos to get involved in the educational planning for their children. "If we are going to have a successful community, I think a school should be within the community and the community could be developed around this particular area."

She then told a story about a BIA-run school in the Steamboat area where the Navajo parents were dissatisfied with the superintendent and the principal. The parents got together at the chapter house and voted 171 to 0 in favor of asking that the school officials be replaced. However, BIA officials at Window Rock told the parents later that the superintendent and principal were protected by civil service regulations. "We, we are beaten, just like on the television, the Indians are always beaten," she said.

She concluded her statement by complaining that the Navajo Tribal Council was never consulted about location when a new elementary school was to be built. Frequently this meant building a large school and then closing down smaller local schools. To fill up the new school, youngsters would either have to be bused long distances or boarded. "That means taking away little kids from other schools, these little tots that should remain at the other area until they reach eighth grade," she added. It cannot be denied that it is best for small children to be at home, she said, and Senator Kennedy concurred that "it is a disgrace."[5]

Annie, of course, had gone off to boarding school at the age of eight. She had sent her own children and the children in her household off to school at St. Michael's Mission outside Window Rock when she was elected to the Tribal Council and they were in the early primary grades. She had seen that while some of the children, such as Irma, had done well in that environment, others, such as her son Franklin and her herder's daughter Lydia, found the experience traumatic.

There were a number of factors, besides the experience of her own children, that could have caused Annie's change of opinion on the worth of boarding schools during the seventeen years between her early speech and her testimony at Robert Kennedy's hearing. At that time the instruction in the government boarding schools was inferior, physical abuse was frequent, and sexual abuse was not unknown. The teachers did not appreciate Navajo culture, and the children were made to behave like white children.

Some of the original reasons for sending Navajo children to boarding school no longer pertained. Roads on the reservation had improved, making the daily transporting of children more feasible. Due largely to Annie's efforts, conditions in many of the hogans were also more sanitary, so that children had better living situations. More hogans had wooden floors and window screens, and there was better access to clean water. More of the parents had high school educations, and they had a better understanding of disease prevention. They were learning that they could challenge the Bureau of Indian Affairs on many fronts, and education was one of them.

Robert Kennedy was assassinated in June of 1968, just a few months after his visit to Flagstaff. The report, which was eventually released in his name, "accused BIA teachers and administrators of being insensitive to cultural differences, providing poor instruction, overemphasizing vocational training at the expense of college preparatory work, and not trying hard enough to alter the boarding system." [6]

HEAD START ON THE RESERVATION

Annie was one of the earliest advocates of the federal Head Start Program on the reservation. Programs were set up in the chapter houses, and the children learned basic skills such as counting and colors and reading readiness in both English and Navajo. With many of the staff and volunteers coming from the children's families, it was seen as a family-oriented program rather than just a program for children. Head Start provided an important transition for Navajo children, preparing those who were growing up in a hogan for life at a modern school and such cultural changes as indoor plumbing.

In May, Annie and forty-eight other members of the Tribal Council went over to the University of New Mexico in Albuquerque to attend a meeting of the Indian Health Committee of the American Academy of Pediatrics to share their experiences and pick up new information.

During the meeting the importance of Annie's earlier lobbying for money for home improvement was affirmed. The delegates learned that Navajo children were generally shorter and skinnier than typical American children. However, Navajo children who came from larger homes and whose homes had inside sanitation and water were generally taller and heavier and had less trachoma and ear infections than children whose homes had outside facilities.

Annie spoke at the conference about the success of the Head Start program on the reservation. With the Navajo families of the children working as volunteers, paid employees, and board members, the program fulfilled a number of goals. "Navajos with at least a high school education are running these schools themselves," she said. "We love it very much because of the family involvement."[7]

A story related by Annie's Navajo friend and neighbor Louise Nelson illustrates the devotion to preschool education of both Annie and her constituents. The residents of Klagetoh had been working on a building for the youngsters. It was early winter, and the men had been doing the work on the foundation, preparing for the cement. When the day ended and the cement had still not arrived, everybody went home. It was dark and the night was very cold when the truck loaded with wet concrete arrived in Klagetoh and was directed to Annie's home. The drivers knocked on the door and asked for instructions for what to do with their load. Annie knew that if she refused the cement they would have to pay for it anyway and then pay for a new batch as well, a situation that would break the budget. She told the drivers to return to the building site and wait for her there. Then she threw on a heavy jacket, knotted her scarf under her chin, and began to go through the neighborhood, stopping at homes. At each, she told of the situation; every man volunteered to help and recruited additional neighbors. When she was confident of having enough workers, she went back to her home and put some tarps into the rear of her pickup on which she piled a grill, firewood, a leg of lamb, some flour, bowls, and her big pot. While the men worked spreading the concrete for the foundation, she built a fire and started cooking. By the time the concrete was nice and smooth, it was very late and the temperature hovered around freezing. But when the volunteers came over to the fire to warm their hands, there was a big pot of bubbling mutton stew and a stack of warm fry bread for them to eat before they went home to the warmth of their beds.[8]

THE STUDENT CLOTHING PROGRAM

Annie was also involved in a project for providing clothing to Navajo school children. The program had begun back in 1954. That September, when it was time for the children to go back to school, it was discovered that 2,500 of the 17,000 Navajo students came from families so impoverished that their parents could not afford to buy them decent school clothes. The issue of how to help these children was discussed at length, but it was Annie, the only woman—and more importantly, the only mother—on the council who understood what it might mean to a child to have to stay at home from school for a lack of clothing. She moved that the council appropriate $350,000 to pay half of the cost of clothing for the students. Later Sears Roebuck offered a 16 percent discount on clothing bought from them, and council members decided to pay the full cost of clothing for those students who needed it. Eventually this seemingly simple and compassionate gesture would end up causing major headaches for the council, but at this point the measure had widespread support.

By 1962 the cost of the program was nearing $1 million annually and eventually would reach $2 million. Annie continually chaffed at the idea of spending so much money for ready-made clothing when there were so many women needing work on the reservation. Every couple of years she brought up the idea of buying sewing machines and having the shirts made by Navajo women. She was never able to gather any acceptance for her idea, and it probably would have led to numerous unforeseen problems.[9]

Even with the outfits coming from commercial sources, by

1968 the program was running into problems of acceptance. The clothing that was provided definitely was not what the older students wanted. Boys wanted to wear only Wrangler jeans, and they tore the heels off the oxfords provided by the program to repair their Western boots. During a meeting, Annie noted that the girls wanted miniskirts and fishnet stockings. "Some of us don't like to see the type of clothing our children wear, but nevertheless, that is the fashion," she said with the wisdom gained from her own years of motherhood.[10]

HEALTHY BABIES AND SMART STUDENTS

Throughout her years on the Tribal Council, Annie was active in issues of Navajo children's health and education, often visiting schools and talking to the youngsters. Because she was frequently seen around the reservation and was heard every week on her radio program, she became known to the young people of her tribe. She let no opportunity pass in her efforts to encourage them.

Early in her tenure, she devised a baby contest to be held every year in late summer at the Navajo Tribal Fair in Window Rock. Round-cheeked babies with coppery skins, black hair, and deep brown eyes are adorable, and the contest was popular. Indian Health Service doctors and nurses got the opportunity to look the babies over to spot such problems as tuberculosis or glaucoma. Without these contests some Navajo babies would never have been seen by a doctor. In those days, of every 1,000 Navajo babies, 55 would die in their first year, a mortality rate twice as high as that for white infants. Babies won the contest for appearing alert and healthy, and their mothers took home prizes of diapers, gift certificates for baby clothes, and, of course, cases of Pet Milk. Annie also set up a booth every year at both the Navajo Tribal Fair and the Gallup Inter-Tribal Ceremonial, with posters, movies, and information on tuberculosis and other health topics. With the many thousands of Navajos who attended both fairs every year, it was a perfect opportunity for education.

Marie Allen recalled a day in the early 1950s when she was an eighth grader who had traveled from the reservation to Phoenix, the state capital, to represent Apache County at the state spelling bee. It was the first time an Indian student had won the spelling bee, and as Marie sat on the stage, she was experiencing not only the normal nervousness of a spelling bee contestant but all the tension brought on by being off the reservation in a big city and knowing she represented her tribe. Then at the back of the room she saw a Navajo woman and recognized Annie, the mother of her friend Irma.

"She came all the way up to the stage and said, 'I heard there was a Navajo girl representing Apache County and I had to see who it was,'" Marie recalled. "She shook my hand and said, 'I want you to try to win the spelling bee. I want you to try very hard. I'm Annie Wauneka and I'm attending a meeting here, but I came over to see you and wish you well.' And she said all that in Navajo and then she left. I was really very pleased that she encouraged me." Although she did not win the bee, Marie learned from Annie the feeling of bringing honor to her tribe.[11]

A few years later, while in high school, Marie would accompany her father, Hosteen Tso, an official from St. Michael's chapter who had no formal education, to sessions of the Tribal Council. She would translate the English sections for him and take notes. Her father always pointed out Annie Wauneka and reminded Marie that Annie was the daughter of the great Chee Dodge. Because Marie and Annie had a clan relationship calling for Annie to address Marie's father as "Dad," the two women called each other "big sister" and "little sister" through what would turn into a decades-long association. At graduation, Marie earned a college scholarship from the tribe and became a public health nurse. She worked in Chinle on a follow-up program to the Many Farms clinic. In 1974, Marie Allen became the Navajo area assistant director for the Indian Health Service, a position that made her the highest-ranking member of her tribe working for the IHS within the Navajo area.[12]

Another young Navajo, Peterson Zah, who would grow up to become chairman of the Navajo Tribe, also first became aware of Annie as he accompanied his father, Henry Zah, an elected representative from Jeddito and Low Mountain, to Tribal Council meetings in the 1950s. Peterson Zah remembers, "I always liked what she had to say because she made things look so simple using native intelligence. Lawyers would come into the council hall and talk about how complicated legal issues are, and after Mrs. Wauneka would listen to them, she could come out and summarize the whole day's meeting into two or three sentences, and she was right on target. She had a beautiful way of talking that made a lot of sense. I was impressed whenever she spoke." [13]

INTERVENING AT PHOENIX INDIAN SCHOOL

A few years later Peterson Zah became a student at Phoenix Indian School. "I remember vividly her coming to Phoenix Indian School when we students staged a demonstration and a walkout because we did not like the quality of food that was given to us by the school," he said. "We had the same thing over and over again. It was government surplus food, whatever the government was trying to get rid of. We got tired of eating it, and we wanted a little more variety and something like we Indian students were used to eating back home—basic foods like corn and meat. We contacted the administration, talked to the superintendent and principal, and our desires were not addressed so we decided to stage a demonstration. The administrator was taken aback by all of that, so they invited some tribal leaders to come down and investigate what was happening. Annie Wauneka came down with the Navajo delegation. They had a student assembly so after one or two days of their visitation and investigation they could present their findings to the student body. I was just a young guy, just a senior sitting in the audience. She was very eloquent. She spoke the truth about what she saw and heard. She was not afraid to tell the administration what they were doing wrong. Most of the other tribal groups that came in, they didn't want to challenge the administration. The superintendent was such an overbearing person to begin with. Annie Wauneka spoke up to him and said, 'We want our children to eat the right food. If they are hungry, you should feed them. Why is the United States now saying that they don't have enough money to feed them?' So she took them on. She was very forceful, and I was impressed with her." [14]

The early summer of 1968 continued to be filled with routine business for the council. Because of the snow there was water in the reservoirs and good grass for the animals, so for once the delegates didn't have to worry about drought. But in August Annie took part in a highly dramatic political event. It took only moments, but in the years to come the memory of those brief minutes by those who were there and those who were not—and the elaboration of that memory—would supersede the decades of her other work on the Tribal Council.

9

Cultural Clashes and Cultural Bridges

LIKE HER FATHER BEFORE HER, Annie Wauneka was admired for her skill as a builder of cultural bridges. She spoke Navajo well and was well grounded in her own culture; she was also fluent in English and comfortable interacting with people off the reservation.

Unlike her father, however, Annie wasn't always diplomatic. She knew that the Navajos had to adapt to the white world in many ways, but she wanted to be met halfway. She expected the white people who worked for and with the Navajos to be respectful. And when she didn't see that, she expressed her opinions, sometimes forcefully.

TED MITCHELL AND THE *DNA*

One white man about whom she had strong opinions was Ted Mitchell, a young Harvard-educated lawyer who was heading a legal services program set up to help low-income Navajos with their off-reservation legal problems. The program, funded by the Office of Navajo Economic Opportunity (ONEO) with federal War on Poverty money, was called Diné Be'iiná Náhiilna Be Aga'dit-t'ahii, which means "attorneys who contribute to the economic revitalization of the people" in Navajo and was quickly shortened to DNA.

Mitchell had worked for the tribe in a small legal aid program under tribal attorney Norman Littell for about fifteen months and then left to head a regional Office of Economic Opportunity program. While with the Navajo Legal Aid program, he had worked hard, had taken on hundreds of cases, and had earned the respect of the Navajo staff. But for all his dedication to serving the Navajos, Mitchell was brash and had a way about him that some perceived as arrogant. When he wanted to come back to the Navajo Reservation and applied for the DNA directorship, Annie and several other council members had tried their best to see that he was not hired. They wrote to the newspaper and protested to the Washington office, claiming Mitchell had left Navajo Legal Aid under circumstances that made him unwelcome on the reservation.[1] He had apparently been vocal in his disagreement with Littell on some matters, and as we have seen previously, Annie was willing to brook no criticism of the older lawyer.

Despite their protests, Mitchell had been hired in December 1966; he proceeded to set up offices and hire attorneys, interpreters, and office staff. The idealistic young group began working to bring social justice to the Navajo Reservation in cases ranging from monetary recovery for sheep hit and killed by speeding cars to school discrimination cases. Navajo tribal advocates (without law degrees) assisted clients when their cases, such as divorces, were heard in the tribal court rather than state or federal courts. That was fine and caused no stir, but they also challenged certain practices of the BIA, defended their clients against the tribal police department, sought welfare benefits for clients whose applications had been denied, and went after a number of local white-owned businesses that had been exploiting their Navajo customers for years.

Unlike the legal aid program for which Mitchell had previously worked, DNA did not get money from the tribe and was not under the control of the Tribal Council. The lawyers saw this as an absolute necessity if they were to retain attorney-client privilege. However, they had to battle continually to keep their status separate from powerful interests in the tribe who wanted a say in what they did and did not do.[2]

According to Mitchell, "If an institution like DNA is to be an agent for change, if it is to modify the existing allocation of power and prestige in the interest of the common, powerless sagebrush-root people, then conflict with the people and the institutions which presently hold and wield power is inevitable." Once the conflict was manifested, Mitchell saw it as his job to stick up for his clients and to intimidate those with power to the extent they would not continue to wield it over the little guy.[3] With the help of the DNA lawyers, ordinary Navajos began to learn that they had legal rights and could exercise them.

But, as is true everywhere, when the rights of the poor are upheld, the powerful frequently feel that their rights are violated. The situation came to a head when two of the DNA lawyers got involved in a dispute in Chinle representing some parents who felt that their children were being discriminated against, and despite many pleas, the school board was not doing anything about it. The school board faction felt DNA should not be involved. Mitchell defended his staff, but Guy Gorman, chairman of the Chinle school board, went to the Advisory Committee and his old friend Annie Wauneka and asked that Mitchell be thrown off the reservation.[4]

DNA was representing the parents, and Annie usually supported parents' involvement with the schools, so her position against DNA here is somewhat unusual, but it was a complicated case, and other loyalties came into play. Also, one of the car dealerships that had been charged with unsavory practices by DNA was the one founded by Annie and Chee's old friend Rico Menapace, and she had no doubt heard of his disgruntlement. So in July 1968, with Annie leading the way, the Advisory Committee passed a resolution that Mitchell leave his job and the reservation.[5]

But Mitchell, feeling that the Advisory Committee did not hire him and therefore could not fire him, did not leave. He and his Navajo supporters, who were numerous, maintained that if the Advisory Committee could fire employees whenever there was a disagreement, the DNA as well as other tribal entities, such as the tribal utility authority, would be hampered in their work.[6] As Mitchell explains: "Annie sensed that she and her allies were threatened with a diminution of their power and she frantically fought back. Her antagonism confirmed the value of DNA's existence and its work. What happened to us was as old as human conflict."[7]

About a week later, Chairman Raymond Nakai sent Mitchell a letter demanding that he comply with the Advisory Committee resolution, but Mitchell told friends he was committed to the DNA and was staying.

A "DIRTY" LAUGH WINS A SLAP

That is the way the situation stood when, on August 5, Duard Barnes, a Washington official, came to Window Rock to explain the provisions of the new 1968 Civil Rights Act and how it applied to the Navajo Nation. During the discussion a paragraph was read that said, "No Indian tribe exercising the right of self-government shall deny any person due process of law."

Annie stood and asked, "Would you clarify this? We have the Treaty of 1868. Within that treaty it says that any non-Indian that comes on to the Reservation and does not behave himself—he or she can be excluded. What happens to our law? Does this kill it? This body has been given authority to exclude any non-Indian. Does this supersede our law?"

Barnes said, "I don't know who you have in mind."

Annie replied, "I don't have anybody in mind."

Mitchell was sitting in the back of the room as an observer. Embarrassed because it was clear to everyone in the room to whom she was referring, he let out a loud guffaw. There followed tittering and a few murmurs from others in the chambers, because it was clear what was on her mind.

Hearing Mitchell's laugh, which so irritated her anyhow, Annie turned around, glared at him, and said, "Ted Mitchell, you behave yourself." [8]

The meeting continued, but that night Annie brooded about the young Harvard lawyer who seemed to be causing so much trouble and had that afternoon given "the silliest, dirtiest laugh" she had ever heard. To her mind, Mitchell had been laughing at her, the members of the Advisory Committee who had voted to expel him, and at Chairman Nakai. Mitchell said he was laughing out of nervousness because it was clear that everyone knew Annie was talking about him.

As usual, Annie was up before dawn the next morning and had plenty of time to go over the previous day's events as she drove from Klagetoh to Window Rock. Mitchell's laugh echoed in her memory, and she fumed. The entire group reconvened to continue the discussion. Annie looked for Mitchell, but he did not appear until later in the afternoon. Annie noticed when he walked into the council room, and she decided to confront him. The legislative secretary was reading aloud the provisions of the Civil Rights Act, and Annie was waiting for a recess. When one of her colleagues asked about the same paragraph Annie had questioned the previous day, she looked back at Mitchell and was enraged to find him smiling again.

At that point Annie was told someone was outside who wished to speak to her, so she made her way to the back to leave, passing Mitchell. "Ted, are you ready to laugh some more?" she asked.

"No more, Mrs. Wauneka. I apologize," Mitchell said.

Annie then said, "I don't need your apologies," and hit him several times on the head and face, yelling at him to get out. Mitchell threw up his arms to protect himself and headed for the door. The rest of the assembled group watched in stunned silence.[9]

The pummeling was not as spontaneous as it might have seemed. Two decades later, Annie would confess to a newspaper reporter that she had wrapped her hand around a pen knife before hitting Mitchell. "I told myself my hands were too soft because I hadn't handled a calf in years," she said.[10] It wasn't until after the heat of the moment that Annie began to consider possible repercussions and wondered if the police would come after her for battery.

ADVISORY COMMITTEE EXCLUDES MITCHELL

By 9:30 A.M. the next day the Advisory Committee had again voted to exclude Mitchell from the reservation, and early in the afternoon the tribal police went to the DNA offices and escorted Mitchell off the reservation, although the officers allowed him to drive his own vehicle.

For the next weeks, the reservation and nearby Gallup were abuzz with talk of the incident. Local newspapers ran long stories, quoting those involved. Annie had had her own altercations with Raymond Nakai, she told a reporter, *but the majority of the people like Raymond Nakai. What did Ted do? He laughed at the Chairman and the leaders of the Tribe. . . . I know what kind of a man Ted Mitchell is and I'm glad Mr. Nakai has found it out. I guess he's been laughing too much over there (pointing over the hill to DNA headquarters), so he decided to come right into this chamber and laugh at us, especially me. . . .*

I, as Mrs. Annie Wauneka, known throughout the country, do not like to slap anybody. A lot of people think I made a mistake. But, no, the time was right. We have non-Indians who are honest and capable. Here we have Ted Mitchell who comes over here and laughs at the people. I'm not going to have Ted Mitchell laugh at me. We're feeding this man. He's making a living off of us. DNA is a good program if it is run right by a good director. But the program is not for Ted Mitchell, it is for the Navajo people. Now he's trying to build an empire. We're not going to allow him to do it.[11]

Mitchell proceeded to run the DNA from an office he set up in the El Rancho Hotel in Gallup. His assistant, Peterson Zah, a Navajo advocate, or legal assistant, ran the Window Rock office. Navajos who supported the DNA passed petitions protesting Mitchell's exclusion. Some of the protestors met with Nakai, who defended Annie, comparing her to a coiled rattlesnake, saying, "If you do not annoy a coiled rattlesnake, it will not strike you. If Ted Mitchell had controlled his emotions this would not have happened. He pushed her too far with that outburst."[12]

SUPPORT FOR MITCHELL

This was a period in American history of unprecedented student activism, and the situation attracted the attention of numerous Navajo university students at the end of summer vacation who joined together, calling themselves Dineh for Justice. They picketed the council hall and eventually were invited in to address the Advisory Committee. They were told to choose two representatives to speak for them. The first speaker asked for an explanation of the exact grounds for the exclusion order. Carl Todacheene, one of the council members, gave an hour-long answer that apparently satisfied the protestors.

Annie was certainly ready to put the incident aside. When

the students were finished, she arose and said, "We would like to thank this group for visiting us. We have heard of these demonstrations elsewhere and now we have had an opportunity to see how they are done. However I am sure you have other important business to attend to, just as we have other important items we must consider. We will now have to go on with other business." [13]

In Gallup, the DNA board, consisting of eleven Navajos and eight white lawyers and professors, voted to support Ted Mitchell and even gave him a raise. Peter MacDonald, executive director of ONEO, cautioned the other DNA employees to avoid further provoking the situation. He also spoke in support of Mitchell, although he had previously been critical of Mitchell. A five-member committee set up to support Mitchell and protest his exclusion included John Dodge, DNA board president and a relative of Annie's, and Dr. Taylor McKenzie, the only Navajo doctor and one of Annie's long-time allies. [14]

Mitchell hired an attorney to defend himself, and a judge ruled that Mitchell could not be excluded from the reservation. The wrangling continued, however. Eventually Mitchell was offered a job heading up Micronesian Legal Services. On February 28, 1970, Mitchell resigned, taking up a position half a globe away from the Navajo Reservation, a position he retained thirty years later.

The slapping incident itself took only moments, and the events before and after it occurred over only three days, yet the story stuck and was forever associated with Annie Wauneka, assuming equal billing with her years of work on eradicating TB and her Medal of Freedom.

SPEAKING UP FOR FRIENDS

Although the incident with Ted Mitchell was certainly dramatic and provided no end of colorful stories, it was not typical of Annie's interaction with the white people with whom she worked, either on the reservation or elsewhere. She was unusually aware of the need for the expertise of outsiders and quick to point out the advantages of cooperation.

In addition to her work on several tribal committees, that

summer Annie took on a new responsibility that thrust her into yet another sphere when she was appointed to the board of directors of the Navajo Tribal Utility Authority. The NTUA had responsibility for providing power, water, and sewer services to the reservation. Just as she had accepted the challenge of learning about the transmission and treatment of tuberculosis years previously, she began to study up on the basics of how utilities are operated. The water utility built upon her long-term work to decrease the incidence of dysentery and other gastrointestinal problems by lobbying to provide safe water sources throughout the reservation.

Although Annie was the most recent addition to the board, she brought a resolution to the full council that the current NTUA manager's contract be renewed and his salary raised. The manager, Mac Eddy, was white and had served in his position for three years. Annie testified that he was competent, capable, and trusted. In the following discussion, those who thought he should not get a raise were mostly those council members whose areas were not yet on the electricity grid. Others thought the job should go to a Navajo, although there did not seem to be any tribal member with the necessary training. Annie told them that Eddy had started the job with a staff of twenty-two white workers and had replaced all but nine of them with Navajos. The council eventually voted overwhelmingly to give Eddy a new contract and the requested raise, with the stipulation that he hire a Navajo assistant and begin training him to take over.[15]

SUPPORT FOR A WHITE MUSEUM DIRECTOR

In one particular case, Annie found it highly useful to have a white person on staff. Martin Link was a white anthropologist who went to the reservation as a volunteer teacher and ended up establishing and running the Navajo Museum. In addition to collecting the usual museum items and documents, if a heavy rain eroded a set of human bones in a cornfield or other spot where people went, it was Link's job to go complete the excavation and take the bones back to the museum. Because of the Navajo fear of anything to do with death, this was a job he had to do himself and could not delegate. Link recalls having to justify his position in front of the Navajo Tribal Council Budget and Finance committee. Annie supported him, saying, "We need at least one *bilagáana* [white man] on the staff who isn't afraid to dig up skeletons."[16]

Link also tells of going with her and other committee members to look over the historic Hubbell Trading Post in Ganado. The Hubbell family wanted to sell the site and had offered the place to the Navajo Tribe. "I looked at it and thought what a horrendous inventory job it would be," Link recalls. "Then there would be maintenance and keeping the whole thing up as a museum. The other committee members were very interested, and the only person that was against it was Annie Wauneka. She said, 'Something of this value and this importance, we Navajo People just don't know how to take care of things like this. It will just go downhill, and they'll be selling trinkets here. If the Park Service wants it, they should have it. They have more money and expertise to maintain it.' When the decision was made to sell it to the National Park Service she supported it down the line."[17]

There were times, however, when Annie adamantly rejected incursions of others onto the Navajo Reservation. One such time was when discussion came up in a January 1965 Tribal Council session on setting up a Job Corps work camp. Annie strenuously objected when it became clear that non-Navajos would be included because the camp was federally funded. "If we approve of this, it means inviting people of the Spanish-American races, the Colored races and others. What would be the reaction on the part of our local community people when they find that we have all these strange races mixing with our young men and women? What you're inviting here is integration, and I don't think this would be acceptable on the part of the Navajos."

Council member Sam Day agreed with her, saying "I'm proud of my Navajo blood. We should all be aware of anything that would break down a race. . . . The more you expose, the more you make an opportunity. Why the very heritage is broken down."[18] Interestingly, neither Annie nor Sam Day were full-blooded Navajo. We have previously discussed the question of Chee Dodge's paternity. Whoever his father was, he definitely was not a Navajo. Sam Day's father had been white.

Martin Link agreed that her behavior was inconsistent. "She had streaks like that. But then other times you'd turn around, and she'd be just the opposite: the more acculturation the better. She was a great one for bringing in aspects of white culture. She was one of those rare people who can take a broad look at somebody else's culture and say I want that and that and half of that and two-thirds of that, and you can keep the rest. We'll pick and choose what's best for us." [19]

10

The Navajo-Hopi Conflict

BY 1970 IT HAD BEEN EIGHT YEARS since the *Healing v. Jones* decision had determined that the Hopis and Navajos should share equally in the 1882 Executive Order Reservation lands. Behind the scenes, the Hopis' lawyers had been busy trying to convince members of Congress to expand the Hopi rights in various ways. From time to time, the Navajos had to spend some time addressing these legal and legislative challenges. Although Annie was not one of the prime players in the Navajo struggle to retain rights to the land involved in what was called the Navajo-Hopi Joint Use Area, as one of the main leaders of the Navajo Nation, she was drawn in to the fray.

Annie poured over all of the proposals and associated paperwork in any policymaking situation in which she was involved. After reading one of the proposals dealing with the Navajo-Hopi conflict in preparation for a Washington trip in January 1970, she bustled into the next Tribal Council meeting concerned about the very term "Joint Use Area."

"I don't think the Hopis are using the area where the court has made a decision, all they have is interest, they're not joint-users," she lectured her fellow council representatives. "To my way of thinking, that's two different words. If we're going to use the 'joint use' kind of language, this group up on the hill in Washington, DC, might believe that the Hopis are actually using it."[1] In fact, only Navajos—about 10,000 of them—had been living on the land, with the Hopi congregating in their villages and adjacent farms in district six.

FRIENDS IN HIGH PLACES

Annie's use of the phrase "on the hill" to describe the Congress of the United States, a term used mostly by news reporters and Washington insiders—and probably not understood by most of the Navajos she was addressing—showed what a product of her many Washington lobbying trips she herself was becoming. She also knew the players on the Washington scene, and they knew her. As she walked down the halls in the Senate Office Building, she was recognized by the senators and their staffs, and she knew them. In some cases, she knew their families. One day Dr. Robert Bergman, an IHS psychiatrist, was showing Dr. Robert Coles, the psychoanalyst and writer, around the reservation. Coles was accompanied by a young man also named Robert. Bergman didn't catch the young man's last name, but the three men joked about all having the same first name. While the men were talking in the IHS offices, Annie dropped by and joined the discussion. After a few minutes she asked to speak to Bergman alone. In the hall she said, "Why didn't you introduce me to that young man. Don't you know that's Robert Kennedy Jr.?"[2]

Although Annie was not an official member of the Navajo negotiating team, because of her familiarity with government officials she accompanied the group to Washington in January in an attempt to lobby for the rights of Navajos who would be affected by the division of what Navajos and their advocates wanted to call the "joint interest area."

MACDONALD WINS CHAIRMANSHIP

In the fall elections of 1970, Raymond Nakai lost the chairmanship to his former friend and employee, Peter MacDonald, who had been heading up the Office of Navajo Economic Opportunity. Despite the previous rancor between MacDonald and Annie, after the election they both put grievances aside, at least on the surface and temporarily. When one contingent of council members wanted to postpone MacDonald's inauguration because of an investigation of possible fund misuse in the ONEO office, Annie cautioned them to listen to the 18,335 people who had voted for

MacDonald, saying that the voters had heard the charges and either didn't listen or didn't care. "The majority of the Navajo people have made their choice," she said.[3]

MacDonald reciprocated by appointing her to the Advisory Committee, a surprising step. He consolidated the Health and Alcoholism Committees and appointed Annie as a member. Three years later, he appointed her health ambassador to the Navajo Nation, an honorary title that recognized her work in this area. On the other hand, he made it more difficult for her to speak in council sessions when he rearranged the seating in the chambers alphabetically, putting "Wauneka" in the dim back of the hall where she had to struggle to be seen and called upon, sometimes standing through several other speakers in order to finally be recognized.

Peter MacDonald was well educated by white standards, moved easily in the white world, and was adamant that the Navajos should have more control over their own destiny—from having a greater say over how federal funds were spent by the BIA and the PHS to renegotiating leases for natural resources found on the reservation. Many of Annie's political activities over the next decade were related to the priorities he set. MacDonald brought in a new lawyer to serve as general counsel for the tribe, and the new administration had to take time to learn about the pending cases, mainly the extraordinarily complex politics of the Navajo-Hopi land situation. The new tribal legal team was stunned to realize that nothing much had been done in the decade after the *Healing v. Jones* decision in essence took away thousands of acres of Navajo land. While they rushed to catch up with the situation, the Hopi faction and their congressional supporters took advantage of what they saw as a temporary weakness and jumped in to try to gain even more of the disputed territory for the Hopis.

Had the land in question offered nothing but the overgrazed grasslands visible to the casual observer, the issue of partition might have continued to simmer for decades. However, the situation took on additional urgency because of the assumption by both tribes and some utility companies that the area contained vast deposits of coal, uranium, and oil. In the early 1970s, the United States was facing an energy crisis, and a number of energy companies were eager to get access to these resources. Some companies saw the Hopis as easier to deal with than the Navajos because Peter MacDonald had made it clear that he was determined to push for higher royalties and more control over mineral production on Navajo land. He was very successful in talking to the press and getting attention for his efforts.

STEIGER BILL CALLS FOR PARTITION

A bill introduced by Representative Sam Steiger, an Arizona Republican, called for immediate partition of the surface rights of the disputed lands, relocation within five years of the Navajos from lands that would be deemed Hopi territory, and immediate reduction of the number of livestock on the entire area. Steiger's plan would be disastrous for the Navajos.

MacDonald saw the need for drastic action. At one point he chartered a converted four-engine propeller-driven World War II cargo plane to fly the whole council and some Navajos living in the Joint Use Area to Washington. The plane was too big to land on the little airstrip in Window Rock so the hundred or so people drove in caravan to the larger airport in Albuquerque and took off from there. They flew all night, and when they arrived at Capitol Hill, they broke up into groups to talk to a list of representatives they deemed crucial contacts.[4]

When Annie went before a House committee to testify against the Steiger Bill in April 1972, she had never been in better form. Although speakers were routinely limited to five minutes, because of her prominence she was accorded unlimited time for her statement. She had to use it well, because with Representative Steiger on the committee, she was eye to eye with her adversary.

"In the first place, this isn't an Indian dispute," she began,

it's a white man's dispute. We Navajos and Hopis, like all neighbors, had our quarrels, but for the most part we lived side by side in peace for 500 years until white administrators, lawyers, and congressmen persuaded some of us that the situation couldn't be tolerated for another five minutes.

The jurisdictional act that authorized the Navajo-Hopi lawsuit of 1962 was a mistake. It was lobbied through by white lawyers and has only benefited white lawyers. The Hopis won and we Navajos lost; but the average Hopi, like the average Navajo, doesn't have one bit better life now than before the lawsuit.

The bill, H.R. 11128 [the Steiger Bill] is even worse than the jurisdictional act. It would provide for the physical removal of 8,000 to 10,000 people from their homes—about the same number of Navajos as were marched to Fort Sumner in 1864 under the Army's bayonets.

There has been nothing like this bill since the Communists overran eastern Europe. A whole area—in the United States of America—is to be cleared of its population in order to be resettled by people of another language. This bill is unbelievable. The Indian Removal Act of 1972.

It's a divide and conquer bill. Of course, it is also a white lawyer's bill. The Indians are to be driven out into the desert, while the lawyers are guaranteed job security by provisions in sections 15 and 16 for at least three monster lawsuits. I say, let us Indians work this problem out ourselves, without lawyers or legislation.

This bill is a perfect example of a white man's solution to the Indian problem. You wonder why the problem never gets solved. It's because every white man is an expert on Indian problems, but nobody listens to the Indians. Now, please tear up this stupid bill and listen to an Indian.

We Indians are poor because we don't have enough land. You white people took too much from us. You took so much you have to pay farmers not to grow crops on it. Why not give some of it back to us?

Why pit Navajos and Hopis against each other to fight over their respective shares of poverty? Why not share a small part of your excessive land with us?

I know it is said that letting Indians have adequate land retards their assimilation. We should be forced into the melting pot, and so forth. You can swallow this rubbish only if you sincerely believe it is better to have an Indian on welfare in a city slum than out in the country making his own living.

We Indians know how to make our living off the land. Don't waste money trying to force us to do something else we don't want when we already have this skill. . . .

You have never tried the real solution: give us enough land. . . . If anyone should give up raising livestock and relocate in the cities it is the non-Indian permittees on the lands the Government stole from us. Which is just what I propose. These people are white, well-educated and affluent. They will have no serious readjustment problem. If they do, pay them the $3,000 per family the Steiger bill would award to displaced Navajos. Or extend relocation services to them. But give us back our land.

Return to us Navajos our original country between the four sacred mountains. After our ancestral lands are returned, the lands outside their borders should be granted to the Hopis. The Navajos are the people who need the land most urgently, for there are 130,000 of us and only 6,500 Hopis.

The Indian Claims Commission has already said we owned much of the land among the sacred mountains. Let the proceedings before that Commission stop where they are. We don't want the value of the area as of 1868, when your ancestors stole it from us, paid like all Indian Claims Commission awards, without interest, dollar for dollar in devaluated inflated 1972 paper money. We want justice, gentlemen. We want our land back.[5]

The tone of this fiery speech contrasted sharply with those she made before some of same lawmakers when she was asking for increases in allocations for Navajo health care. In that case she was asking for a portion of the federal budget, which, although mandated by the Treaty of 1868, had to be carved out in competition with other national interests. Here she was pleading for a return of what the Navajos regarded as their spiritual as well as physical home, given to them by the Holy Ones for all time.

PSYCHOLOGICAL EFFECTS OF PARTITION

But Annie knew that appeals to historic justice were not enough to sway the legislators. In an attempt to get more hard data on the effect of relocation, Annie asked the Mental Health Branch of the Public Health Service to study the probable psychological effects on families forced to leave their traditional homes. The study was designed by Dr. Robert Bergman and carried out by

Annie's Navajo friend Ellouise De Groat, who was then assistant director of the Navajo Area Indian Health Service mental health program. By mid-September she and Ellouise were in Washington presenting their findings to the House and Senate committees. The surveys showed that the average Navajo family in the joint interest area had occupied its own piece of land for fifty-five to sixty years and that removal would cause family disorganization and increased rates of depression, suicide attempts, and violent crime.

"So make a careful decision now," Annie cautioned the Senate committee at the conclusion of her testimony presenting the findings of the study. "I have spoken to you from my heart and with a true tongue."[6]

Navajo representatives lobbied fiercely against the bill that would move Navajo families out of their hogans and off of their traditional grazing lands. They enjoyed the support of a large group of traditional Hopis who also opposed partition. But the BIA, the commissioner of Indian affairs, and the secretary of the interior all weighed in for the Steiger Bill. By 1974 the nation and Congress had become consumed with Watergate scandals, and the lawmakers' interest in the Navajos' problems dropped to near zero. Yet they resisted making that decision themselves. That December, Congress passed the Navajo-Hopi Indian Land Settlement Act giving the tribes one last chance to negotiate a compromise on the Joint Use Area with the help of a federal mediator. President Gerald Ford signed the bill while in Vail, Colorado, on a ski vacation.[7]

In January of 1975, Annie was nominated to serve on the Navajo delegation to the negotiations. She was not enthusiastic, citing the fact that she would miss all her other obligations, and she was uncertain that she wanted the responsibility of removing people from their land. She was also clearly aware that her strengths were as a fighter, not a negotiator, and that she tended to get hot under such pressure. "I'd like to advise the council that perhaps I might, if selected, destroy your position and your purpose," she said. "You know me as one who is ready to argue points and I don't think you want a person like that. You notice how the Chairman is very calm and businesslike in these proceedings. Some of us have tried to put him down, but he responds in a very cool-like manner and I think you need those types of people here." [8]

DISTRUST OF HOPIS

Although Annie had indicated to the House committee that some Navajos and Hopis who were neighbors got along fairly well, there is ample evidence that she distrusted Hopis. When she spoke with the Chanins in the early 1970s, she related the story of how her father had been orphaned when his mother had gone to the Hopi mesas to try to get food and never came back, presumably killed by the Hopis. "When they have an enemy come to their mesas, they take you way up to the highest point and feed you just as much as you want to eat," she said, "and when you are ready to go they blindfold you and throw you off the cliff. And that's the end of you . . . I don't know if they still do it or not." [9] Clearly any Hopi who pushed someone off a cliff in the 1970s would be tried for murder, and it would be in all the local papers. There was no reason to suggest that the practice was a current one.

A few years later in discussing the Navajo-Hopi problem with Shirley Witt, a professor and human rights advocate, Annie said, "There is a 'life estate program' which can allow the older Navajo residents to live where they are until they die, under certain circumstances. . . . But that concept is very alien to the Navajo— death and dying. They tell each other that if you stay here, when you die, the Hopi will dig up your bones and throw them over the partition fence." Annie finished her comment with a laugh and a shrug.[10]

Harriet Bock, wife of Dr. George Bock, the head of the Navajo Area Indian Health Service in the early 1970s, was a good friend of Annie's. She recalls that she had two prints hanging over her buffet, one of a Navajo, the other of a Hopi. Whenever Annie came to visit, she always asked Mrs. Bock why she had that picture of a Hopi in her home. "I always explained that we had friends who were Hopis," she indicated, "but Annie was clearly disapproving."[11]

After many months of wrangling, the tribes were not able to work out a compromise, and in 1975 the line separating Navajo and Hopi territory was drawn. Navajos faced a forced removal from what they considered their land.

11

More Washington Lobbying

CONCURRENTLY WITH HER INVOLVEMENT on the land issue, Annie continued working on health care reform during the 1970s. Her efforts mainly involved securing adequate funding for Navajo health care as well as striving to set up ways in which the Navajo People could participate more fully in the administration of their own health care. Now that the Navajos had accepted modern medicine, they wanted more say in how it was delivered.

Although this kind of work did not offer the same level of excitement as Annie's earlier campaign for tuberculosis eradication, it made use of the more mature governing skills she had acquired over the previous two decades of political life. And because of the dedication she had to her job, it took no less of her time.

At times other members of the Navajo Tribal Council had the title of chair of the Health Committee, but in fact it was usually Annie who drove the engine and kept it fueled. When she went to out-of-town meetings, she routinely arrived early and stayed to the end. In her subsequent report to the Tribal Council after a meeting, she occasionally mentioned that she was sure the chair of the Health Committee had been there, but she had not seen him. One can imagine that a new chair, even if well intentioned, would have felt deep in her shadow at such meetings. By having worked in the field for nearly two decades, she knew the movers and shakers, she knew the issues, and she was an effective speaker. Furthermore, whenever she walked into a room, she dominated it simply by her presence. Taller than most Navajos and with a take-charge bearing, she was in command of any situation.

WORK WITH THE INDIAN HEALTH SERVICE

Annie had been instrumental in bringing to the reservation a new program in which community health representatives, who came to be known as CHRs, served as liaisons between the Navajo People and health professionals. The CHRs were selected by their chapters and were paid by the tribe through a Public Health Service grant. After a ten-week training course, the first CHRs, enthusiastic and idealistic, went back to their communities and began to help their people understand the role of the IHS, served as health educators, and assisted the other health professionals. They also communicated community needs to the IHS. Eventually, Annie went to Washington to testify about how well the program worked.

After the CHR program was running, she then moved her attention to the establishment of a Health Advisory Board made of up Navajos who would work with the IHS. In accordance with treaties, Congress annually appropriated money for Indian health care. But how that money was spent was determined by employees of the Public Health Service under their Indian Health Service wing. Very few of these employees were Navajos or other Indians. Annie had learned that eight other tribes had such boards when she attended a meeting in Reno early that year as part of the surgeon general's advisory board. Because Congress had been cutting the budget of the Indian section of the Public Health Service to the point that it was severely impacting services, the eight tribes that had already instituted the boards had decided to go to Washington to lobby for larger appropriations. Knowing of Annie's lobbying abilities, they invited her to accompany them.

Because these other tribes had health advisory boards that were working well, Annie became determined that the Navajos needed such a board. At her prodding and with her assistance, the chairman of the Health Committee and the other members of the Tribal Council worked for months on the proposal for a Navajo Health Advisory Board. The plan was that board members would meet every month with the director of the Navajo Area Indian Health Service and would be charged with knowing that body's policies, programs, and budgets. They were to keep the tribe informed through the Tribal Council and the chapters and would visit schools and encourage students to pursue courses of study in health fields. They would also lobby the national Department of Health, Education and Welfare for sufficient funds. Annie gave a long impassioned speech to the other Tribal Council delegates supporting the measure. The council delegates had already learned that due to budget cuts the numbers of doctors and nurses had dropped so low in the IHS hospitals that wards had been closed in two reservation hospitals, and that several hospitals were so old they were crumbling. The measure passed unanimously.[1]

SUGGESTING REFORMS

This was a particularly significant step for the Navajos. Now that they were accepting mainstream American medical practice, they could begin to have some say in the way money appropriated for their health care was actually spent, rather than having to rely on a system they considered paternal. Also, the PHS administrators did not tolerate criticism or suggestions from their own employees, and there is some indication that public health nurses may have been fired for complaining about the conditions at one of the reservation hospitals. The Health Advisory Board provided a way for Navajo staff to suggest reforms through people who could not be fired.

Under Annie's leadership, alcoholism was identified as a first priority for the board. She had been working on the problem for years now without much success; this was another way to attack the problem. She reminded the board members that 75 percent of all motor vehicle accidents were linked to excessive drinking, as were 83 percent of all arrests by the Navajo police, 31 percent of child abuse cases, and 51 percent of reports of violent acts. Infant deaths were rising due to alcoholic parents. Alcohol abuse was a well-documented threat to stable family life among the Navajos.[2]

The Public Health Service did not adopt all of the suggestions from the Health Advisory Board wholesale, but it did try to incorporate their ideas into its planning. The advisory board also gave the Navajos more responsibility for making sure that the congressional committees responsible for appropriations knew of their needs. Annie had been traveling to Washington to lobby and testify for years, but she had frequently expressed irritation that other Navajo leaders were not willing to participate.

WHAT IS A HOGAN?

The need to educate the members of Congress voting on the appropriations was continual and substantial. In early 1970, Annie headed a group of six Navajos testifying before Senate and House appropriations subcommittees. The Senate committee was chaired by Senator Alan Bible of Nevada. An example of the basic background information she needed to provide is the following exchange that took place when she was telling of current reservation conditions and requesting additional health programs:

Annie Wauneka: Transportation problems many times keep sick people from getting prompt medical care. Navajos have walked many miles carrying sick children to hospitals or clinics. Many Navajos do not have jobs and the average yearly income is $3,000, much below the poverty level. The average family of five or six persons lives in a one-room hogan.

Senator Bible: What is a hogan? Is it a tent? Is it like an igloo?

Annie Wauneka: It is a log structure.

Senator Bible: I know it is your house.

Annie Wauneka: It is a conical-shaped structure.

Senator Bible: If you have a picture, give it to me.

Annie Wauneka: We will send you a picture of it.

Senator Bible: We have a lot of Paiutes up our way, but not any hogans.

At that point, finished with the discussion of hogans, Annie continued with her prepared report detailing the need for more health care workers in the hospital and field and more funds for equipment, supplies, and repairs.[3] (When Annie returned months later to testify on another matter, she took along a reference book she left with Senator Bible with an artist's drawing of a hogan.) Apparently she and the other Navajos who traveled with her to Washington had made their case well, for in July 1971, Dr. George Bock reported to the Tribal Council that the efforts of Annie and the others had nearly doubled the Navajo Area Public Health Service budget from the previous year. He congratulated the group and reminded them that their success was the result of everyone working together.[4]

THE "DO-FOR-ME" PEOPLE

Although Annie was constantly working to get Congress to provide money for programs to improve her people's lives, she was concerned about the fact that too many of the Navajos were relying on welfare without showing any enterprise. Because she thought the idea of "free money" ruined the work ethic, she was always eager to get her constituents into the ONEO Work Experience programs, for which they were paid. "I try to tell the people to make use of this money—build their homes, buy lumber, buy whatever you think you can for your children. And they're buying lumber by the load and we're happy about it," she told a meeting of the Tribal Council. To another friend she said, "My people have had too much given to them. They need to take responsibility for themselves and not look to the federal government and the tribal government for everything."[5] She called able-bodied Navajos who were relying on welfare "the do-for-me people."[6]

The issue of the need for welfare on the reservation, as elsewhere, was complex. Even hard-working Navajos found it difficult to make a living on the reservation. Annie's stand on this issue is interesting. Although she had clearly had a strong streak of industriousness from childhood, she had also had the privilege of a good education and of growing up in one of the two or three wealthiest households on the reservation. She and George were not scraping together a living by grazing a few dozen sheep on a plot of sandy sagebrush but had the benefit of the range Chee had staked out at Tanner Springs.

As Annie became more prominent in the tribe, she frequently encountered a situation that had also faced her father—clan relatives asking to borrow money. In the Navajo culture it is expected that wealthier family members will be generous with their poorer kin. Sharing is an expectation, not an obligation. For those who do not share their wealth in culturally appropriate amounts there are sanctions, including accusations of witchcraft. Although nowhere near as wealthy as Chee Dodge, Annie and George were relatively well off. Their stock operation at Tanner Springs was well managed and profitable. Annie's salary as a council member started off low in 1952 — just $8 per meeting day plus mileage and per diem. But by the early 1970s the annual council salary had risen to $9,000 plus per diem and travel and with extra pay for committee work. Compared to the typical Navajo family income, this was a fortune.

Annie had made it clear that although she would fight to give anyone an opportunity, she was opposed to handouts. Once when she visited her friend Lawrence Huerta in Tucson, she brought along a large collection of outstanding rugs that Huerta says she had taken as collateral for cash loans she had made. Navajos were used to leaving rugs and jewelry as pawn for loans at the trading posts, but not with their relatives. Annie attempted to sell these unredeemed rugs to the Amerind Foundation east of Tucson, but the buyers there thought the price she wanted for the rugs was unrealistic, and she ended up taking them back home with her.[7]

THE IDEA FOR A MEDICAL SCHOOL

Hoping to influence more young people to study for health careers, the Health Advisory Board and the Tribal Council began talking about the need for an American Indian Medical School. In part, they were responding to President Nixon's address to Congress on July 8, 1970, in which he stated, "Only 2.4 percent of HEW's Indian health programs are run by Indians. . . . We are presently able to identify in this country only 30 physicians and fewer than 400 nurses of Indian descent. To meet this situation, we will expand our efforts to train Indians for health careers."

This was just the kind of challenge that Annie had needed. The alcohol problem on which she'd been working seemed intractable. Here was something new into which she could throw her energy. A medical school especially for American Indians would be a culmination of all the projects on which she'd worked over the last twenty years with the aim of improving the health of the Navajos. And this project appeared to be backed by the president of the United States.

Less than a year later, in June 1971, the Tribal Council sent a resolution to Elliot L. Richardson, secretary of health, education and welfare, asking him to conduct a planning study for the establishment of a medical school and related facilities on the Navajo Reservation. It also asked him to find the funding. Annie followed up with a letter stating, "We call on your Department to help us obtain a full commitment of the Federal Government to provide us with an American Indian Medical School which will give our people the necessary training at all professional levels and the essential tools and facilities to accomplish the paramount objective—the care by Indians of our peoples' health."[8]

By March of the following year the committee to whom Secretary Richardson had delegated the study reported back favorably on the possibility of the medical college. On the same day Annie stood up in front of her fellow Tribal Council delegates and exhorted them to support the study and vote to move ahead with the project by committing tribal funds to the effort. "I want my Councilmen to think strong and diligently look ahead. What are we going to do for these youngsters? When we get our youngsters trained they'll be taking the place of the professionals in the health careers. . . . Let's take this courageous step and approve this resolution today. . . . I ask for your favorable vote and let's get going. . . . We've got all kinds of problems in the world and maybe we'll solve some of this by educating our own Navajos."[9]

THE NAVAJO HEALTH AUTHORITY

In June the Tribal Council pledged $50,000 a year for two years to help get the medical college off the ground and also established the Navajo Health Authority to work on many fronts to dramatically increase the number of Native Americans trained in the health fields. Chairman Peter MacDonald named Annie to the board of commissioners.

The president of the board of directors of the Navajo Health Authority was Dr. Taylor McKenzie, the first Navajo doctor. McKenzie had returned to the reservation in 1964 after his surgical residency and had been working since then for the Indian Health Service at the Gallup Indian hospital and at the Shiprock hospital. But he left those positions to spend years trying to get the new medical school established.

Taylor McKenzie and Annie Wauneka had met shortly after his arrival back on the reservation when one of the IHS administrators took him to meet the members of the Health Advisory Board. He said Annie looked him up and down, and he looked her up and down, and finally she broke the ice by shaking hands. Actually, it was not the young doctor's first encounter with Annie.

"I was in junior high in Shiprock on vacation from boarding school, and I was practicing shooting baskets in my yard," he recalls. "I was listening to music on my battery-operated radio when the program changed, and this lady came on talking about tuberculosis. I'd never heard of it, and I was listening with one ear while I continued to shoot baskets. Then finally I stopped what I was doing and just listened for about 30 minutes. After that I used to hear her talking about various things on the radio. She got me to thinking about health matters. When I finally met her, I thought, so, this is the lady with the voice." [10]

Now Annie and McKenzie began working together to establish the medical school. This was not idle talk, but an all-out effort. With members of the board, they went to visit other Indian tribes to enlist their support for the idea and traveled to Washington to lobby for money. During a meeting with an appropriations subcommittee in Washington, Annie brought up the plans for the medical school as evidence that the Navajos were working to train their own medical personnel. When the committee members raised cautions regarding the overwhelming cost of establishing such a school, Annie was adamant that there was a need and they would push ahead.

AFFILIATIONS AND MONEY FOR THE MEDICAL SCHOOL

Establishing a medical school in a relatively remote area was an audacious idea. It was clear there was insufficient infrastructure on the reservation to support a medical school, so the board traveled around the Southwest establishing affiliations. They went to Northern Arizona University in Flagstaff to arrange for the first two years of basic science training to be conducted in the science laboratories there. Annie had never seen such facilities before and was fascinated. Because Flagstaff hospitals lacked the patient load needed to train medical students, they visited several big hospitals in Phoenix, including the Maricopa County Hospital, and arranged for students to have their third-year clinical training there. During the tours Annie asked a few questions, but mainly she listened closely, trying to grasp the new and unfamiliar information on the training of medical students. The plan was for medical students to travel to various reservation IHS hospitals for their fourth year. In addition to the conventional medical studies, they would also have courses through a Department of Native Healing Sciences that would incorporate the traditional medical practices of the various tribes.[11]

As the plans for the medical school moved ahead, Annie made it her personal mission to encourage young Navajos already trained and just starting out in the health care field. John Hubbard became head of the Navajo Health Systems Agency, a spinoff of the Navajo Health Authority, shortly after completing graduate school. She counseled him that he had a big job and should not get discouraged. She encouraged everyone to take responsibility for the success of any committee on which they sat. Hubbard remembers, "During meetings she would make a point of being very precise, and as we were going through the minutes she would check to see if we had followed up on things we'd said we were going to do. She'd look intensely at each person and ask, 'Have you done that?'"[12]

Throughout the decade the various health committees worked to establish the American Indian School of Medicine. McKenzie got pledges of money from corporations and foundations and needed only another $27 million from the federal government, which funds most medical schools. Apparently at one point Annie assumed the school was nearly a reality. Dr. Marlene Haffner, who served as the IHS director on the Navajo Reservation from 1974 to 1981, recalls being at a ceremony to dedicate an addition to the Gallup Indian Hospital when Annie stepped to the microphone and thundered, "When are you white doctors going to go home?"[13]

Unfortunately, after five years of work, the plan faltered. Chairman Peter MacDonald decided that he wanted the school to be for Navajos only, so the other tribes lost interest, and the federal government turned down the proposal as being unworkable. Annie had worked so hard for this and was deeply disappointed. But, true to form, she didn't dwell on the lost opportunity. Dr. Robert Bergman, a former IHS physician who worked on the reservation, remembers that he had warned Annie that the chances for the establishment of the medical college were slight. "Of course, I know that," she told him, "but think of what they'll have to give me to make me feel better about not getting it."[14]

"LET'S TALK LEGISLATION"

During these years, Annie was traveling to Washington so often, either to lobby or to testify in front of Senate and House committees, that she became well known to many elected representatives and their staffs. Once she arrived a day late for hearings, but the committee reconvened just to hear her testimony. She was an effective lobbyist. Sometimes delegations were prepared for trips by being given cards on various members of Congress labeled "tough," "receptive," or "favorable" according to their current opinions on pending legislation affecting the Navajos. Annie did not shy away from the more challenging assignments, and after taking several cards labeled "tough," she returned them to headquarters with the notation "tenderized" in her beautiful script.[15]

In counseling a younger friend, Louise Nelson, who was considering a career in Navajo politics, Annie told the young woman that she always approached the senators and representatives respectfully. "You don't just go in there and say, 'This was our land.' The Eastern senators don't even know that we exist, that there are a people called the Navajo that reside in the Southwest. So you have to introduce yourself and present yourself that you are human too, and you are the first Americans, and go about it in a professional manner and a business atmosphere and explain to them fully what you are there for. You address a young man as your son, a young lady as your daughter, an elderly man as your grandfather, and an elderly woman as your grandmother. Everyone is your family. Especially if you are a woman, everybody rests on your shoulders. Everybody walks with you." [16]

It was rare that Annie was caught off guard. She researched topics and was prepared for most every question asked of her. Once she and five other members of the Education Committee were in Washington to lobby members of Congress to exempt some BIA teachers from a hiring freeze. When they stopped by the office of a California congressman, he asked why he should help them. Annie and the others were prepared with an answer: "Because we lease our coal mines at low royalties so your people can have power. We give out water rights so your people can farm. We help you. Can you help in return?" The congressman admitted he did not know that and was glad to find out. He also promised to do what he could to help them. [17]

Another California congressman who was not particularly sympathetic to Native American causes needed a tougher approach. Having arrived in his Washington office to let him know the Navajo position on a particular issue, Annie was surprised when he told her to "quit playing Indian." When she asked him what he meant, he indicated her outfit of a long tiered skirt and velvet overblouse, which she always wore.

"Congressman," she replied, "I even sleep in these. I didn't come here to talk about your clothes, so you ignore mine and let's talk legislation."

They got down to work, and when they concluded their business, Annie presented him with a pin that had upraised horns as part of the symbol. Then she told him that she would be watching him from the gallery in the House when the vote on the bill was taken.

He glanced up when he walked onto the House floor, and

Annie waved to him. Instead of waving back, the man placed his hands at the sides of his head with his fingers pointing up like horns. When the time came, he voted in favor of the Navajos.[18]

EXPLAINING HER APPEARANCE

Annie's Native dress and hairdo, combined with her otherwise powerful appearance, caused much attention when she traveled off the reservation. Occasionally someone would approach her and ask about her clothing and her jewelry. She was always gracious and took the opportunity to tell those who inquired about the Navajos. Frequently in her travels she was accompanied by Ellouise De Groat, the Navajo social worker who had held various management positions in the Navajo Area Indian Health Service. "In the 1970s not as many foreigners used to travel in the United States," De Groat recalls, "so people weren't used to seeing anyone who looked unusual. So we'd get on the plane, and people would look at her and ask why she was dressed like that. She didn't feel reluctant to tell them that was her Native way of dressing. They'd ask, 'Do the Navajos still fight?' And she'd say, 'No, we don't fight. We're far from fighting. We're just typical American citizens.' People would be amazed at the way she dressed and even more amazed when she spoke English, because she spoke it so perfectly. They'd ask, 'How did you learn to speak English?' and she'd say, 'Taxes went to pay for my education through what is known as the Bureau of Indian Affairs boarding school.'"[19]

SURPRISED SHE SPOKE ENGLISH

One time when De Groat and Annie were in Washington together, they decided to go out for dinner with a social worker friend of De Groat's who lived in the area. She knew of an elegant restaurant near the Potomac. They made reservations, and although De Groat and her friend wore nice dresses appropriate for the occasion, Annie as usual got dressed in her best velvet blouse and draped herself in a huge silver and turquoise squash blossom necklace and thick silver concho belt.

"When we walked in, everyone looked at us," De Groat said. "The menu was all in French. The waiter finally arrived at our table with his tuxedo and black bow tie. He asked what Marilyn wanted and what I wanted, and we ordered. Then he looked at Annie and asked us, 'What does she want?' Immediately she boomed, 'Why don't you ask me?' He was so surprised, he jumped. She ordered something off the menu, then joked with the waiter, saying, 'If it's not what I like, if it's not tasty like mutton, I'm going to have you send it back and get something else.'" Then she let out one of her booming laughs.

"That happened a number of times when I was with her," De Groat recalled. "They looked to me to answer for her or translate for her, and they'd get real surprised that she was able to do it for herself."[20]

Although Washington DC can be a somewhat dangerous place if you're walking on the streets at night, that didn't deter Annie. One evening, growing bored by sitting around in the hotel, she suggested to a fellow Tribal Council delegate that they go out and walk around. Despite her many trips to the nation's capital, she never tired of seeing the sights. He demurred, citing the danger about which they had been warned. She told him they had nothing to worry about, opened her capacious purse, and withdrew what he described as a "watermelon knife." Once when she was traveling to Washington with Dr. George Bock to testify on health care appropriations, she was relieved of such a knife when it showed up in her purse on the airport security scanner.[21]

She was always interested in taking advantage of the cultural opportunities of the big city. Occasionally she would stay in Washington with Lawrence Huerta, the Yaqui Indian who had filled a number of positions on the reservation and was now working for the federal government. He took her to see the musicals "Annie" and "Jesus Christ Superstar."

TAKING THE RANCH TO WASHINGTON

Annie's constant traveling between the reservation and Washington DC required navigating between two almost separate worlds. She would leave a land where indoor plumbing, paved roads, and heat from anything other than a wood fire were rare. After a few short hours on a plane, she would land in a world capital where every modern luxury was common, and where lawyers made more money in a week than some Navajo families saw in a year.

One morning she drove from Klagetoh to the ranch at Tanner Springs to confer with George before leaving on a trip. As usual, much of their conversation concerned the sheep, and they went down to the corral to check on the condition of some of the animals. All of a sudden, Annie became aware of the hour. She had just enough time to drive back to Klagetoh and change her clothes. Then it was back into her pickup to drive at her usual breakneck speed for three hours through Window Rock, Gallup, and on past the red buttes and mesas that line the long valley along the highway to Albuquerque. At the airport, she parked and hustled to the check-in counter, barely making it onto the plane for Washington. As the plane leveled off, and people began to settle in their seats, she stretched her legs out, finding a comfortable position for the long ride. Suddenly, she caught a whiff of a distinctly barnyard smell, not an unusual odor on a sheep and cattle ranch, but quite odd on a commercial airliner. When she glanced down in the direction of the smell, she was horrified to realize that while she had changed her other clothing, she had forgotten to replace her shoes, which were caked with manure. Slowly she drew her feet up under her seat and sat with them that way the rest of the trip.[22]

12

The Final Term

BEGINNING IN JANUARY 1976, everyone involved with Navajo politics began a wild roller coaster ride of emotional experiences. First, a small plane carrying two council members and an interpreter crashed into the side of a canyon between Albuquerque and Gallup. In traditional Navajo belief, bad things do not happen just randomly but are the result of a taboo being broken or a witch having summoned the supernatural to influence events. Because of the fear that these supernatural conditions might be lingering in the council chambers, Chairman Peter MacDonald hired a medicine man to cleanse the headquarters of any residual bad spirits, an act that helped to lessen lingering concern over possible reasons for the disaster.[1]

GRAIN AND MONEY DISAPPEAR

Next, there was the matter of more than seven million pounds of donated grain that had disappeared—it was unaccounted for and probably was stolen.[2] Just one week after that, a management consultant who had been hired to look at tribal organization delivered a report in four large volumes that gave only a partial explanation for the grain problem. The report maintained that the executive officers had little accountability and cited lack of communication between the committees and the operating departments. Constituents whom Annie had not seen in years came to her office and jammed her phone, looking for an explanation. The other council members were seeing a similar reaction, and five of them stood up during the next session to request the chairman's resignation. Annie cautioned restraint. Despite her own suspicions, she suggested that everyone take the volumes home to study over the weekend. "I don't think we should be hasty," she said. "Let's do what is right." The discussion went on in the council chambers for several days until one delegate remarked that it cost the tribe $3,700 every day the council met, and they were accomplishing nothing.[3]

A few days later the reservation was rocked once more when it was announced that a grand jury would be investigating election procedures and financial matters in the MacDonald administration. Reaction on the reservation was mixed, even within the Wauneka household. George heard Peter MacDonald deny all the charges on the radio and believed the tribal leader. Annie was sure something was up. After a rousing argument, they decided to leave it to the judge to make a decision. In the council session Annie requested that Peter MacDonald step down and allow the vice chairman or someone else to conduct the meeting while he discussed the situation. He ignored her request and calmly continued running the session.[4]

If that were not enough excitement, only five days after that, the auditors' report showed that the tribal budget had been overspent by $13 million, although the 1975 budget had been $23.46 million, the highest ever for the tribe. That sent Annie over the top. "Members of the Navajo Tribal Council, I'm talking to you," she thundered in the next session. "That $13 million over expenditure here. I keep thinking about it. I wonder what it's been spent for; how did we define that? All these expenditures, unauthorized expenditures. Why did it happen and how and where did it go?

"We've got to satisfy ourselves to give a better report to our constituents whom we represent. . . . I'm kind of worried about this whole thing now. What should we do?"[5]

A year earlier Annie had been concerned about apparent budgetary problems and the expansion of the government. Unable to get information locally on what was being spent, she and twenty-four other council members petitioned the secretary of the interior, who had to sign off on all Navajo spending, to give an accounting. She wrote a letter to Senator Barry Goldwater, asking him to intercede, but since the request did not come from the entire council, he declined to help her, citing a reluctance to get involved in tribal affairs. Now it appeared that her suspicions were proving right.[6]

In February 1977, the grand jury investigating Peter MacDonald charged him and several aides with a number of counts, including defrauding Tucson Gas and Electric Company out of $7,400 and irregularities in his 1973 federal income tax return. Although many Navajos were sure from the start that he was guilty, MacDonald managed to convince a great many of them that this was merely a case of whites persecuting him because he was trying to get a better deal on the leasing of natural resources and in other ways was flexing the economic muscle of the tribe. Thirty-one of the 102 chapters passed resolutions supporting Peter MacDonald, and the Tribal Council voted to spend $70,000 to hire the noted attorney F. Lee Bailey to defend him, although the Navajo court eventually disallowed the expenditure.

The federal court convened to hear his case in Phoenix in early May 1977. After a week-long trial the jury was deadlocked, and the judge threw out the case for insufficient evidence.[7] It would be fifteen years before MacDonald was actually convicted of the numerous illegal acts he committed during his four terms of office, but for the moment the judge's decision reaffirmed MacDonald's belief that he was above the law.

Throughout the United States, the 1960s and 1970s were a time when ordinary people, both youth and older adults, rose up to protest what they saw as wrongdoing. On the Navajo Reservation people caught the fever of the times. A substantial number of Navajos agreed with Annie that Peter MacDonald should not have been exonerated. She was happy to learn that Navajo legal advocate Peterson Zah, who was now heading the DNA legal services, was planning to lead a group of 350 Navajos in a march from the fairgrounds to the Tribal Council chambers to present a petition listing concerns about kickbacks and conflicts of interest involving millions of dollars in federal and tribal funds and calling for a reorganization of the tribal government and the resignation of all persons implicated in wrongdoing, including the chairman. When the marchers reached the council building, some 300 more protesters joined them. They were supported by a number of council delegates, including Annie. She told a reporter, "the council has been kept in the dark about alleged mismanagement and misuse of funds earmarked for reservation education, housing and employment programs." She endorsed the march as "the only way to make the leaders listen."[8]

INVESTIGATING THE STATUS OF NAVAJO WOMEN

Another sociological marker of the mid-1970s was the women's liberation movement, and this, too, made its way to the Navajo Reservation. Annie was an obvious and outstanding example of what women could accomplish if they were willing to step out of the mold of what was expected. She was appointed to a new women's commission and began to travel the reservation looking into the status of Navajo women.

In a discussion in October 1975 on how she tackled the new assignment, she explained, "I go out and hold these meetings [with women], what are their special problems? At first they thought, 'Well, what does she mean about special problems? What is she gonna do with us?' . . . So I explained it to them that women must speak up now in their behalf, and maybe they never presented their problems to anybody within their chapter meetings and so forth, and finally they came through." Once the women realized what they were being invited to do, they talked about the difficulties of inadequate housing, insufficient medical treatment, alcoholism in their families, and unemployment. The women wanted to work, but the few jobs on the reservation required more education and training than they had.[9]

Although Navajo women traditionally had considerable personal power within the family structure—owning the family hogan and their own herds—their opportunities in the broader world were limited. Annie told of being called to Tuba City to meet with the elected officials to explain her activities with the women's commission. When she walked in the room she began to feel uneasy because the crowd was almost completely men. "All these elected officials . . . from the chapter level up to the tribal council, they were there, and then I thought, 'They're men, how could they understand what I'm sayin'?' Sure enough, they didn't understand it. They said, 'Maybe we ought to call a meeting for the women.' . . . I said, 'No, I'd rather have the women call their own meeting. . . . I told them that they could not call a meeting for women of this area.' " Actually, she told them, the Tuba City women were already making plans for their own meeting.

The man chairing the meeting did not allow questions during the session, so two men came up to Annie in the hall afterward. "What do you mean having these women's conferences?" they asked. "What are they supposed to do?"

"They talk about their problems," she answered. "Women are supposed to speak up about their own problems, not the men's problems, their problems."

"Women have no business talking about themselves," one of them said. "We men, we take care of their problems."

"Hopefully you do," Annie the diplomat answered. "But they must talk."

"I had fun with them," Annie said. "Very interesting. I enjoy it very much." [10]

Annie was a guest speaker at the first Southwest Indian Women's Conference in October 1975 and addressed the more than eight hundred attendees. Her message challenged the women but also laid blame for the difficult plight of Indian women on the intervention of white culture into the traditional Navajo social system.

"Ever since the development of political machinery and bureaucratic organizations among Indians, there has been a sudden perspective of women—and the roles of women—as second-class citizens. The basic reason for discrimination against Indian women stems from the Federal government's intervention in Indian affairs," she said.

"To offset the second-class role, Indian women must become more active in politics and become aware of the educational opportunities open to Native American women."

However, she made it clear that she felt that women's quest for equality should not end up as a battle between the sexes. The struggle to maintain Indian tribal self-identity superseded equal opportunity for women.[11]

She reiterated this strong belief in the statement she submitted to the National Commission on the Observance of International Women's Year as a member of the women's commission. She had been assigned to the committee called Special Problems for Indian Women and Minority Groups. Her report began, "No role for the American Indian women on the reservation in America can be discussed without first addressing issues related to equal treatment, opportunity and recognition of the Indians and the Tribal Government. . . . It is apparent more and more today that 'equal opportunity' for Indians cannot be realized until the unique legal status of the American Indian tribe is reaffirmed and strengthened by the federal government. Only after this is done can the role of the American Indian women on the reservation be assessed fairly." [12]

She listed issues that Indian women saw as critical: protection of Indian land as a means of maintaining the language, spirit, emotional ties, and tribal values of each group; protection of the land's resources; strengthening of tribal government; reaffirmation of the tribal-federal relationship; and the ability of the tribal government to negotiate for federal funds and use them for effective programs and services. None of these issues were solely for the benefit of women, but Annie was trying to stress that without attention to such issues, women would suffer.

Annie was the keynote speaker at the first Navajo Women's Conference, where the participants discussed integrating traditional and modern values for Navajo women. She suggested that women should not compete with Navajo men but should strive to become equal partners. She also urged women not to settle for clerical jobs but to seek work at the decision-making levels in administration.[13]

She countered critics who worried that Navajo women belonged in the hogan and would loose something essential if they took jobs. "I see a lot of these educated Navajo girls typing," she said. "They went to school. As secretaries they have been taught to use shorthand, they have been taught to use typewriters. . . . And she has been paid. This is done for economy reasons.

"And she has been taught to live in a nice house where you just touch the walls and the lights come on. Where you touch a certain metal, turn it, and the water is running. Yet she is an Indian. Her belief is within her. Her heritage is within her. . . . She is a Navajo and will always remain an Indian."[14]

A SHEAF OF HONORS

After twenty-five years of service to the Navajo Nation and at age sixty-four, Annie was beginning to think of retirement. She had been amply recognized for her work and accomplishments. In 1976 the readers of the *Ladies Home Journal* had voted her a Woman of the Year in the inspirational and educational leadership category. Other honorees in other categories were First Lady Betty Ford, Margaret Mead, Ella Grasso, Betty Furness, and Maya Angelou.

It was only the most recent item of the sheaf of honors she had been collecting since the Medal of Freedom had been presented by Lyndon Johnson in 1964. Among her many awards was one from Project Hope for encouraging Navajos to become trained nurses. Others came from the North American Indian Women's Association, the Girl Scouts of America, Project Concern, the Public Health Service, and the National Community Health Representatives. She also received the highest award given by the Society of Public Health Educators, the Will Ross Medal from the International Lung Association Conference in Montreal, and an honorary doctorate in humanities from the University of New Mexico in Albuquerque. Such doctorates are taken seriously on the reservation, and after she received this award in 1972 she always signed her letters "Dr. Annie Wauneka." Senators and other government officials addressed her as "Doctor" in hearings, although given that she was always testifying on health matters, it is unclear if they knew that the degree was honorary rather than medical. Children were also sometimes confused. When she visited a school and was introduced as Dr. Wauneka, one little boy asked if she were there to give them shots. She replied, "No, I'm just a talking doctor."[15]

THOUGHTS OF RETIREMENT

As early as October 1975, and again the following summer, she had told interviewers that she was planning on retiring, citing a desire to spend more time with George and her children and grandchildren.[16] By this time, Irma had three sons, and Lorencita had married Edmond Cohoe and had two sons and a daughter. Annie loved having the children around.

Peter MacDonald had also decided to leave office and had chosen Dr. Taylor McKenzie as his successor—that is, until McKenzie announced Milton Bluehouse Sr. as his running mate. McKenzie was a good friend of Annie Wauneka's through their work on health care over the years; Milton Bluehouse was her son-in-law, married to her daughter Irma. Annie joined in the campaign with great enthusiasm.

Unwilling to see his office go to a contingent with whom he disagreed, Peter MacDonald reentered the race and was challenged by former chairman Raymond Nakai. In the primary, the McKenzie-Bluehouse ticket lost out.

RUNNING ONCE AGAIN

At some point, Annie decided to make a bid to keep her own seat. For once, she did not campaign for the position. She was gratified that supporters had urged her to run again. She had become a fixture in the Tribal Council, and she was busy serving on many committees, working long hours for improvements in health and education. But this time, unlike in previous races, her opponent had considerable popular support. Running against her was Jimmie Nelson, a well-known member of the Native American Church and an advocate of the ritual use of peyote. Nelson wanted to win and campaigned seriously throughout the Wide Ruins and Klagetoh chapters, saying that Annie had gotten so important that her traveling to Washington and Phoenix and Santa Fe removed her from her constituents.

Some of her constituents also had begun to see her as too

strong and overbearing. Annie usually attended mass at St. Anne's Mission in Klagetoh, and after church she was always the main speaker at the coffee break. She would give out the news and encourage people to vote, attend chapter meetings, and take care of their health—all information she thought was important for them to have. Though the other parishioners respected her, some of them found her pushy and resented the way she dominated the gatherings. It is a cultural trait among Navajos not to wish to stand out and to view with suspicion those who do. Some of the people in her area were terrified of her and dared not oppose her for fear of getting on her bad side. Fear of witchcraft remains very strong on the Navajo Reservation. Despite the feelings of some of her constituents, it was Annie's clear dedication to the welfare of her people that helped her maintain her popularity.

During the campaign, Jimmie Nelson also got support from Peter MacDonald and MacDonald's lawyer, George Vlassis, who saw Annie as an obstacle to the chairman's agenda. They claimed that Annie was too old, had been around too long, and was out of touch with what was needed on the reservation.

THE WINDOW ROCK SEVEN

Interestingly, there was a confrontation brewing that would demonstrate just how willing Annie was to become involved in contemporary events. Also on the ballot for Tribal Council in the Shiprock area was a young half-black, half-Navajo named Donald Benally, a friend of Annie's and a vocal opponent of Peter MacDonald. The tribal rule was that delegates had to be at least thirty years old. Although Benally was only twenty-five, the Navajo Court of Appeals decided that he could remain on the ballot. There was a legal tussle with a body called the Supreme Judicial Council, a group of council members organized by MacDonald to watch over the courts, which ruled that Benally could not run. In this period of great political interest among the young throughout the country, this denial of the chance for youthful representation lit the fires of rebellion on the Navajo Reservation. Other Navajos, including Annie, were opposed to the Supreme Judicial Council, seeing it as a challenge to the separation of the legislative and judicial bodies. With the complaints against Mac-Donald mounting, and with what they saw as the arrogance of the Supreme Judicial Council, lack of an independent judiciary, and other concerns throughout the reservation, a group of seven young men had tolerated enough.

Calling themselves the Diné Bii Coalition (Coalition of the People), they tried to get answers from the Tribal Council. Annie never talked to them but knew who they were, having had them pointed out to her from a distance. A fighter all her life for justice and one who would frequently stand alone to follow her beliefs, she wondered about these young people, particularly since they shared some of her beliefs.

When the Diné Bii Coalition was not allowed to speak to the council, the young men made alternate plans to be heard. Just as the day was beginning to lighten at 7 A.M. on November 13, the day before the election, they arrived at the government complex at the base of the famous Window Rock and entered the tribal administration building, taking it over. They demanded a public apology from both Peter MacDonald and Raymond Nakai for the violence during the campaign. The also demanded that the Supreme Judicial Council be abolished and that the tribe's white attorneys be removed. The FBI was called, and because two loaded rifles and a .357 magnum were found inside, the young men were accused of the overblown charges of kidnapping and assault with a deadly rifle. They were taken to jail in Gallup, and a hearing was scheduled for the next day.[17]

On that Tuesday afternoon, as Navajos were flocking to the polls and with her own seat on the line, Annie and her daughter Irma drove to Gallup for the hearing. The gray-haired sixty-eight-year old who had been accused of being out of touch was the only council member present, the only one to show concern about what the young Navajos, who had gained the name "The Window Rock Seven," had on their minds.

During the hearing, the U.S. magistrate listened to the young men's story and then sent them back to their cells. However, their attorney had recognized Annie Wauneka and asked if she would intervene. She said she would consider it, but only if she could talk to the young men alone. This was agreed to, and she was led to the jail through two locked doors, which were then locked behind her.

Of course the young men knew who she was when she appeared in their cell, and they addressed her respectfully as "mother" or "grandmother." Later she reported, "I talked to them like their mother. I told them: 'You behave yourselves, don't do this, don't do that,' as any mother talks to her children. They seemed so innocent and friendly." Although she was not taking personal responsibility for the group, she decided that she would be willing to lend her name to their release.[18]

When a reporter approached her just after the men were released from jail, she initially declined to talk, saying, "Why are you so interested in me? You should be talking to them." Later, however, she said, "People out there [on the reservation] are so concerned and interested in this. You hear so much about it and it sounds so dangerous, so I decided to come in and find out what was going on. No other councilman seems to take an interest.

"If the tribal leaders did the right thing in explaining to them in the first place, maybe these things wouldn't happen. Maybe they're doing it wrong, but they're just trying to get information."

When the hubbub died down, Annie turned to her daughter and said, "Let's go. I just signed my life away." And they drove back to Klagetoh to await the election results.[19]

A SURPRISING ELECTION OUTCOME

The next morning politicians and ordinary Navajos alike heard the news. Despite his numerous legal difficulties, Peter MacDonald had won a third term. Everyone was stunned to hear that Annie Wauneka had lost to Jimmie Nelson by thirteen votes. His message had convinced just enough people to gain him the seat that Annie had held since 1951. That morning's paper also carried a condemnation of Annie by Peter MacDonald, who was angered by her involvement with the Diné Bii. "The news media creates events rather than reporting them," he was quoted as saying. "Unfortunately Mrs. Annie Wauneka, who at one time in her career was a true leader of her people, has also become a media creation. The kindly old grandmother, the Navajo Golda Meir or Indira Gandhi, is a fable created by the press who like to have good pictures." His interview was given before the results of the election were known, when it looked like Annie would still be a daily thorn in his side.[20]

But the new council would not take over until after the first of the year, and Annie held her seat for another month. The present council still had to deal with the unrest and the demands by the youthful demonstrators. About two weeks after the election, some of the young men who had been arrested along with some young women demonstrated again under the Window Rock, still seeking information and a chance to address the council. Twenty-one of them were arrested, although they were eventually released. Annie was out of town that day, but on her return she urged the council and the chairman to allow the group to speak and to address their concerns. "They're not a bunch of mobs, they're our young people," she said. "You can use the police force to put these people in jail, but that is no answer."[21] Because of her defense of the militants, other council members began calling her "Annie Get Your Gun" and "AIM [for American Indian Movement] Annie" behind her back.

Eventually on December 12, a bitterly cold and damp day, a small group of the Diné Bii Coalition was allowed to speak along with a pro-MacDonald group called the Navajo Nation Grievance Association. Although it was Annie who had fought for their right to speak to the council, the members of the latter group used part of their time to condemn her. However, their remarks were made in Navajo and neither reported nor translated. When Larry Anderson, one of the Window Rock Seven, was given the floor, he stood up for Annie, saying that the Navajo Nation Grievance Association had ridiculed an outstanding woman and should reconsider its allegations.[22] In fact, were it not for Annie's work, many of her young accusers would not have been alive—either they or their parents might have died from tuberculosis, gastrointestinal disease, malnutrition, or a host of other ailments about which she had educated the Navajo People.

HAPPY TO HAVE SERVED

For two days the two groups had the floor, stating their positions. Then, at last, Annie had a chance to rebut. She used most of her time addressing the groups' requests regarding the elections in Shiprock and Donald Benally's candidacy, urging the council and administration to look further into the problems. But, still reeling from her unexpected defeat, she was stung by the undeserved criticism and defended herself. "I've been accused of many things throughout my life. I served 27 years here, you can read my record, and I think I have a wonderful record throughout the Nation. . . . With these little abuses, it makes no difference. I'm sorry to say that I imagine some time they'll come around and say, I need your help and I'm willing to help. So that doesn't bother me at all. I think that's the way it's been planned. Pour everything on Mrs. Wauneka, that doesn't bother me at all, ladies and gentlemen. I'll walk out of here as a person who's always been proud, dignified and go back to my community and I'll probably say the same things that you people are saying to whoever are the leaders. If the things aren't done right, they'll hear from me, like you folks are doing here. It'll be my privilege and I'm very happy to have served here."[23]

Although her decades as a politician had put her in the middle of many bitter debates and she had remained standing through many tougher fights, there can be no doubt that this final council meeting was a sad ending to her years as a delegate.

The loss of her position on the Tribal Council brought up the question of her occupancy of the house in Klagetoh. It had been given to her in connection with her job as the area's council delegate. She asked the community what she should do. Did they want her to move out? The residents of Klagetoh would not hear of it. "You are our mother," they told her. "You stay right there."[24]

III

The Post-Council Years

13
Traveling Near and Far

WHEN THE COUNCIL SESSIONS RESUMED after the first of the year, it was painful to Annie to be excluded. It was not as if she did not have work to do, however. She was serving on the Navajo Area Health Board, the Navajo Health Authority Board of Directors, and the governing board of the Navajo Health Systems Agency, which was charged with putting together a master health plan for the area and which was established by the National Health Planning Act. She was also on the board of the Navajo Nation Health Foundation that was set up to earn funds for the Sage Memorial Hospital in Ganado, where Annie and so many members of her family had been treated.

Dr. Marlene Haffner, head of the IHS in Window Rock, recalled, "I seldom made any major decisions without her input. I valued her judgment." However, Annie could be difficult to work with. "The PHS leaned on her so heavily that we created a certain imperiousness in her. She was used to being deferred to and consulted," Haffner said.[1]

RELYING ON OLD HABITS
Frequently Annie drove into town just out of habit, to see what was going on in local affairs. Then, as now, the restaurant at the Window Rock Motor Inn (now called the Navajo Nation Inn) served as the town square for this spread-out reservation. If one is in government, it is *the* place to see and be seen. People observe who is lunching with whom, who is visiting the reservation, and who stops to shake hands at what table. They try to be inconspicuous as they strain to overhear snatches of conversation when interesting situations are developing. Over the two and a half decades Annie Wauneka had served on the council,

she had lunched there hundreds of times and discussed politics over countless cups of coffee with every mover and shaker on the reservation and lots of friends and people who just wanted her ear.

The habits of all those years were not easily put aside. Now, although she was not involved in Tribal Council affairs, she would stop by the Inn before or after a meeting to hobnob or to catch up on the news. There were endless post-election discussions — why she had lost, how her replacement was doing, why he was not reporting back to his chapter constituents.

Annie and George celebrated their fiftieth wedding anniversary in 1979 with a mass at the mission church at St. Michael's that included a papal blessing. Many guests, grateful for her help over the years, showered her and George with gifts. Theirs had been an unusual relationship, with Annie living in Klagetoh, frequently gone from the reservation, and George content to stay at the ranch and watch over the children and livestock, but the marriage was strong, and they were both happy with the arrangement.

She spent more time with friends. Despite her work and family responsibilities through the preceding years, she had frequently made time to drop in on friends and relatives. On the Navajo Reservation that could mean a long drive, but she would show up for birthday parties or ceremonies or just to share a cup of coffee. Her desire for connection with other people superceded her need or desire for rest, and her unflappable energy supported her need.

SPENDING TIME WITH A NEW FRIEND

Once out of office, Annie also filled her time with even more traveling — for pleasure as well as official business. One of her traveling companions was a young white former sociology professor named Ron Faiche, who had been hired some years before to work with the census bureau to develop enumeration district lines for the upcoming 1980 census. He had first met Annie when she heard that he had been out to her area with his maps, talking to people in the chapter about the boundaries. Her son

Franklin had represented the family at a meeting at the chapter house and reported back that the chapter line agreed upon in the meeting had been drawn too far to the east. Annie and Franklin, who was of considerable height and girth, then tracked Faiche down in his office and demanded the line be changed. The two of them together were imposing. "Annie was very demanding . . . she seemed very cold," Faiche remembers. "She was getting hot, and you could tell this was important to her. She left, but I knew I was going to see her again." Eventually, after some time and some legal wrangling, the line was drawn to Annie's satisfaction, and Faiche and Annie became friends, exchanging frequent telephone calls. Sometimes they would talk for an hour in the evenings. Eventually they began meeting for lunch.

It was an unexpected alliance. Faiche appeared on the scene when Annie was looking for causes and events to fill her time. Annie's friendship was most welcome to Faiche, who was alone on the reservation. In long talks, she helped him understand what was going on in Navajo politics beneath the level of what was apparent to him as an outsider.

One of these events took Faiche deeply into the Navajo culture with Annie as a guide. One day he had left his office briefly and forgotten his lighter on his desk. When he came back, it was gone. Although he saw it as petty thievery, Annie said, "I don't think that it was just somebody who wanted your lighter. I think it is somebody who wishes you bad things. Maybe somebody from one of the chapters that lost out on one of the disputes didn't get the line they wanted. This is not good." She explained that Navajo witches gather personal items from those they wish to harm. When Faiche asked if it was serious enough to pack his bags and leave the reservation, she said "Oh no, no. We'll deal with it. I want us to go see a medicine man who will say some prayers for you. That will help counter things. I'll talk to him. I'll get in touch with him through his daughter. He's up in the Shonto area, and we'll get it set up."

The instructions came back from the medicine man that Faiche had to go out late at night with a coffee can and gather up a number of items including some dirt from outside the office windows of Chairman Peter MacDonald and the general counsel. After Faiche had gotten what was necessary, they drove to the hogan of an old medicine man wearing long turquoise earrings. He had a pipe with "Navajo tobacco"—herbs from the Four Sacred Mountains. The medicine man mixed the dirt with water and herbs, began a chant, and lit the sacred tobacco. He then instructed Faiche to take the dirt, now a paste, out to his Monte Carlo and rub it on all four of his tires. The ceremony seemed to do the trick, as no calamities befell Faiche, and life continued as before.

Eventually Faiche and Annie became so close that they talked on the phone three or four times a week if they were not getting together. The two also traveled together just to see the area. George was happy staying at the ranch, Annie's daughters were busy with their jobs and families, and Annie found it was pleasant to have a companion on trips to Monument Valley and Glen Canyon Dam. Like many others before and after him who spoke of Annie dropping by for birthdays or holidays or just to say hello, Faiche discovered that she was willing to put in considerable time and energy to stay connected to those she cared about. Years later, Faiche would say, "She was the best friend I ever had."[2]

Although Annie may have seemed driven and restless to an outsider, her constant moving about was not particularly unusual in her culture. Navajos like to travel, and they have a vast reservation. It is not unusual for a Navajo man or woman to hop in a pickup and drive to Gallup or Flagstaff for groceries or drive a hundred miles to visit a relative on a whim. In fact, the Navajo creation myth is one of movement from one world to the next, ever upward, until The People—or Diné—arrived on the face of the earth.

A TRIP TO CHINA

In 1980 a travel opportunity arrived that eclipsed everything previous, including her trips to Alaska and Hawaii. Most anthropologists believe the Indians arrived in the Americas from Asia, migrating across a land bridge in the Bering Strait, although the Navajos believe that their ancestors emerged from the underworld in the Four Corners area where they live now. The Chinese government invited a delegation of American Indians to visit in the hopes of building an alliance between the two groups. If one concurs with the anthropologists, it was a bringing together of long-lost cousins.

Both Annie and her friend Ellouise De Groat, the IHS administrator, were invited to represent the Navajos, joining about two dozen other Native Americans. They got their passports and protective shots. Annie also decided to opt for some Navajo-style protection and hired a medicine man to perform a traditional ceremony for herself.

The trip took place in August. They flew first to San Francisco and then transferred to a Chinese airplane. In China, their home base was Shanghai. When they arrived there was much curiosity on both sides. The Chinese found Annie most interesting, with her voluminous skirt, her silver and turquoise jewelry, and her scarf tied under her chin. The Indians were surprised at how people in China all seemed to dress alike. Annie and De Groat marveled at how much the Chinese looked like Navajos, pointing out particular individuals to each other and comparing them to friends and acquaintances they knew back home. "We had carbon copies over in China," De Groat recalls.[3]

The similarity they saw was not a fantasy on their part. Dr. Clarence Salsbury, who had come to Sage Memorial Hospital in Ganado after twelve years as a medical missionary in Hainan, China, wrote in his autobiography how he thought many Navajos had an Asian look about the eyes.[4]

Shortly before the group was to visit the Great Wall outside of Bejing, Annie's knee, which frequently bothered her, began to act up. She was taken to a hospital and had a chance to closely observe one aspect of Chinese medical care as the doctors gave her an acupuncture treatment. De Groat received treatment as well because she was coming down with a cold. The acupuncture treatment worked for both of them. "The day we went to the Great Wall, she outran me," De Groat remembers. "I was huffing and puffing, but she went up there with no problems. She had no pain in her knee, and when we came back, still no pain."

In the mornings, Annie arose at dawn as usual and went outside to do her prayers with corn pollen. At that time the streets in China are full of people, many of them doing t'ai chi exercises. She was invited to join them and did so.

Before she had left the reservation for China, a medicine man visited her and told her of a place he had heard about in China where a waterfall flows into a river and there is a perpetual rainbow. The rainbow is an important symbol for the Navajos, and he asked her to bring him back some of the soil from the area. Annie arranged to visit the spot and, after asking permission from a Chinese official, bought back a little handful of the dirt in a plastic bag.[5]

EXCHANGING CULINARY TRADITIONS

As the group traveled around, there was always an opportunity for cultural exchange. When the Americans visited an area where the people were sheepherders, Annie was surprised to find that many of the sheep looked like the Karakul breed that Chee Dodge raised. Interestingly, this breed did originate in Asia. She was also surprised that the Chinese boiled their mutton when preparing it. During her part of the cultural exchange at that stop, she butchered a sheep while the curious Chinese formed a crowd behind her, watching her technique, as she cut off the head first, then slit the hide down the belly and peeled away the hide from the flesh. Wanting them to taste Navajo-style roasted mutton, she built a fire and roasted the ribs over the coals. Then, in order to finish the Navajo meal, she asked for flour, mixed it with water and fat, and made tortillas to go along with the ribs. To make the event complete, she thought it would be good to have some typical Navajo entertainment, so she enlisted Philip Cassadore, an Apache medicine man who was also on the trip, to play the drum, and she taught the Chinese to do a round dance like the one Navajos do at the Enemy Way ceremony. "I gained such popularity," she later told her friend Louise Nelson. "Now I know how movie stars feel!"

On another night, the American delegation was served a typical Chinese banquet with dish after dish of exotic foods. Ellouise

De Groat found everything delicious and ate some of each dish, but Annie was suspicious of one of the offerings. She asked an interpreter what it was, and when she learned it was camel, she ate no more.

Although Annie was open to new cultural experiences, save camel meat, she really drew the line at activities that violated her most deeply held beliefs. Because of her typical Navajo reticence to have anything to do with the dead, she did not visit any of the famed tombs nor go to see Mao's body in its glass casket. Soon the trip was over, and after a short stop in Japan, it was back to the reservation to see what the rest of life had to offer.

When Annie returned to the reservation, she had another sing as a cleansing ritual. Later, when De Groat developed problems with her liver and had to have a transplant, Annie was sure that her visits to the tombs had contributed to her illness.[6]

CORN POLLEN AND CATHOLICISM

Just as Annie straddled white and Navajo culture in the political and medical arenas, she managed to practice both Catholicism and her Native religion. Once, when driving Annie to the Sage Hospital, Sallie Lippincott Wagner, the trader at Wide Ruins, asked Annie if she was a Presbyterian. She answered, "I was baptized a Christian, but I'm really corn pollen."[7] Yellow corn pollen, a symbol of female fertility, is a highly sacred item to Navajos. Annie always began her day with a prayer and a sprinkling of corn pollen. Such prayers are private, but a typical one might be, "Very early at dawn with corn pollen in my hand, I raise my corn pollen to the east. I am within my four sacred mountains. I know the four sacred mountains will hear my daily prayer and answer me."

Annie tried to explain her feeling for her religion to a writer.

What is it . . . this corn pollen, which is very sacred in the beginning of life of a Navajo—what is it? What are the sacred mountains? What are the connections with nature? Why is the corn planted—the yellow corn and the white corn?

And the Sacred Songs are pertaining to these corns. And the Sacred Songs are sung to the Sacred Mountains. To the Sun. To the Mother Earth. To the Great Bodies of Water.

And the prayers are performed at a certain hour of the day, or a certain hour of the night. Not usually at the hand of the clock. But it's at the movement of the stars. Or the movement of the Sun or the movement of the Moon.

These are connections that are made. There are long stories connected with these things. Many connections. . . . There are many sacred things within the Navajo country. It is very hard for a non-Navajo to understand some of these beliefs.[8]

HELPING THE NAVAJO NATION HEALTH FOUNDATION

Particularly satisfying for Annie was her work with the Navajo Nation Health Foundation, which had taken over the running of Sage Memorial Hospital in 1974. For decades, she had chafed watching federal agencies such as the Bureau of Indian Affairs and the Public Health Service, which were dominated by white personnel, control the spending of money allocated for Native American benefit in such areas as health and education. Now new policies under the Indian Self-Determination Act of 1975 called for more Indian involvement in these federal programs. In Washington, testifying before Senate and House appropriations committees, Annie described the Navajo Nation Health Foundation as the first comprehensive health care program to be controlled by Indians. Although the hospital was privately run, it served a poverty-stricken population and relied on the fact that the federal government was legally obligated to pay for Indian health care. (One official characterized the Indian arm of the Public Health Service as a sort of HMO for Indians, for which they had paid the premiums in advance with their land.) The foundation had a contract with the PHS to provide health care to Navajos in the south-central area of the reservation—1,200 square miles with about 12,000 residents. Annie explained the role of the foundation, stressing the need for about $3 million above the PHS contract to cover the cost of care for the more than 40,000 patients seen at the hospital and field clinics.

The services available at Sage Memorial were, in fact, an alternative to the federally imposed Public Health Service, and Annie let the lawmakers know that in the future the foundation would prefer to receive the money directly through block grants rather than through the phs as a way of reducing overhead. "We can manage our own affairs and we ask you to help us make Indian self-determination mean something," she told the committee members. "Please do not turn us down."[9]

ON THE CAMPAIGN TRAIL AGAIN

When election year came around again in 1982, Annie was anxious for Chairman Peter MacDonald to leave office, and she let it be known that she was looking for another candidate to support. Peterson Zah had decided to run for the chairmanship, and one of his friends who thought the two would mesh served as a go-between. Zah's friend told Annie that Zah would like to have her come to his home and meet his family. He would even do the cooking. Annie had known about him for years—they had been on the same and differing sides of many issues during his work at dna.[10]

"She came, she was very pleasant, and we got acquainted," Zah remembers.

She knew about my family and my father. She asked some questions, one of which was how I felt about the Treaty of 1868. Had I read and studied the implications of that treaty? The other was about the direction in which I would lead the Navajo Nation. How did I feel about the court system? She asked if I was willing to tackle that issue so that we didn't have a Tribal Council that was supposed to be a law-making body always involved in everything. I told her what my plans were, that we did need to overhaul the whole judicial system and come in with a system that included separation of powers. Her third concern was education and youth and how they needed to be taught about their own culture, their own history, and their Navajo language. She was concerned about the health of the Navajo People and thought that they needed to watch their diet more, and they needed to take care of their spiritual well-being also.

At the end of our meeting that day, she said, "I've made up my mind. I'll support you. Where is your schedule? Where are you going to go?" So I gave her the schedule, and I think the next day I was going out to Crownpoint, way out east of Window Rock—about a three-and-

a-half-hour drive. She read through the list of appearances and said, "Okay, I'll help you get elected."

On the day of his get-together with Annie, Zah was recovering from an all-night meeting the previous evening. After she left, he went to another meeting that lasted past midnight and kept him out until about 2 A.M. by the time he drove home. He was still deep in sleep at 6 A.M. when Annie was knocking at his door.

"Son, I'm ready to go," she said. "Let's go campaign." She always addressed younger people as son or daughter, and as spoken in Navajo, the words conveyed both respect and affection.

"But the meeting isn't until noon," Zah explained, sleepy-eyed.

"Well, we'll drive on over. I've got a lot to tell you along the way," she said.

"So I got in my car with her, and we drove," Zah said. "She knew all the back roads. She'd say she'd been through there thirty, forty, fifty years before. She remembered the families, she'd spent the night with some of them." [11]

EDUCATING A YOUNG POLITICIAN

"There was so much education, so much that I got from her," Zah recalls.

She would say that when you go before a Navajo crowd, the first thing is to tell people what clan you are. Every Navajo person belongs to four clans, and you have to say them in this order: your clan, your father's clan, your mother's father's clan, and your paternal grand-mother's. Those four clans make you a person. The second thing you say is who you are married into, what clan—your wife's clan and your wife's father's clan and how many children you have. Then where your mother and father come from. Do you have any livestock? Are you a landowner? Do you have a grazing permit? Those are the most important things in campaigning. You may have all these wonderful ideas about the judicial system, Tribal Council reorganization, the BIA, and what Congress is doing—those are all secondary. Because when you are elected, your whole family goes with you and is being elected, so people have to know what clan you are. The older folks aren't going to refer to you as Mr. Chairman, they are going to refer to you by your clan relationships, such as my son, or my grandson. Government is a foreign thing. That was an invaluable lesson.

Annie also taught the young candidate how to talk to a Navajo audience. "You can think in English, but when you face an audience of traditional Navajo people, you have to be very eloquent in the Navajo language, using Navajo analogies and native intelligence," Zah said.

She was my teacher in that situation. Simple things like when you are campaigning and shaking hands, you have to look them right in the eye as you answer their question. Don't grin, don't look around, you have to focus all of your attention to that one individual who is shaking your hand. You have to give them that time that they are looking for from you.

She also said that when you are talking to a traditional Navajo audience, you have to put them at ease by telling them some Navajo jokes. Navajos are pleasant people, and they have to know you have a sense of humor because you're going to need a sense of humor in that job.

Annie's early arrival that first morning of campaigning was just a taste of what was to come. She was seventy-two years old, but she nearly ran the much younger candidate to exhaustion. Another day at the end of the campaign, they had visited the Whitehorse Lake chapter house until early afternoon and then went to another chapter house until past midnight. When they arrived in Window Rock, Zah went home to bed, and Annie had to drive on to Klagetoh. But there were still two more chapter houses to visit. Zah remembers, "The next morning she was knocking at my door at 7 o'clock, saying, 'We've got to go. You want to win this election? We've got to get on the road.' She had an unbelievable amount of energy!" [12]

WORKING FOR THE ZAH ADMINISTRATION

Whether it was Annie's help or whether the Navajo People were tired of Peter MacDonald and ready to try someone else, Peterson Zah won the election in November of 1982 by receiving 29,203 votes to MacDonald's 24,658. Before he was even installed, Zah created a nine-member committee to recommend to him sweeping changes in how the tribal government should operate. Annie, of course, was a member of the committee.

As soon as Zah was sworn in as chairman, he appointed Annie to be his adviser and the health ambassador to the Navajo Nation. "In that position I didn't want her to come to work and punch in a clock from 8 to 5," he explains. "She was free to rove around, talk to youth groups and other people. She went to Washington to represent us. She was an excellent adviser and ambassador because people respected her and what she said. She was walking dignity." [13]

Although she may have been dignified, she certainly was not stuffy. On a trip to a conference in Las Vegas, when Ellouise De Groat was unable to accompany her, the IHS sent along a young man to help her with her suitcase and papers and oversee the travel arrangements. The agency instructed the aide to save all his receipts, and they would reimburse his expenses when he got back. This young man had worked for the IHS for only a week; he was short on cash and apparently did not have a credit card. After he and Annie had been installed in their rooms, she called him and said she was hungry and wanted to go to dinner. He told her that he didn't have much money and that they'd have to choose a modest restaurant.

When they met in the lobby, they had to walk by all the slot machines to get out. Annie had never played one of them before, so she decided to use up the quarters she had to try her luck. She put in a few quarters and got a few back. She fed those back in until the fruit symbols lined up and the quarters started tumbling out, and out, and out. When they were all counted, she had won about $1,800. Taking her winnings, she turned to her young escort and, all thoughts of economizing gone, declared, "Sonny, let's go get us a steak!" [14]

Annie spent a great deal of time in her new job driving around to the schools, speaking to classes of youngsters about their culture, their history, their motivation, and their problems. Accord-

ing to Peterson Zah, when she walked onto school grounds anywhere on the reservation, activity stopped. Young people could
be running about, yelling, chewing gum, but when Annie Wauneka arrived, "it was as if time froze." [15]

She was particularly concerned about the difficulties the
youngsters faced in mixing the white culture's ways that they
saw on television with the traditional Navajo culture. "I ask them
what's the biggest problem they see on the reservation," she said.
"They don't wait two or three minutes. They say, 'alcohol, drugs.'
I turn around and say why is that problem here? Who's bringing
in the problem? It's for you to decide. Whether you're going to
join the crowd. You're going to be the leaders of tomorrow. You're
going to do it with a good mind." [16]

PASSING THE HAT FOR NAVAJO WAY
Another new challenge Annie took on was as a board member of
the Navajo Way, an agency similar to the United Way. Everywhere
she went on the reservation she talked up the need for contributions to support the good work of the agency. "My job now is
campaigning for Navajo Way," she told a group in Los Angeles
in April 5, 1984. "I use the words 'share and care.' So far we've
raised a little over $100,000. When I get back, I'll have to go out
and work to get some more money." [17]

Asking for money had become routine for Annie, who more
than twenty times had stood before the lawmakers of Washington and without hesitation looked them in the eyes and asked for
tens of millions of dollars. She rarely had gotten all she asked for,
but the IHS and the tribe clearly thought it was worth the invest-
ment in her expenses to send her to Washington, for with her
testimony they would end up with more money than they could
have expected otherwise.

As she traveled throughout the reservation, even doing personal errands, she was recognized and honored. Peter Iverson,
who spent time doing research in the area, noted that whenever
Annie walked into a bank where there was a long line of customers, she was immediately ushered to the head of the queue.

ENJOYING GRANDMOTHERHOOD

Despite her many official obligations, Annie now had more time for her grandchildren. Milton Bluehouse Jr., Irma's youngest son, lived not far from his grandmother and spent a great deal of time with her, beginning around the time she lost her council seat. She'd drive up to the Bluehouse home in a cloud of dust and call for her daughter Irma and grandson. "Sonny Boy, get your stuff together and comb your hair; we're going," she'd announce.

"The world was a blur when I traveled with Grandma, because she usually sped across the reservation around eighty miles an hour," Milton remembers. "Trees whizzed by, animals ran, scurrying across the road, and passed cars grew smaller by the second in the side-view mirror." A pile of papers would be stacked beside her, matters to be looked into wherever they were going. Whether they ended up at the council chambers in Window Rock or a remote chapter house, Milton was surprised and uneasy to hear men he knew to be corrupt address his grandmother as *Shimá*, meaning "mother" or "mom" in Navajo.

The prominent older woman and the young child came from different worlds in dozens of ways, but they loved their time together as they drove.

Grandma would ask me what I was thinking about, and we'd laugh because I told her about the "I Love Lucy" episode where Lucy is working in the chocolate factory. . . . If in the distance there was a mountain, or a land formation, Grandma would tell the story of that particular place, how it was created and the belief behind it. She'd tell it in a way that as you are listening to her you are getting the facts first. But sooner or later the story changes and exactly as you were forming the question as to why that particular land formation was there, she'd begin to answer it. Navajo stories are like that; first the facts of the story and answers to "why" at the exact moment "why" is forming. I never asked Grandma questions, because it wasn't polite. It was like an affront to their credibility or a doubt of their intelligence. So you never asked questions of older folks in Navajo country. Sooner or later the answers you want will become apparent. After her story we'd sit quietly, driving along, the quietness letting the story enter my soul, so I would never forget. If there was no story to tell, Grandma would sing

*old Navajo songs, sacred songs or the usual summer songs. I'd help
her sing a few too, and then I would introduce a song I'd learned—
the Mickey Mouse Club song. This was how we traveled, both enjoying
each other's company.*[18]

Milton remembers that he took every chance he could to accompany his grandmother down to Tanner Springs, or Round
Tree, as they sometimes called it, to visit his grandfather. They'd
take groceries and laundry, which was easier to do in town since
the ranch didn't have running water. Their arrival generally involved some fireworks.

*As we'd get closer and closer to the ranch, we'd see evidence of trees
being chopped down. My grandma would give a really big sigh. Of
course, my grandpa was cutting down the trees. That just set the stage.
My grandmother and grandfather really did get along. They loved each
other, but they used to argue a lot. I never heard the opening barrage
of words, but somehow I instinctively knew Grandma started it. The
reason I never heard the opening was because I was sent to put up the
potatoes, cases of soda pop, and canned goods that we'd brought. So by
the time my mission was accomplished and I entered "no man's land,"
only a few stray rounds were being fired. It was here, after the skirmishes, that Grandpa did the most peculiar thing. He winked at me,
smiled, and gave me the thumbs up signal, all while Grandma's back
was turned, of course. There was always this constant battle between
them, but when we left, they were always on good ground.*[19]

After the groceries were put up and Annie and George had
settled the issue of the day, she and Milton would get back in the
pickup and drive around the ranch. "We used to drive up on top
of the ridge," he says, "and she'd tell me stories of Chee Dodge and
say that once there were thousands of cattle there. Sheep as well.
We just pondered a lot of things. Drive around, get out and look,
get back in the car. Drive around again. It was a normal every-
other-week thing. It wasn't like you were expecting the answers
to life every time you were with Grandma. But I got the answers
just by watching her; it was her presence and the way she carried
herself."

One day when Annie had several of her grandchildren in her

pickup, they decided they would be tourists and would drive to the nearby Painted Desert and Petrified Forest National Monument. Milton remembers his grandmother being fascinated by all the exhibits, including evidence of dinosaurs; she would study them with concentration and would urge her grandchildren to look closely at them. Back in the parking lot she unwrapped some charcoal she'd packed in aluminum foil, and they all rubbed some on their feet to cleanse them of the spirits of the dinosaurs that might still be lurking about. Afterward they piled back in the pickup to drive more than a hundred miles into the town of Flagstaff so she could take the kids out for what she considered to be really good hamburgers.

She was always willing to give a hand when her grandchildren needed her. One day she found young Milton struggling up the hill with his injured dog in a wheelbarrow. The dog had been attacked by the neighbor's bulldog and was in bad shape. Annie said she'd drive them both to Gallup to the veterinarian. They put the dog in the back of the pickup but then decided it would be too cold for the dog. They moved the bleeding animal into the cab and flew off down the road at even a little faster than her usual speed. It was closing time by the time they got to Gallup, but because it was Annie, the vet motioned them in. The dog's injuries were too grave, however, and after he died, Annie and Milton made the sad trip home. Later, in recounting the story, Annie said, "I never cried over an animal in my life, but I sure cried over that dog." One suspects it wasn't so much the dog that prompted her grief but seeing her beloved grandson so bereft that brought on her tears.[20]

The time grandmother and grandson spent together did not always involve driving around. Sometimes they stayed at her home in Klagetoh. "When I'd spend my summer days at Grandma's house, sometimes she'd sit quietly and she'd have her right elbow in her left hand and her chin in her hand," Milton recalls. "She'd have this faraway, distant look. She wore glasses, so the light reflecting off the outside window would reflect off of her glasses. It was like she was seeing something on the inside of her glasses, something very important. She was so quiet. I always wondered what she was thinking about.

"I didn't know she was famous until about my senior year in high school. Before that, I figured that she was just my grandmother. I thought, grandmothers do these things. They jump in their trucks and go everywhere."[21]

A SPECIAL BIRTHDAY PARTY

In truth, no other Navajo had done all that Annie did. And in early 1984 Chairman Peterson Zah decided that the tribe should give a special recognition to the woman to whom they all owed so much. More than forty people were involved in planning the celebration, which evolved into an entire day of events in honor of Annie's seventy-fourth birthday. Both Arizona and New Mexico proclaimed "Annie Wauneka Day," and a scholarship fund was established in her honor.[22]

On the day before the ceremony a nasty spring storm swept across the reservation with rain, snow, and sleet, not the best weather for the lunchtime barbecue that was planned. But, undaunted, Annie took charge. Later, she confessed she had looked up to clouds and said, "Tomorrow you're going to behave, because tomorrow's my day." Sure enough, April 10 dawned sunny and warm, with temperatures in the high sixties, a perfect day. Whoever the Navajo spirits are who oversee such matters, they complied on that day and did as they were told.

School buses brought children from across the reservation, and car license plates indicated the visitors had come from as far away as Mississippi to attend the ceremonies. Presidential candidate Walter Mondale sent his daughter Eleanor to represent him, delegates came from other tribes, and national and local officials from the BIA and IHS joined the crowd. The Window Rock crossroad, usually so sparsely traveled that a flock of sheep could wander across it in safety, was crowded with vehicles. Firemen were brought in to help police officers direct the traffic.

The celebration began with a song and flag raising; then it was on to a two-hour Tribal Council meeting in which Annie was hailed as "Our Legendary Mother" and Chairman Zah placed the

Navajo Medal of Honor, the highest award given by the Navajo Nation, around her neck.

Blinking back tears and with a catch in her usually strong voice, Annie said she was accepting the medal "in honor of my better half, George Wauneka, my family and the memory of my father, Chee Dodge, who greatly influenced my life and in honor of the people who have worked with me." At this point she had to take off her glasses and borrow a handkerchief from someone in the audience to wipe her eyes. Pointing to the murals on the council chamber walls surrounding the crowd, she indicated the section depicting her father signing the first oil leases for the tribe, and she said she'd looked to him for counsel on difficult decisions. "When the debate gets hot, when the decision gets to the point where I don't know how to vote, I'd look up there and ask him to give me the best advice. He passed on the legacy of leadership to me." She called the Navajo medal the most meaningful of all her awards. At the end of her speech she walked to George, bent over, and hugged him, saying in Navajo, "And what about you? What about you?"[23]

After the lunch barbecue, Annie gave out prizes to Navajo students who had won contests run in conjunction with the Navajo Youth Conference and Annie Wauneka Day.

A CELEBRATION DINNER

The day concluded with a sold-out banquet and more speeches in the evening. A banner behind the head table proclaimed, "I go forth to move about the earth in wisdom, courage and peace." Throughout the day Annie had been dressed in a colorful print skirt and a bright purple velvet tunic adorned with three silver and turquoise pins, one as big as the rim of a teacup, a heavy squash blossom necklace, a heavy silver concho belt, and her Medal of Freedom in addition to the new medal. She wore large silver and turquoise bracelets on her wrists and several rings on each hand. In the evening, she added an oversize corsage of red roses. Not many gray-haired grandmothers could have moved with that much metal weighing them down nor stood up to that quantity of decoration, but on her it seemed natural. George, seated next to her, sported a blue ribbon on his sport coat, an acknowledgment from the organizers that without his help and quiet concurrence, Annie's career would not have been what it was.

Dr. Theodore Marrs, former IHS director on the reservation and former special assistant to President Gerald Ford, gave the keynote speech, opening with, "Dr. Wauneka has never solicited my assistance, she has demanded it." He concluded, "She's never lost sight of the cycles of the moon, but she's learned the cycles of the budget in Congress. She's remained a shepherdess, but her flock is the people of the Navajo Nation. Strong men look to this shepherdess. They call her 'mother.' Rough kids actually look on her with respect. Chairmen, chiefs, presidents are all included in her flock. She has put love into politics."

Then followed a series of testimonials from many of the people Annie had worked with over the years. Alyce Rouwalk, president of the Council for Navajo Women, told how grateful she and other Navajos who had lost touch with the culture were that Annie had reached out to them, never ridiculing them for their inability to speak Navajo or their lack of knowledge of Navajo traditions. "She is the mother who teaches us how to be a Navajo—the most lasting influence on our lives," she said.

Then followed the presentation of a stack of telegrams from well-wishers, including President Ronald Reagan, and a $1,000 check to use for a vacation. But the organizers did not figure Annie quite right. "Mr. Zah has said many times that money that comes out of the reservation should remain on the reservation," Annie announced. "So it will be spent on the reservation. Anyway, George Wauneka wouldn't want to get away for even one mile." She concluded, "This [award] does not mean I want to stop here. When I get up in the morning, I want to go and do more." Grasping the messages in her hand she added, to knowing laughter, "I want to get all these telegrams so I can use them . . ."[24]

BEGINNING TO FEEL THEIR AGE
And she did keep on traveling the reservation, speaking to school children, raising money. Six weeks later, she was in Tucson to

speak at a hearing by the Senate Special Committee on Aging and the House Committee on Interior and Insular Affairs looking into long-term care for the elderly Indians. She reminded the elected representatives once more of their federal trust responsibility and treaty obligations while discussing the complications of working with the three separate state systems—Arizona, New Mexico, and Utah—under which various parts of the Navajo Reservation were governed and coordinating those regulations with the federal guidelines.

The issue of care for older Navajos soon became personally relevant. George, who in 1989 was eighty-six years old, was failing. The once strong, handsome rancher who had overseen the livestock operation while also caring for his disabled sons was beginning to forget important things, like turning off the gas. It was decided that he could no longer fend for himself or his sons, who were by now grown men. George, sons Marvin, Henry, George, and Timothy, and daughter Sallie went into the nursing home at Toyei near Greasewood. George wept at leaving the ranch, but his easy-going nature prevailed, and he eventually made a good transition to his new home. The Waunekas' youngest son, Franklin, who had helped his father at Tanner Springs for years, took over the day-to-day running of the ranch.

Annie, too, began to slow down. A series of tragic and unpleasant events happened over the next few years. Her daughter Georgia Ann and her husband, Ed Plummer, who had served the tribe and the BIA in many capacities, were sideswiped in a traffic accident. Ed was badly injured and, after lingering for some time, died. Annie had been very close to him and grieved at his passing. Around this time, Lorencita was also widowed. The tribal government changed character again as Peterson Zah lost his bid for reelection to Peter MacDonald.

TESTIFYING AGAINST MACDONALD

Shortly after MacDonald began his fourth term of office, he was accused of taking bribes from Navajo and non-Navajo contractors in exchange for guaranteed work on the reservation. Beginning in 1988 three separate grand juries looked into his affairs but did not indict him. Eventually a U.S. Senate committee decided to look into MacDonald's activities and held hearings in Washington. Annie was invited to testify. The senators, including two of her old friends from Arizona, Dennis DeConcini and John McCain, were most respectful of her, and their staff members were impressed with her poise and dignity. But the transcript of her testimony shows that she was removed from what was going on and vague about many of the matters about which they questioned her.[25]

Because of the charges against Chairman MacDonald, the Tribal Council took over the government in February 1989 and put MacDonald on leave. He refused to leave gracefully and put the entire government in an uproar for months. Eventually a march on tribal headquarters by his supporters led to a riot that resulted in the death of two of the protestors and severe injuries to three protesters and three police officers. At the end of that year, Peterson Zah was voted back in and took over in 1990. The office was changed from chairman to president, and the duties were curtailed somewhat. Eventually, Peter MacDonald was convicted and sent to jail on the reservation for bribery; later he was transferred to federal prison for multiple charges of corruption.[26]

As the new decade began, Annie became more forgetful and would leave her home in Klagetoh and walk and walk until someone would find her and guide her home. The state of Arizona suspended her driver's license, but sometimes she got in her truck to go to Window Rock for lunch anyhow. She'd stop in to see Ellouise De Groat and complain of her failing memory. De Groat noticed that Annie was repeating herself, but she was gentle with her old friend. When De Groat asked her why she was risking driving without a license, Annie's response was, "Well, there's not a policeman on every corner."[27]

THE LAST WASHINGTON TRIP

Then in early 1992 came word that Annie was to receive a special Indian Achievement Award in Washington. Her friend, neighbor, and clan daughter Louise Nelson was chosen to accompany her. They had a good time as they drove to Albuquerque to catch the plane, but during the flight Louise noticed that Annie became confused easily, questioning the flight attendants when Nelson left her seat to use the restroom.

During their three days in Washington they did some sightseeing, and Annie was given VIP treatment wherever she went. Senator DeConcini gave them passes to the Senate Dining Room. Every once in a while, however, Annie would imagine people calling the room when no call had been made. Nelson began to worry about what might happen during the awards ceremony.

"The next day, I realized that she was a very powerful woman," Nelson recalls now. "They took us by limousine to the awards banquet, and her table was already reserved. We sat with President and Mrs. Zah, Senator McCain, and Senator Dominici at a circular table right near the platform. Alan Houser, the Indian sculptor who made the award, was at our table, too. I was worried she might trip or stutter, but as we entered that banquet hall, she just came alive. Something happened that she blossomed there. She was very alert. James Watt came by and the Cherokee chairperson Wilma Mankiller, and she remembered every one of them and greeted them. All the national Indian leaders were there from all over the United States. Her conversation was bright, she joked as if she hadn't aged, gabbing with all the congresspeople. When she went up to receive her award she had her written speech, but she'd just glance at it. That was her turf, her territory."[28]

14

A Life Assessed

THE WASHINGTON AWARDS CEREMONY marked the end of Annie's public life. Shortly after that trip, she was diagnosed with Alzheimer's disease and entered the nursing home at Toyei in 1993 with George, Sallie, and her sons. Her daughters and friends would stop by to take her on rides to the Tanner Springs ranch and to Sonsola Buttes, her father's old home near Crystal, but eventually these outings became more confusing than pleasant for her.

George's condition worsened, and he was moved to a nursing home in Chinle, where he died in August 1994.

At its spring commencement of 1996, the University of Arizona awarded Annie Wauneka an honorary doctor of laws, her third honorary doctorate, but her condition had deteriorated so much that she did not attend the ceremony. Her beloved grandson Milton Jr., at the time a University of Arizona student, accepted the award for her.

SEEKING CHEE'S APPROVAL

It is unfortunate that this cruel disease robbed her of the chance to look backward at the immense changes that had happened over her lifetime and to savor her role in the advancement of the Navajos. Just as Chee's striving for ever-increasing wealth seems to have been propelled by a desire to overcome the severe deprivations of his childhood, Annie's relentless drive to serve, to help, to know, appeared to be motivated as a way to prove herself to an adored father who, when she was young, seemed to hold her in less regard than he did his older children.

As a young woman, Annie did what was expected of her: helped during the flu epidemic, made good grades at Albuquerque Indian School, with her husband George ran the Tanner

Springs ranch for her father, had a large family, and was a good cook and mother. But her intelligence and her curiosity drove her beyond what was expected. During meetings at the Tanner Springs ranch house, she was unwilling to merely cook the stew and boil the coffee. She wanted to know what was going on when her father and other leaders gathered to talk. When Chee chided her for not offering her services as a translator during a local gathering regarding stock reduction, she accepted his challenge and became more bold.

Throughout her life, Annie idolized Chee Dodge and identified with him. Although it appears that toward the end of his life Chee grew to respect the strengths of his youngest child, the psychological need to prove herself worthy seems to have been indelibly laid upon her. Whenever she faced a difficult decision, she always tried to imagine what Chee would have done in that circumstance.

STRIKING OUT ON HER OWN

Yet Annie did not let her life be defined by Chee's—and she struck out into political territory where he had not ventured. When the opportunity arose for her to get involved with the chapter, to run for office, to head up the Health and Welfare Committee, to lead the fight against alcoholism, to lobby for an Indian medical school—she did not hesitate, although no one had defined the path before her. When asked in her first term to form a new Health and Welfare Committee, she could have done much less—perhaps studied the issue and presented her findings to the rest of the council. It was her idea to visit the patients in their scattered hospitals, to take them news of home, and to explain their illness. She could have left the health education regarding gastrointestinal disease and trachoma to the government nurses. But she went out to visit the poorest hogans in the furthest canyons. She wore out tires and rattled the bolts from her pickups until they had to be traded in after only two years. For much of her work she asked no reimbursement.

It is unclear how much her childhood experience of helping to nurse other students during the great flu epidemic influenced her later interest in health issues. Exposure to that much death certainly was a traumatic experience for an eight-year-old. But in telling the tale in later years, only a hint of bitterness crept in as she focused on what she had done to help, and the satisfaction she gained from the experience, even in light of learning that her siblings had all been gathered into the big house near Crystal, out of the reach of infection.

What is apparent is that spending so much of her life in the company of her powerful and charismatic father prepared her to deal forthrightly with other powerful men and not be cowed by their positions. If she could confront the autocratic Chee Dodge, she certainly would not be intimidated by local Bureau of Indian Affairs officials—especially since she was of the mind that they worked for the Navajo Tribe and were assistants rather than overseers, an opinion they seldom shared. When she had complaints about one of President Johnson's appointees, she wrote directly to him at the LBJ Ranch in Texas. She had met Johnson at the White House. He was a Westerner, a rancher, a leader—just like her father. That was enough to convince her that she should take her case to him.

"When she set her mind to do something, she was unafraid," recalled her son-in-law, Milton Bluehouse. "She knew how to conquer fear, which is the first enemy on the path to wisdom. It gave her the courage to confront stubborn bureaucrats, the courage to face every obstacle placed in the path of the People." [1]

BROADENING THE ROLE OF MOTHERHOOD

Since Annie still had a household of children ranging in age from seventeen to just over one year when she was became a Tribal Council delegate in 1951, she owed some of her ability to concentrate on her new job to effective childcare arrangements and household help. With no running water or electricity, even the most basic housekeeping chores were laborious and time consuming. Hired helpers and extended family members pitched in. Many of the children went to Catholic boarding school in St. Michael's. But the element that made it all work was George Wauneka's willingness to play both mother and father to his children, particularly his disabled sons. Although it is not unusual for Navajo men to cook or clean up from time to time, or to care for and play with their children, his taking on all of those responsibilities to the extent that he did was remarkable.

After her election to tribal office Annie expanded her mothering role from her immediate family to all of the Navajos. Annie was always interested in the children of the tribe. She worked to provide layettes for newborns, established the healthy baby contest, promoted the importance of inoculations against childhood diseases, fought for money to upgrade homes so children could grow up in a healthy environment, investigated conditions in both reservation and off-reservation schools, and lectured about Navajo values in schools whenever she had the chance. Many of the young people she influenced grew up to become leaders among their people. Among them were Peterson Zah and Albert Hale, who each were elected president of the tribe, Taylor McKenzie, who was the first Navajo medical doctor and, later, vice president of the tribe, and Marie Allen, who became a public health nurse and eventually Navajo area assistant director of the Indian Health Service. When Annie no longer held office, she became more involved in school affairs, and every graduation season brought her more invitations to speak than she could honor. When these students became grownups, they would remember her visits and would speak of her as a role model, as someone who had compassion for all the Navajo People, whatever their age or need, whether they were traditional sheepherders or young adults who had returned to the reservation after years away, unable to speak the language but looking for belonging.

The mothering role she had played for thousands of Navajos was acknowledged at the seventy-fourth birthday party when she was called "Our Legendary Mother."

THE INDISPENSABLE LINK

Though Annie Wauneka was at ease doing business in the white world, she was Navajo to the core. She spent years urging Navajos to seek out white doctors for tuberculosis and infections, yet she frequently consulted medicine men for their help in matters of the spirit. She was able to move comfortably on Capitol Hill during lobbying trips. As was necessary in the whirl of Washington life, when visiting the offices of senators and representatives she came directly to the point of her visit in a very few minutes and looked them directly in the eye, as no polite Navajo would do to another. Yet a world away on the Navajo Reservation, where time moved more with the seasons than with the second hand on the clock, she exhibited every subtle nuance of expected courtesy when she visited a hogan, observing a ritualized inquiry about the health of the family and livestock before addressing the reason for the call. And she always had plenty of Navajo jokes to warm up a crowd she was addressing. As one of the doctors with whom she worked said, she became "the great communicator, the indispensable link."

FOLLOWING CHANGING WOMAN

In the mid-1970s, when feminism was a new and popular movement, she was the obvious role model when the movement reached the Navajo Reservation. Hundreds of young women crowded to hear her speak at conferences. Her message was somewhat different from that of the white feminists who did a fair amount of male-bashing. "Son, that's not me," she told Peterson Zah during a conversation on the subject. "I'm not going to carry the flag that way."[2] When Annie spoke on the role of women, she emphasized integrating the role of traditional and modern values and of the importance of Navajo men and women working together. She reminded the younger participants that although Navajo women had not been tribal leaders, they had always held a strong role in the family, they could own their own property, and their views and opinions were respected. She urged them to emulate the values of Changing Woman, their creator, and to follow her teachings.

EFFECTIVE THROUGHOUT HER LIFE

Frequently biographies of well-known people concentrate on their earlier years since the majority of people make their greatest contributions when they are young and vigorous. Once they have attained success, they either keep doing more of the same or begin a decline.

As Julian Barnes writes in the *New York Times Book Review,* "the account of a life that has become successful somehow assumes that it could not have been otherwise: that the obstacles overcome were always bound to have been overcome. Whereas the first part of a life is full of implicitly narrative risk. Logically, we know that our hero is going to make it; but at the same time rival possibilities—which seem like probabilities to our hero—loiter like footpads."[3]

It is true that Annie's early work of traveling over the reservation to urge people with tuberculosis to seek treatment and convincing the medicine men to refer their patients with tuberculosis to the white doctors is a dramatic story. But once that problem was under control, she continued her vigorous work well into her seventies, shifting her focus to alcoholism and education. It was in these endeavors that she was not so successful. Excess alcohol consumption continues to this day to be a major problem on the Navajo Reservation. Unlike the situation with tuberculosis, no miracle drug has been discovered to help conquer the much more complex issue of alcoholism. Although Annie won numerous small battles to improve education on the reservation, it must have been a bitter disappointment when she and her friend Taylor McKenzie could not bring a medical school to the Navajo Reservation. Had she been able to do so, it would have been an enormous capstone to her career.

As the issues with which she dealt became more complex, both those wholly on the reservation and those that required federal intervention, Annie grew more politically sophisticated. With her increasing power, she also became more embroiled in intratribal difficulties. Because over the years she traveled so frequently to Washington to lobby for Navajo issues or to testify in front of House and Senate committees, she was recognized by the elected officials and their staffs, and she came to know who among them she could rely on to support her causes. She testified more than two dozen times in front of congressional committees. Sometimes the senator or representative conducting the hearing would waive the time limit for her, telling her that they wanted to hear all that she had to say.

Her sheer physical energy far exceeded that of many younger Navajos. Peterson Zah praised her stamina when he described the time that he and Annie had both addressed some students in San Juan, Utah. Afterward, he flew home; she drove. But the next morning when he was still in bed, she was attending a function in St. Michael's.[4]

LOSING THE LAST ELECTION

However, her stridency built up over the years and eventually contributed to the loss of her seat on the Tribal Council. She had a hard time realizing that at coffee hour after church people just wanted to drink coffee and catch up with each other. They did not want a lecture on health care, nor did they care so very much what was going on in Washington. Annie knew that decisions made far away could impact profoundly the lives of the Navajos—and their children and grandchildren. She wanted her neighbors to care as much as she did. But when she took over the floor Sunday after Sunday, some of the other parishioners at the Catholic mission in Klagetoh resented it. They said that she was so identified with Washington she'd lost touch with the reservation. Some of her constituents found her manner and her power terrifying, and there were whispers of witchcraft.

She also lost votes on the basis of her decades-long battle against peyote. Although some of her constituents saw the hallucinatory cactus as a legitimate adjunct to their spiritual practice in the Native American Church, Annie never considered it anything but a harmful drug.

POST-COUNCIL WORK

The loss of her Tribal Council seat did not deter Annie from continuing to work for the tribe, both as an employee under Peterson Zah and as a volunteer on numerous boards. As the honors and awards began to mount as a testimony to her work, she always ended her acceptance speech at any presentation ceremony by assuring the audience that this acknowledgment would not cause her to rest but would push her to continue. As she said in accepting the Navajo Nation Medal of Honor, "I think at night, I'm going to get up tomorrow to go and do more." And she did.

THE WHOLE TRIBE MOURNS

In early October of 1997, having lived in the nursing home at Toyei for about four years, Annie became ill. After some weeks, the doctors at Sage Memorial finally diagnosed her illness as leukemia and transferred her to a hospital in Flagstaff. Her children and grandchildren traveled back and forth from their homes to spend as much time with her as possible. Although she had not spoken much for years, at the end she looked at Irma and said clearly in Navajo that she knew that it was the end. She died on November 10. Navajo Nation President Albert Hale, whom she had saved from death as a child, proclaimed that the government would shut down for a day to mourn.

Annie Wauneka's body was taken to a mortuary in Gallup, where a rosary was said on November 12, 1997. The next day, a funeral mass was held at Mary, Mother of Mankind Catholic Mission in St. Michael's, the same church from which her beloved father had been buried. Her pallbearers were all commissioned officers in the Navajo office of the Indian Health Service, wearing their uniforms. Although Dr. Taylor McKenzie was by then retired from the IHS, he dug out his uniform and joined the younger men. The church was filled with those who had worked with her, those who had benefited from her public service, and those who, as children, had heard her speak in their schools. They took every seat in the pews, crowed the aisles, and spilled out onto the worn sandstone stairway that leads into the church.

The Arizona and New Mexico papers carried full obituaries and feature stories about her life. The *New York Times* carried her picture along with an obituary, and National Public Radio noted her passing. All of the tributes mentioned her years of service to the Navajo Tribe and her contribution to the bringing of modern medicine to the reservation. They told of her long years fighting tuberculosis and alcoholism. Interestingly, several of them also mentioned her altercation with Ted Mitchell, the young DNA lawyer. The incident had taken only a few moments; the ramifications had played out in about a year. Compared with the twenty-six years Annie spent on the Tribal Council and her years of work for the Navajos both before and after her council tenure, the affair had been merely a passing flash of anger in a career of disciplined reason. Perhaps it was that the outburst seemed so out of character, so unusual coming from a woman described as "walking dignity," that the memory of the event lingered for decades.

Having begun life as the least regarded of her famous father's children, it was she who, on his death, took up the banner and carried on his message and his work with much the same flair as the Old Mr. Interpreter himself. In the end, she was not the least of his children, but the best.

Annie Dodge Wauneka's family decided to bury her at the Tanner Springs ranch in a private family ceremony. With her grandsons bearing her casket, she was put into the sandy reddish-brown earth in a slight depression on the side of a rise just below the La Pinta Mesa among the juniper and sagebrush. It is a place of quiet and peace, looking north to the lush forests of the Fort Defiance plateau and west to the soft blue and lavender mesas and Painted Desert.

Because the depression concentrates the moisture, the grass grows greener and more lush in that spot, where sheep often gather to graze. It is a fitting place for someone who called herself "just a sheepherder with a little more education."

Notes

INTRODUCTION

1. Howells, "Mildred Howells," p. 2.
2. Riley, "American Indian Women," pp. 43–70.
3. Munker, "Enchantment and Passion," pp. 377–97.
4. Sally McBeth, in the introduction to *Essie's Story*, discusses in detail the differences between Native American biography and autobiography and the role of the non-Indian in the production of these works. Those interested in this issue should find her thoughtful review illuminating.

1. AN ILLUSTRIOUS FATHER

1. Reichard, *Social Life*, p. 134.
2. Underhill, *Navajos*, p. 100.
3. Robert Roessel, "Navajo History," p. 507.
4. Brophy, "Indian Service."
5. Brugge, "Henry Chee Dodge," p. 92.
6. Evers, *Between Sacred Mountains*, pp. 136–40.
7. Evers, *Between Sacred Mountains*, pp. 136–40.
8. Brugge, "Henry Chee Dodge," p. 93.
9. Underhill, *Navajos*, p. 124.
10. Kelly, *Navajo Indians*, p. 6.
11. Benedek, *Wind Won't Know Me*, pp. 22–23.
12. Van Valkenburgh, "Henry Chee Dodge," p. 6.
13. Davis, "Navajo Indians."
14. Borgman, "Henry Chee Dodge," p. 91.
15. Thomas Dodge, "Chee Dodge."
16. Augustus Dodge, letter to Honorable E. P. Smith.
17. Brugge, "Henry Chee Dodge," p. 93.
18. Chee Dodge, testimony on boarding school case.
19. Brugge, "Henry Chee Dodge," p. 95.
20. Van Valkenburgh, "Henry Chee Dodge," p. 6.

21. Van Valkenburgh, "Henry Chee Dodge," p. 6.
22. Van Valkenburgh, "Henry Chee Dodge," p. 6.
23. Hoffman and Johnson, "Henry Chee Dodge," p. 199.
24. Hoffman and Johnson, "Henry Chee Dodge," p. 199.
25. Patzman, "Henry Chee Dodge," p. 37.
26. Underhill, *Here Come the Navajo!*, p. 219.
27. Chee Dodge, testimony on land dispute case.
28. Hoffman and Johnson, "Henry Chee Dodge," p. 200.
29. Brugge, "Henry Chee Dodge," p. 96.
30. McNitt, *Indian Traders*, p. 281.
31. Brugge, "Henry Chee Dodge," p. 96.
32. Acrey, *Navajo History*, p. 115.
33. Hoffman and Johnson, "Henry Chee Dodge," p. 204.
34. Hoffman and Johnson, "Henry Chee Dodge," p. 205.
35. Witherspoon, *Navajo Kinship and Marriage*, p. 27.
36. Underhill, *Navajos*, p. 167.
37. Acrey, *Navajo History*, p. 174.
38. Hoffman and Johnson, "Henry Chee Dodge," pp. 206–8.

2. THE FAMILY SHEEPHERDER

1. Brugge, "Henry Chee Dodge," pp. 99–100.
2. Yazzie, note to Chee Dodge.
3. Kelledy, letter to Anselm Weber.
4. "Dr. Annie D. Wauneka Day," videotape, comments of Dr. Theodore Marrs.
5. "Dr. Annie Dodge Wauneka Day."
6. Hart, "Legendary Mother," p. 1.
7. R. Collier, *Plague of the Spanish Lady*, p. 305.
8. Trennert, *White Man's Medicine*, p. 125.
9. Wauneka, interview by Chanin and Chanin.
10. M. Nelson, *Annie Wauneka*, p. 24.
11. Wauneka, interview by Chanin and Chanin.
12. R. Collier, *Plague of the Spanish Lady*, pp. 68–70.
13. Leighton and Leighton, *Navajo Door*, p. 76.
14. Trennert, *White Man's Medicine*, p. 126.
15. Wauneka, interview by Chanin and Chanin.
16. Trennert, "Indian Sore Eyes," p. 126.
17. "Henry Chee Dodge," pp. 5–7.
18. Borgman, "Henry Chee Dodge," p. 91.
19. Wilken, *Anselm Weber O.F.M.*, p. 91.

20. Wauneka, interview by Chanin and Chanin.
21. Shirley, interview by author.
22. Wauneka, interview by Chanin and Chanin.
23. Roland, "Annie Wauneka."
24. Chee Dodge, letter to Frank Lane.
25. Iverson, *Navajo Nation*, p. 21.
26. Bailey and Bailey, *History of the Navajos*, p. 122; Acrey, *Navajo History*, p. 200.
27. M. Nelson, *Annie Wauneka*, p. 27.
28. Wauneka, interview by Chanin and Chanin.
29. M. Nelson, *Annie Wauneka*, p. 30
30. Milton Bluehouse Jr., "I Remember," p. 8.
31. Reichard, *Social Life*, p. 140.
32. M. Nelson, *Annie Wauneka*, p. 35.
33. Irma Bluehouse, interview by author.
34. Wauneka, interview by Chanin and Chanin.
35. Irma Bluehouse, interview by author.
36. Menapace, interview by author.
37. Wauneka, interview by Chanin and Chanin.

3. THE AGONIES OF STOCK REDUCTION
1. Downs, *Animal Husbandry*, p. 18.
2. Underhill, *Here Come the Navajo!*, p. 235.
3. "Range Management Report," p. 8.
4. J. Collier, *From Every Zenith*, p. 241; Kelly, *Navajo Indians*, pp. 159–60.
5. Parman, *Navajos*, pp. 41, 65.
6. Aberle, *Peyote Religion*, p. 86.
7. Aberle, *Peyote Religion*, p. 87.
8. Witt, "Interview with Annie Dodge Wauneka," p. 64.
9. Hoffman and Johnson, "Henry Chee Dodge," pp. 209–10.
10. Acrey, *Navajo History*, p. 234.
11. Milton Bluehouse Jr., interview by author.
12. Wauneka, interview by Chanin and Chanin.
13. Borgman, "Henry Chee Dodge," p. 89.
14. Frisbie and McAllester, *Navajo Blessingway Singer*, pp. 250–55.
15. Menapace, interview by author.
16. Menapace, interview by author.
17. Salsbury, *Salsbury Story*, p. 209.
18. Tom Dodge, letter of resignation to John Collier.

19. Irma Bluehouse, interview by author.
20. Irma Bluehouse, interview by author.
21. Brugge, "Henry Chee Dodge," p. 97.
22. Benedek, *Wind Won't Know Me*, p. 84; "Chee Dodge Dies," p. 5.
23. M. Nelson, *Annie Wauneka*, pp. 44–45.
24. Don Dodge, interview by author.
25. Hobson, "Navajo Acquisitive Values," pp. 18–19.
26. Tsosie and Parker, letter to Navajo Tribal Council.
27. Wauneka, interview by Chanin and Chanin.
28. Wagner, interview by author.
29. Chee Dodge, letter to House Committee on Indian Affairs.
30. Langley, "Chief of the Navajo," p. 21.
31. "Chee Dodge Dies," pp. 1, 5.
32. Wagner, interview by author.
33. Salsbury, *Salsbury Story*, p. 209.
34. Hoffman and Johnson, "Henry Chee Dodge," p. 96.
35. Wyman, "Navajo Ceremonial System," p. 537.
36. Huff, "Chee Dodge."
37. Irma Bluehouse, interview by author.
38. Resolution to Navajo Tribal Council.
39. "Monument Is Placed."

4. A BATTLE AGAINST TUBERCULOSIS

1. Minutes of the Navajo Tribal Council, Feb. 16, 1962.
2. Irma Bluehouse, interview by author.
3. Wagner, *Wide Ruins*, pp. 45–46.
4. Whiterock, interview by author.
5. Ruth Roessel, *Women in Navajo Society*, p. 133.
6. Ruth Roessel, *Women in Navajo Society*, p. 133.
7. Stewart, *Voice in Her Tribe*, p. 61.
8. "List of Successful Candidates."
9. Lawler, "Tribal Officers Take Oath."
10. Wauneka, "Navajo and His Future."
11. Minutes of the Navajo Tribal Council, Jan. 15, 1952.
12. Minutes of the Navajo Tribal Council, April 14, 1952.
13. Minutes of the Navajo Tribal Council, April 25, 1952.
14. Minutes of the Navajo Tribal Council, Aug. 14, 1952.
15. Good Tracks, "Native American NonInterference," pp. 55–56.
16. Minutes of the Navajo Tribal Council, April 15, 1952.
17. Shirley, interview by author.

18. Whiterock, interview by author.
19. "Navajos and Annie Wauneka."
20. Wauneka, interview by Chanin and Chanin.
21. Minutes of the Navajo Tribal Council, July 27, 1953.
22. Navajo Health Education Project, *Orientation to Health*, pp. 15-17.
23. Leighton and Leighton, *Navajo Door*, pp. 56-59.
24. Trennert, *White Man's Medicine*, p. 196.
25. Parman, *Navajos and the New Deal*, p. 13.
26. Friggens, "Annie Wauneka," p. 11.
27. "Navajos and Annie Wauneka."
28. Friggens, "Annie Wauneka," p. 11.
29. Minutes of the Navajo Tribal Council, Oct. 17, 1953.
30. Minutes of the Navajo Tribal Council, Aug. 14, 1953.
31. Krug, *Navajo*, pp. 18-19.
32. McKinley, interview by author.
33. "Navajos and Annie Wauneka."

5. THE TUBERCULOSIS CAMPAIGN INTENSIFIES

1. Hale, interview by author.
2. Minutes of the Navajo Tribal Council, Feb. 12, 1954.
3. Wauneka, interview by Chanin and Chanin.
4. Minutes of the Navajo Tribal Council, Jan. 13, 1955.
5. Minutes of the Navajo Tribal Council, May 13, 1954.
6. Adair and Deuschle, *People's Health*, p. 32.
7. Irma Bluehouse, interview by author.
8. Stewart, *Voice in Her Tribe*, p. 57.
9. Wauneka, interview by Chanin and Chanin.
10. Minutes of the Navajo Tribal Council, July 15, 1955.
11. Minutes of the Navajo Tribal Council, April 8, 1955.
12. Proceedings, Second Working Conference on Services for Patients, passim.
13. Adair and Deuschle, *People's Health*, p. 33.
14. Adair and Deuschle, *People's Health*, p. 52.
15. Adair and Deuschle, *People's Health*, p. 88.
16. Minutes of the Navajo Tribal Council, Oct. 11, 1955.
17. Wauneka, interview by Chanin and Chanin.
18. Wauneka, interview by Chanin and Chanin.
19. Wauneka, interview by Chanin and Chanin.
20. Friggens, "Annie Wauneka," p. 13.
21. Wauneka, interview by Chanin and Chanin.

22. Hart, "Legendary Mother."
23. Minutes of the Navajo Tribal Council, Oct. 30, 1956.
24. Friggens, "Annie Wauneka," p. 12.
25. Lamphere, *To Run after Them*, pp. 36, 57.
26. Minutes of the Navajo Tribal Council, Jan. 31, 1957.
27. Wauneka, testimony before Senate Committee on Appropriations, Labor, Health, Education and Welfare, April 1–May 19, 1958.
28. Minutes of the Navajo Tribal Council, Jan. 15–16, 1959.

6. ALCOHOLISM AND PEYOTE

1. Minutes of the Navajo Tribal Council, Aug. 25, 1961.
2. Adair and Deuschle, *People's Health*, p. 127.
3. Wauneka, "Helping a People," pp. 88–90.
4. "Arraign Goana in Ben Dodge Killing."
5. Minutes of the Navajo Tribal Council, April 26, 1962.
6. Minutes of the Navajo Tribal Council, Dec. 10, 1962.
7. Kunitz and Levy, *Drinking Careers*, p. 17.
8. Levy and Kunitz, *Indian Drinking*, p. 24.
9. Kunitz and Levy, *Drinking Careers*, p. 18.
10. Levy, interview by author.
11. Levy and Kunitz, *Indian Drinking*, p. 24.
12. Kunitz and Levy, *Drinking Careers*, pp. 25–26.
13. McKinley, interview by author.
14. Wauneka, testimony before Senate Committee on Appropriations, Interior Department, March 20, 1963.
15. Kunitz, *Disease Change*, p. 121.
16. Minutes of the Navajo Tribal Council, June 2, 1954.
17. Brugge, *Navajo-Hopi Land Dispute*, pp. 100–101.
18. Minutes of the Navajo Tribal Council, Aug. 16, 1963.
19. Irma Bluehouse, interview by author.
20. Kennedy, telegram to Annie D. Wauneka.
21. Wauneka, telegram to John F. Kennedy.

7. AWARDS AND ACRIMONY

1. Brugge, *Navajo-Hopi Land Dispute*, p. 102.
2. Irma Bluehouse, interview by author.
3. "Pawhuskan's Sister to White House."
4. Johnson, remarks at presentation.
5. Johnson, remarks at presentation.

6. "Navajo Annie D. Wauneka."

7. Minutes of the Navajo Tribal Council, Dec. 9, 1963.

8. Minutes of the Navajo Tribal Council, June 19, 1961.

9. Kammer, *Second Long Walk*, pp. 26–36.

10. Kammer, *Second Long Walk*, pp. 46–48.

11. Brugge, *Navajo-Hopi Land Dispute*, p. 89.

12. Minutes of the Navajo Tribal Council, Aug. 9, 1964.

13. Minutes of the Navajo Tribal Council, Dec. 12, 1964.

14. Wauneka, letter to Lyndon B. Johnson, Dec. 12, 1964.

15. Beaty, letter to Lee C. White.

16. "Udall-Littell Case Climax."

17. White, letter to Annie D. Wauneka.

18. Minutes of the Navajo Tribal Council, March 23, 1965.

19. *Littell v. Udall*, 242 F. Supp. 635 (1965).

20. Wauneka, letter to Lee C. White; White, letter to Annie D. Wauneka.

21. George Bock, interview by author.

22. Proceedings, Third National Conference on Indian Health, passim.

23. MacDonald, *Last Warrior*, p. 135.

24. Richardson, "Navajo Way," p. 4.

25. Iverson, *Navajo Nation*, p. 86.

8. OVERSEEING BABY CONTESTS AND STUDENT PROTESTS

1. New York Times Oral History Program, "Annie Wauneka, Navajo," p. 16.

2. Milton Bluehouse Jr., interview by author.

3. "Deadly Windfall"; "Cry for Help."

4. Wauneka, "Navajo and His Future."

5. Wauneka, testimony, Senate Committee on Labor and Public Welfare, March 30, 1968.

6. Iverson, *Navajo Nation*, p. 114.

7. Proceedings, Indian Health Committee.

8. L. Nelson, interview by author.

9. Minutes of the Navajo Tribal Council, Feb. 19, 1962.

10. Minutes of the Navajo Tribal Council, April 12, 1968.

11. Allen, interview by author.

12. Allen, interview by author.

13. Zah, interview by author.

14. Zah, interview by author.

9. CULTURAL CLASHES AND CULTURAL BRIDGES

1. Iverson, *Navajo Nation,* p. 93.
2. Blue, interview by author.
3. Mitchell, e-mail to author.
4. Hardwick, "Board Backs Mitchell."
5. "Ted Mitchell."
6. "Ted Mitchell."
7. Mitchell, e-mail to author.
8. "Ted Mitchell."
9. "Ted Mitchell."
10. Hart, "Legendary Mother."
11. Rushton, "Advisory Committee."
12. Rushton, "Nakai Meets Students."
13. "Dineh for Justice."
14. Lincoln, "DNA Board."
15. Minutes of the Navajo Tribal Council, July 23, 1969.
16. Link, interview by author.
17. Link, interview by author.
18. Minutes of the Navajo Tribal Council, Jan. 14, 1965.
19. Link, interview by author.

10. THE NAVAJO-HOPI CONFLICT

1. Minutes of the Navajo Tribal Council, Jan. 22, 1970.
2. Bergman, interview with author.
3. Minutes of the Navajo Tribal Council, Dec. 7, 1970.
4. MacDonald, *Last Warrior,* p. 188.
5. Wauneka, testimony, House Subcommittee on Indian Affairs, April 18, 1972.
6. Wauneka, testimony before Senate Subcommittee on Indian Affairs, April 14, 1972.
7. Churchill, *Struggle for the Land,* p. 157.
8. Minutes of the Navajo Tribal Council, Jan. 23, 1975.
9. Wauneka, interview by Chanin and Chanin.
10. Witt, "Interview with Annie Dodge Wauneka," p. 66.
11. Harriet Bock, interview by author.

11. MORE WASHINGTON LOBBYING

1. Minutes of the Navajo Tribal Council, May 2, 1970.
2. "Vocational Rehabilitation Services Plan," p. 29.
3. Wauneka, testimony, Department of Interior and Related Agencies Appropriations, April 17, 1970.

4. Minutes of the Navajo Tribal Council, July 17, 1971.

5. Goosen, interview by author.

6. De Groat, interview by author.

7. Huerta, interview by author.

8. Navajo Health Authority, *Capsules of History*, p. 1.

9. Minutes of the Navajo Tribal Council, March 9, 1972.

10. McKenzie, interview by author.

11. McKenzie, interview by author.

12. Hubbard, interview by author.

13. Haffner, interview by author.

14. Bergman, interview by author.

15. "Pawhuskan's Sister."

16. L. Nelson, interview by author.

17. "Annie and the Congress."

18. "Pawhuskan's Sister."

19. De Groat, interview by author.

20. De Groat, interview by author.

21. Milton Bluehouse Sr., interview by author.

22. Irma Bluehouse, interview by author.

12. THE FINAL TERM

1. Minutes of the Navajo Tribal Council, Feb. 3, 1976.

2. Minutes of the Navajo Tribal Council, Feb. 3, 1976.

3. Minutes of the Navajo Tribal Council, Feb. 10, 1976.

4. Minutes of the Navajo Tribal Council, Feb. 15, 1976.

5. Minutes of the Navajo Tribal Council, Feb. 20, 1976.

6. Wauneka, letter to Barry Goldwater; Goldwater to Annie Wauneka.

7. "MacDonald Trial Begins; Feder, "MacDonald Acquitted."

8. Lichtenstein, "Members of Navajo Tribe."

9. New York Times Oral History Program, "Annie Wauneka, Navajo," p. 17.

10. New York Times Oral History Program, "Annie Wauneka, Navajo," pp. 18–19.

11. "Women's Meeting Slams Discrimination."

12. Wauneka, "Dilemma for Indian Women."

13. Arviso, "Workshop Directs Awareness."

14. Steiner, *New Indians*, p. 225.

15. De Groat, interview by author.

16. Roland, "Annie Wauneka"; New York Times Oral History Program, "Annie Wauneka, Navajo," p. 5.

17. Orr, "Navajo Council Coalition."
18. Irma Bluehouse, interview by author.
19. Irma Bluehouse, interview by author; "WR Seven."
20. "MacDonald Scolds Media."
21. Minutes of the Navajo Tribal Council, Dec. 8, 1978.
22. Minutes of the Navajo Tribal Council, Dec. 12, 1978.
23. Minutes of the Navajo Tribal Council, Dec. 13, 1978.
24. Locke, "Zah Applauds Wauneka."

13. TRAVELING NEAR AND FAR

1. Haffner, interview by author.
2. Faiche, interview by author.
3. De Groat, interview by author.
4. Salsbury, *Salsbury Story*, p. 108.
5. De Groat, interview by author.
6. De Groat, interview by author.
7. Wagner, interview by author.
8. Steiner, *New Indians*, p. 165.
9. Wauneka, testimony, House Subcommittee on Interior Appropriations, Feb. 23–24, 1982.
10. Zah, interview by author.
11. Zah, interview by author.
12. Zah, interview by author.
13. Zah, interview by author.
14. Milton Bluehouse Sr., interview by author.
15. "Arizonans to Remember."
16. Saltzstein, "Wauneka Proud of Past."
17. Penney, "Building a Future."
18. Milton Bluehouse Jr., "I Remember," passim.
19. Milton Bluehouse Jr., interview by author.
20. Milton Bluehouse Jr., interview by author.
21. Milton Bluehouse Jr., interview by author.
22. Saltzstein, "Tribe Prepares Birthday Bash."
23. Locke, "Zah Applauds Wauneka"; Saltzstein, "Wauneka Proud of Past."
24. "Dr. Annie D. Wauneka Day," videotape.
25. Wauneka, testimony, Senate Special Committee on Investigations of Select Committee on Indian Affairs, Feb. 9, 1989.
26. "Navajo Ex-leader Convicted."

27. De Groat, interview by author.
28. L. Nelson, interview by author.

14. A LIFE ASSESSED

1. States, "Nation Loses Annie Dodge Wauneka."
2. Zah, interview by author.
3. Barnes, "Love Affair with Color."
4. Locke, "Zah Applauds Wauneka."

Bibliography

Aberle, David. *The Peyote Religion among the Navajo.* Chicago: Aldine, 1966.

Acrey, Bill. *Navajo History: The Land and the People.* Shiprock NM: Department of Curriculum Development, Central Consolidated School District no. 22, 1979.

Adair, John, and Kurt Deuschle. *The People's Health.* New York: Appleton-Century-Crofts, 1970.

Allen, Paula Gunn, and Patricia Clark Smith. *As Long as the Rivers Flow.* New York: Scholastic, 1996.

"Annie and the Congress." Undated and unidentified newspaper clipping. Special Collections, AZ 500, Box 42, University of Arizona Main Library, Tucson.

"Annie Wauneka Is Given Public Health Educators Honorary Fellow's Award." *Window Rock AZ Navajo Times,* Nov. 15, 1973, pp. 3–4.

"Annie Wauneka of Navajo Council Receives Medal of Freedom Award." Undated and unidentified newspaper clipping. Tom Dodge Papers, Arizona Collection, Arizona State University, Tempe.

"Annie Wauneka Receives Presidential Freedom Award." *Amerindian,* July–Aug., 1963, pp. 1–2.

"Arizonans to Remember: Names We Should Know." *(Phoenix) Arizona Republic,* Jan. 1, 2000, p. B9.

"Arraign Goana in Ben Dodge Killing." *Gallup NM Independent,* June 26, 1957, p. 1.

Arviso, Millie. "Workshop Directs Awareness among Women." *Window Rock AZ Navajo Times,* Nov. 30, 1978, pp. 17–18.

August, Jack. "The Navajos and the Great Society: Ted Mitchell and Dinebeiina Nahiilna Be Agaditahe." Unpublished manuscript. 1981. Arizona Collection, Arizona State University, Tempe.

Bailey, Garrick, and Roberta Glenn Bailey. *A History of the Navajos: The Reservation Years.* Santa Fe NM: School of American Research, 1986.

Barnes, Julian. "A Love Affair with Color." *New York Times Book Review*, Nov. 26, 1998, p. 6.

Bataille, Gretchen, ed. *Native American Women: A Biographic Dictionary*. New York: Garland, 1993.

Benedek, Emily. *The Wind Won't Know Me: A History of the Navajo-Hopi Land Dispute*. New York: Alfred Knopf, 1992.

Beveridge, W. I. B. *Influenza: The Last Great Plague*. London: Heinemann, 1977.

Bluehouse, Milton, Jr. "I Remember." Unpublished manuscript. Copy in author's collection.

Borgman, Rev. Francis o.f.m.. "Henry Chee Dodge—The Last Chief of the Navajo Indians." *New Mexico Historical Review* 23 (April 1948): 81–93.

Brophy, William A. "The Story of the Indian Service." Speech given at Department of Interior, Aug. 20, 1946. Tom Dodge Papers, Box 8, Folder 10, Arizona Collection, Arizona State University, Tempe.

Brugge, David M. "Henry Chee Dodge, From the Long Walk to Self Determination." In *Indian Lives: Essays on Nineteenth- and Twentieth-Century Native American Leaders*, ed. L. G. Moses and Raymond Wilson. Albuquerque: University of New Mexico Press, 1985.

———. *The Navajo-Hopi Land Dispute: An American Tragedy*. Albuquerque: University of New Mexico Press, 1994.

Chanin, Abe, with Mildred Chanin. *This Land, These Voices*. Flagstaff az: Northland Press, 1977.

Chanin, Abe, and Mildred Chanin. "Annie Wauneka's Fight for Anglo Medicine." *Window Rock az Navajo Times*, Nov. 24, 1977, p. 1.

"Chee Dodge Dies." *Gallup nm Independent*, Jan. 7, 1947, pp. 1, 5.

Chisholm, James S. *Navajo Infancy: An Ethnological Study of Child Development*. New York: Aldine, 1983.

Churchill, Ward. *Struggle for the Land*. Monroe me: Common Courage Press. 1993.

"Closing Arguments Are Heard in MacDonald Conspiracy Trial." *(Tucson) Arizona Daily Star*, Oct. 14, 1992, p. 3b.

Collier, John. *From Every Zenith: A Memoir*. Denver: Sage Books, 1963.

Collier, Richard. *The Plague of the Spanish Lady: The Influenza Pandemic of 1918–1919*. New York: Atheneum, 1974.

Crosby, Alfred W. *Epidemic and Peace, 1918*. Westport ct: Greenwood Press, 1976.

"Cry for Help from the Proud Navajo." *Life*, Jan. 5, 1968, pp. 14–23.

Davis, Emily C. "Navajo Indians at Last Can Learn to Read and Write in Own Language." *Kansas City Star*, Feb. 27, 1940.

"Deadly Windfall." *Time*, Jan. 5, 1968, p. 23.

De Groat, Ellouise. "A Tribute to Dr. Annie Dodge Wauneka, Appreciation and Birthday Celebration." Unpublished manuscript. April 10, 1978.

"The Dilemma over DNA." *Window Rock AZ Navajo Times*, July 18, 1968, p. 2.

"Dineh for Justice Students Picket Tribal Council Again," *Gallup NM Independent*, Aug. 16, 1968, p. 1.

Disney, Loren. "Navajo Mother, Tribal Leader to Receive Presidential Medal." *Tulsa Daily World*, Aug. 6, 1963, p. 10.

Dodge, Thomas H. "Biographical Note." Tom Dodge Papers, MSS-033, Box 1, Arizona Collection, Arizona State University, Tempe.

———. "Chee Dodge Still Most Powerful Navajo Leader." Tom Dodge Papers, MSS-033, Box 1, Arizona Collection, Arizona State University, Tempe.

Downs, James F. *Animal Husbandry in Navajo Society and Culture.* Berkeley: University of California Press, 1964.

———. *The Navajo.* New York: Holt, Rinehart and Winston, 1972.

"Dr. Annie D. Wauneka Day." Videotape. April 10, 1984. Irma Bluehouse's private collection.

Evers, Larry, series ed. *Between Sacred Mountains: Navajo Stories and Lessons from the Land.* Vol. 2. Tucson: Suntracks and University of Arizona Press, 1984.

Feder, Wendy. "MacDonald Acquitted." *Window Rock AZ Navajo Times*, May 19, 1997, p. 1.

"Former Navajo Leader Convicted." *New York Times*, Nov. 15, 1992, p. A40.

Friggens, Paul. "Annie Wauneka: Great Lady of the Navajos." *Empire Magazine, Denver Post*, Nov. 1, 1970, pp. 8–13.

Frisbie, Charlotte J., and David P. McAllester. *Navajo Blessingway Singer: The Autobiography of Frank Mitchell, 1881–1967.* Tucson: University of Arizona Press, 1978.

Good Tracks, Jimm G. "Native American NonInterference." *Social Work*, Nov. 1976, pp. 30–34.

Hardwick, Dick. "Board Backs Mitchell." *Window Rock AZ Navajo Times*, July 25, 1968, p. 1.

Hart, William. "Legendary Mother Still Helping Navajos." *(Phoenix) Arizona Republic*, June 19, 1988, p. 1.

Heath, Dwight B. "Prohibition and Post-Repeal Drinking Patterns among the Navajos." *Quarterly Journal of Studies on Alcohol* 25 (March 1964): 119–35.

"Henry Chee Dodge." *Padres' Trail,* Feb. 1947, pp. 4–7.

Hobson, Richard. "Navajo Acquisitive Values." *Papers of the Peabody Museum of American Archaeology and Ethnology, Harvard University.* Vol. 42, no. 3. Reports of the Rimrock Project, Value Series no. 5. Cambridge MA: Peabody Museum, 1954.

Hoffman, Virginia, and Broderick H. Johnson. "Henry Chee Dodge" and "Annie Dodge Wauneka." In *Navajo Biographies,* vols. 1 and 2. Chinle AZ: Dine and Board of Education, Rough Rock Demonstration School, 1974.

Horne, Esther Burnett, and Sally McBeth. *Essie's Story: The Life and Legacy of a Shoshone Teacher.* Lincoln: University of Nebraska Press, 1998.

Howells, Polly. "Mildred Howells: The Dilemma of the Father's Daughter." Paper presented at Women Writing Women's Lives seminar, New York, Nov. 2, 1998.

Huff, J. Wesley. "Chee Dodge, Old Mr. Interpreter, Is Laid to Rest." *Gallup NM Independent,* Jan. 10, 1947, p 1.

"Indian Achievement Award Goes to Annie Wauneka." *Amerindian,* Sept.–Oct., 1959, p. 1.

Iverson, Peter. *The Navajo Nation.* Westport CT: Greenwood Press, 1981.

Johnson, Lyndon B. Remarks at Presentation of Medal of Freedom Awards. Press release, Dec. 6, 1963. Heckscher File, Presidential Papers, White House Staff Files, Box 40, Folder: Medal of Freedom, Lyndon Baines Johnson Library and Museum, Austin.

Kammer, Jerry. "A Legacy of Healing." *(Phoenix) Arizona Republic,* Dec. 7, 1997, p. H1.

———. *The Second Long Walk: The Navajo Hopi Land Dispute.* Albuquerque: University of New Mexico Press, 1980.

Kane, Robert L., and Rosalie A. Kane. *Federal Health Care (With Reservations!).* New York: Springer, 1972.

KARV, Arizona Radio and Television. "Memorial Broadcast—Chee Dodge." Tom Dodge Papers, MSS-033, Box 7, Arizona Collection, Arizona State University, Tempe.

Katz, Jane. *Messengers of the Wind: Native American Women Tell Their Stories.* New York: Ballantine, 1996.

Kelly, Lawrence C. *The Navajo Indians and Federal Indian Policy, 1900–1935.* Tucson: University of Arizona Press, 1968.

Kluckholn, Clyde. *Navajo Witchcraft*. Boston: Beacon Press, 1944.

Krug, J. A. *The Navajo: A Long Range Program for Navajo Rehabilitation*. Typed report. March 1948. Arizona State Museum Library, Tucson.

Kunitz, Stephen J. *Disease Change and the Role of Medicine: The Navajo Experience*. Berkeley: University of California Press, 1983.

Kunitz, Stephen J., and Jerrold E. Levy. *Drinking Careers*. New Haven: Yale University Press. 1994.

Lamphere, Louise. *To Run after Them*. Tucson: University of Arizona Press, 1977.

Langley, Dama. "Chief of the Navajo." *Desert Magazine*, Feb. 1946, pp. 20–21.

Lawler, Joe. "Tribal Officers Take Oath at Window Rock Ceremonies." *Gallup NM Independent*, March 21, 1951, p. 1.

Leighton, Alexander H., and Dorothea C. Leighton. *The Navajo Door: An Introduction to Navajo Life*. Cambridge: Harvard University Press, 1944.

Levy, Jerrold E., and Steven J. Kunitz. *Indian Drinking, Navajo Practices and Anglo American Theories*. New York: John Wiley and Sons, 1974.

Lichtenstein, Grace. "Members of Navajo Tribe Hold Protest on Alleged Fund Misuse." *New York Times*, May 19, 1976, p. 10.

Lincoln, Abraham. "DNA Board Supports Mitchell, Board Seeks to End Exclusion." *Window Rock AZ Navajo Times*, Aug. 22, 1968, p. 1.

"List of Successful Candidates in Navajo Tribal Council Poll." *Gallup NM Independent*, March 8, 1951, p. 1.

Locke, Patrice. "Annie Dodge Wauneka: An American Original." *Indian Trader*, Dec. 1984, pp. 4–6.

———. "Zah Applauds Wauneka: The Young Lady Leader." *Window Rock AZ Navajo Times*, April 11, 1984, pp. 1, 5.

MacDonald, Peter, with Ted Schwarz. *The Last Warrior: Peter MacDonald and the Navajo Nation*. New York: Orion Books, 1993.

"MacDonald Scolds Media." *Window Rock AZ Navajo Times*, Dec. 14, 1978, p. 1.

"MacDonald Trial Begins." *Window Rock AZ Navajo Times*, May 12, 1977, p. 1.

Mankiller, Wilma, and Michael Wallis. *Mankiller: A Chief and Her People*. New York: St. Martin's Press, 1993.

McNitt, Frank. *The Indian Traders*. Norman: University of Oklahoma Press, 1962.

"Mitchell Gets DNA Support." *Gallup NM Independent,* Aug. 18, 1968, p. 1.

"Monument Is Placed over the Grave of Chee Dodge." *Gallup NM Independent,* May 27, 1949, p. 1.

Munker, Donna. "Enchantment and the Biographical Passion." *American Imago* 54, no. 4: 377–97.

"Navajo Annie D. Wauneka Presented Freedom Medal." Associated Press clipping, n.d. Tom Dodge Papers, MSS-033, Arizona Collection, Arizona State University, Tempe.

"Navajo Ex-leader Convicted." *New York Times,* May 29, 1992, p. A13.

Navajo Health Authority. *Capsules of Navajo Health Authority History.* N.d. Navajo Nation Library, Window Rock AZ.

Navajo Health Education Project. *Orientation to Health on the Navajo Indian Reservation.* U.S. Department of Health, Education and Welfare. Rev. ed. Washington DC: U.S. Public Health Service, 1960.

Navajo Tribal Council. Minutes of meetings, 1951–1977. Microfiche collection, Navajo Tribal Office of Records, Window Rock AZ.

Nelson, Mary Carroll. *Annie Wauneka: The Story of an American Indian.* Minneapolis: Dillon Press, 1972.

New York Times Oral History Program. "Annie Wauneka, Navajo." Listening to Indians, Glen Rock, New Jersey. Typescript. Oct. 19, 1975. Labriola National American Indian Data Center, Arizona State University, Tempe.

Orr, John. "Navajo Council Coalition to Talk." *Gallup NM Independent,* Dec. 6, 1978, p. 1.

Parman, Donald L. *The Navajos and the New Deal.* New Haven: Yale University Press, 1976.

Patzman, Stephen N. "Henry Chee Dodge: A Modern Chief of the Navajos." *Arizoniana: The Journal of Arizona History* 5 (spring 1964): 35–41.

"Pawhuskan's Sister to White House to Receive Freedom Medal." Undated and unidentified newspaper clipping. Tom Dodge Papers, MSS-033, Arizona Collection, Arizona State University, Tempe.

Penney, Rada. "Building a Future for American Indians." Los Angeles: Indian Centers, 1982.

Proceedings of the Indian Health Committee of the American Academy of Pediatrics. University of New Mexico, Albuquerque, May 23, 1968. Navajo Nation Library, Window Rock, AZ.

Proceedings of the Second Working Conference on Services for Hospitalized Navajo Tuberculosis Patients. Sponsored jointly by the Navajo Tribe, Navajo Agency, and American Indian Development. Gallup NM, April 29-30, May 1, 1955. Arizona State Museum Library, Tucson.

Proceedings of the Third National Conference on Indian Health. Held under the auspices of the National Committee on Indian Health. New York, Nov. 19, 1964. Arizona State Museum Library, Tucson.

Qoyawayma, Polingaysi. *No Turning Back: A True Account of a Hopi Indian Girl's Struggle to Bridge the Gap between the World of Her People and the World of the White Man.* As told to Vada F. Carlson. Albuquerque: University of New Mexico Press, 1964.

"Range Management Report." Land Management Unit 17, p. 12. AZ 124, vol. 41, Special Collections, University of Arizona Main Library, Tucson.

Reichard, Gladys. *Navajo Religion: A Study of Symbolism.* New York: Bollingen Foundation, 1950.

————. *Social Life of the Navajo Indians.* New York: Columbia University Press, 1928.

Resolution to Navajo Tribal Council on the death of Chee Dodge. Jan. 7, 1947. Special Collections, AZ 500, Box 42, Folder 1, University of Arizona Main Library, Tucson.

Richardson, Cecil Calvin. "The Navajo Way." *Arizona Highways,* April 1995, pp. 2-4.

Riley, Glenda. "The Historiography of American Indian and Other Western Women." In *Rethinking American Indian History,* ed. Donald Fixico, pp. 43-70. Albuquerque: University of New Mexico Press, 1997.

Roessel, Robert A. "Navajo History, 1850-1923." In *Handbook of North American Indians,* ed. William C. Sturtevant. Vol. 10. Washington DC: Smithsonian Institution, 1983.

Roessel, Ruth. *Women in Navajo Society.* Rough Rock AZ: Navajo Resource Center, 1981.

Roland, A. L. "Annie Wauneka, a True Humanitarian." *Window Rock AZ Navajo Times,* June 10, 1976, p. 2.

Rushton, Ted. "Advisory Committee Reaffirms Mitchell Exclusion." *Gallup NM Independent,* Aug. 9, 1968, p. 1.

————. "Nakai Meets Students to Discuss Ted Mitchell." *Gallup NM Independent,* Aug. 13, 1968, p. 1.

Salsbury, Clarence G., with Paul Hughes. *The Salsbury Story—A Medical Missionary's Lifetime of Public Service.* Tucson: University of Arizona Press, 1969.

Saltzstein, Kathie. "Tribe Prepares Birthday Bash." *Gallup NM Independent,* April 7, 1984, p. 1.

———. "Wauneka Proud of Past." *Gallup NM Independent,* April 10, 1984, p. 2.

Sekaquaptewa, Helen, as told to Louise Udall. *Me and Mine: The Life Story of Helen Sekaquaptewa.* Tucson: University of Arizona Press, 1969.

Shaw, Anna Moore. *A Pima Past.* Tucson: University of Arizona Press, 1974.

States, Janel. "Nation Loses Annie Dodge Wauneka." *Flagstaff AZ Navajo-Hopi Observer,* Nov. 19, 1997, p. 1.

Steiner, Stan. *The New Indians.* New York: Harper and Row, 1968.

Stewart, Irene. *A Voice in Her Tribe: A Navajo Woman's Own Story.* Socorro NM: Ballena Press, 1980.

"Ted Mitchell, Director, Expelled Following Disturbance in Hall." *Window Rock AZ Navajo Times,* Aug. 15, 1968.

Trennert, Robert A. "Indian Sore Eyes: The Federal Campaign to Control Trachoma in the Southwest, 1910–40." *Journal of the Southwest* 32, no. 2 (summer 1990): 121–46.

———. *White Man's Medicine: Government Doctors and the Navajo, 1863–1955.* Albuquerque: University of New Mexico Press, 1998.

"Udall-Littell Case Climax." *Window Rock AZ Navajo Times,* Feb. 11, 1965.

Underhill, Ruth. *Here Come the Navajo!* Washington DC: U.S. Indian Service, 1953.

———. *The Navajos.* Norman: University of Oklahoma Press, 1956.

Van Valkenburgh, Richard. "Henry Chee Dodge—Chief of the Navajo Nation." *Arizona Highways,* June 1943, pp. 5–7.

"Vocational Rehabilitation Services Plan of the Navajo Nation." 1977. Goldwater Collection, Box 3, Folder 17, Arizona State University, Tempe.

Wagner, Sallie Lippincott. *Wide Ruins: Memories from a Navajo Trading Post.* Albuquerque: University of New Mexico Press, 1997.

Wauneka, Annie. "The Dilemma for Indian Women." *Wassaja,* Sept. 1976, p. 8.

———. "Helping a People to Understand." *American Journal of Nursing,* 62, no. 7, July 1962.

————. "The Navajo and His Future." Speech given at Roundtable Conference. El Morro Theater, Gallup NM, Aug. 10, 1951. Special Collections, AZ 500, Box 42, University of Arizona Main Library, Tucson.

Wilken, Robert L. *Anselm Weber O.F.M.: Missionary to the Navaho, 1898-1921.* Milwaukee: Bruce, 1955.

Witherspoon, Gary. *Navajo Kinship and Marriage.* Chicago: University of Chicago Press, 1975.

Witt, Shirley Hill. "An Interview with Dr. Annie Dodge Wauneka." *Frontiers* 6, no. 3: 64-67.

"Women's Meeting Slams Discrimination." *Window Rock AZ Navajo Times,* Oct. 2, 1975.

Woodman, Marion. *Leaving My Father's House: A Journey to Conscious Femininity.* Boston: Shambala, 1993.

"WR Seven Released after Annie Wauneka Pledges Guidance." *Window Rock AZ Navajo Times,* Nov. 16, 1978, pp. 3-4.

Wyman, Leland C. "Navajo Ceremonial System." In *Handbook of North American Indians,* ed. William C. Sturtevant. Vol. 10. Washington DC: Smithsonian Institution, 1983.

INTERVIEWS

Allen, Marie. Interview by author. Fort Defiance AZ, August 1995.

Arthur, Claudine Bates. Interview by author. Window Rock AZ, Aug. 1995.

Bergman, Robert, M.D. Telephone interview by author. Oct. 1997.

Blue, Martha. Telephone interview by author. 1998.

Bluehouse, Irma. Interview by author. Ganado AZ, Aug. 1995, May 1996.

Bluehouse, Milton, Jr. Interview by author. Tucson, May 1996, March 1997, March 1998.

Bluehouse, Milton, Sr. Interview by author. Tucson, May 1996.

Bock, George, M.D. Interview by author. Tucson, Sept. 1996.

Bock, Harriet. Interview by author. Tucson, Sept. 1996.

De Groat, Ellouise. Interview by author. Window Rock AZ, Aug. 1995.

Dodge, Don. Interview by author. Window Rock AZ, July 1995.

Faiche, Ron. Interview by author. Albuquerque, Aug. 1995.

Goosen, Irvy. Telephone interview by author. Oct. 1997.

Haffner, Marlene, M.D. Telephone interview by author. July 2000.

Hale, Albert. Interview by author. Window Rock AZ, Aug. 1995.

Hubbard, John. Interview by author. Window Rock AZ, Aug. 1995.

Huerta, Lawrence. Interview by author. Tucson, Nov. 1995.

Levy, Jerrold E., Ph.D. Interview by author. Tucson, June 1996.

Link, Martin. Interview by author. Gallup NM, Aug. 1995.

McKammon, Charles, M.D. Telephone interview by author. July 2000.

McKenzie, Taylor, M.D. Telephone interview by author. July 1999.

McKinley, Howard. Interview by author. Fort Defiance AZ, Aug. 1995.

Menapace, Alan. Interview by author. Gallup NM, Aug. 1995.

Nelson, Louise. Interview by author. Window Rock AZ, Aug. 1995.

Perkins, Warren. Telephone interview by author. July 2000.

Shirley, Ann. Interview by author. Sawmill AZ, Aug. 1995.

Wagner, Sallie Lippincott. Telephone interview by author. April 1999.

Wauneka, Annie. Interview by Abe Chanin and Mildred Chanin. Scottsdale AZ, mid-1970s. Unpublished manuscript. Copy in author's collection.

Whiterock, Lydia Yazzie. Interview by author. Chambers AZ, Aug. 1999.

Zah, Peterson. Interview by author. Tempe AZ, June 1996.

LETTERS, TELEGRAMS, E-MAIL

Beaty, Orren, Jr., Letter to Lee C. White, Feb. 10, 1965. EX IN/Navajo, Container 3, Lyndon Baines Johnson Presidential Library and Museum, Austin.

Dodge, C. H. Letter to E. P. Smith, Commissioner of Indian Affairs, regarding Chee Dodge, Feb. 1, 1875. Historical File, Octavia Sellin Public Library, Gallup NM.

Dodge, Chee. Letter to Committee on Indian Affairs, U.S. House of Representatives, Sept. 12, 1944. Special Collections, AZ 500, Box 42, Folder 2, University of Arizona Main Library, Tucson.

———. Letter to Frank K. Lane, Secretary of the Interior, Feb. 2, 1914. Historical File, Octavia Sellin Library, Gallup NM.

Dodge, Tom. Letter of resignation to John Collier. Tom Dodge Papers, MSS-033, Box 1, Folder 16, Arizona Collection, Arizona State University, Tempe.

Goldwater, Barry. Letter to Annie Wauneka, Jan. 31, 1972. Arizona Collection, Arizona State University, Tempe.

Kelledy, L. J., S.M. Letter to Anselm Weber, July 9, 1912. Special Collections, AZ 500, Box 42, Folder 2, University of Arizona Main Library, Tucson.

Kennedy, John F. Telegram to Annie D. Wauneka, July 1, 1963. White House Central Subject File, Box 512, Folder MA 2-10, John Fitzgerald Kennedy Library and Museum, Boston.

Mitchell, Ted. E-mail to author. Jan. 9, 1998.

Tsosie, Anna M., and Mary Agnes Parker. Letter to Navajo Tribal Council, Sept. 10, 1951. Special Collections, AZ 500, Box 28, Folder 4, University of Arizona Main Library, Tucson.

Wauneka, Annie D. Letter to Barry Goldwater, Jan. 18, 1975. Arizona Collection, Arizona State University, Tempe.

————. Letter to Lee C. White, June 10, 1965. EX IN/Navajo, Container 125, Lyndon B. Johnson Library and Museum, Austin.

————. Letter to Lyndon B. Johnson, Dec. 31, 1964. EX IN/Navajo Container 3, Lyndon B. Johnson Library and Museum, Austin.

————. Telegram to John Fitzgerald Kennedy, July 5, 1963. White House Central Subject File, Box 512, Folder MA 2-10, John Fitzgerald Kennedy Library and Museum, Boston.

White, Lee C. Letter to Annie D. Wauneka, Feb. 15, 1965. EX IN/Navajo, Container 3, Lyndon B. Johnson Library and Museum, Austin.

————. Letter to Annie D. Wauneka, June 21, 1965. EX IN/Navajo, Container 125, Lyndon B. Johnson Library and Museum, Austin.

Yazzie, Hataty. Note to Chee Dodge. AZ 500, Box 42, Folder 2, University of Arizona Main Library, Tucson.

SENATE AND HOUSE OF REPRESENTATIVES TESTIMONY
Dodge, Chee. Testimony on boarding school case. Affidavit. Office of Indian Affairs, Record Group 75, File Mark 8271/March 10, 1888, National Archives, Washington DC.

————. Testimony on land dispute case. Undated transcript. Hubbell Working Papers, Hubbell Trading Post, Ganado, Arizona.

Wauneka, Annie. Testimony, U.S. Senate, Hearings before Committee on Appropriations, Labor, Health, Education, and Welfare, fiscal year 1959, April 1–May 19, 1958, Y4.Ap6/2:L11/1959, p. 1178.

————. Testimony, U.S. Senate, Hearings before Committee on Appropriations, Interior Department and Related Agencies Appropriations, fiscal year 1964, March 20, 1963, Y4.Ap6/2:In8/964, p. 1498.

————. Testimony, U.S. Senate, Hearings before Senate Committee on Labor and Public Welfare, Special Subcommittee on Indian Education, part 3, Flagstaff AZ, March 30, 1968, Y4.L11/2:In2/2/pt.3, p. 998.

————. Testimony, U.S. Senate, Hearings before Subcommittee on Department of Interior and Related Agencies Appropriations, fiscal year 1971, part 4, April 17, 1970, Y4.Ap6/2:In8/971/pt.4, pp. 4310–21.

————. Testimony, U.S. Senate, Hearings before Subcommittee on Department of Interior Appropriations, fiscal year 1973, April 14, 1972, Y4.Ap6/2:In8/973/pt.4, pp. 3783–93.

————. Testimony, U.S. House of Representatives, Hearings before Subcommittee on Indian Affairs, on partition of Navajo and Hopi 1882 Reservations, April 18, 1972, Y4.In8/14:92–44, pp. 88–92.

————. Testimony, U.S. House of Representatives, Hearings before Subcommittee on Interior Appropriations, fiscal year 1983, part 4, Feb. 23–24, 1982, Y4.Ap6/1:In8/6/983/pt.4, pp. 572–78.

————. Testimony, U.S. Senate, Hearings before Special Committee on Investigations of Select Committee on Indian Affairs on Federal Relationship with Indians, Feb. 9, 1989, Y4.In2/11:5, HRG 101-26/pt.2, pp. 193–201.

Index

In the AMERICAN INDIAN LIVES series

I Stand in the Center of the Good
Interviews with Contemporary Native American Artists
Edited by Lawrence Abbott

Authentic Alaska
Voices of Its Native Writers
Edited by Susan B. Andrews and John Creed

Dreaming the Dawn
Conversations with Native Artists and Activists
By E. K. Caldwell
Introduction by Elizabeth Woody

Chief
The Life History of Eugene Delorme, Imprisoned Santee Sioux
Edited by Inéz Cardozo-Freeman

Winged Words
American Indian Writers Speak
Edited by Laura Coltelli

Life, Letters and Speeches
By George Copway (Kahgegagahbowh)
Edited by A. LaVonne Brown Ruoff and Donald B. Smith

Life Lived Like a Story
Life Stories of Three Yukon Native Elders
By Julie Cruikshank in collaboration with Angela Sidney,
Kitty Smith, and Annie Ned

LaDonna Harris
A Comanche Life
By LaDonna Harris
Edited by H. Henrietta Stockel

Essie's Story
The Life and Legacy of a Shoshone Teacher
By Esther Burnett Horne and Sally McBeth

Song of Rita Joe
Autobiography of a Mi'kmaq Poet
By Rita Joe
Catch Colt
By Sidner J. Larson

Alex Posey
Creek Poet, Journalist, and Humorist
By Daniel F. Littlefield Jr.

Mourning Dove
A Salishan Autobiography
Edited by Jay Miller

I'll Go and Do More
Annie Dodge Wauneka, Navajo Leader and Activist
By Carolyn Niethammer

John Rollin Ridge
His Life and Works
By James W. Parins

Singing an Indian Song
A Biography of D'Arcy McNickle
By Dorothy R. Parker

Crashing Thunder
The Autobiography of an American Indian
Edited by Paul Radin

Telling a Good One
The Process of a Native American Collaborative Biography
By Theodore Rios and Kathleen Mullen Sands

Sacred Feathers
*The Reverend Peter Jones (Kahkewaquonaby) and
the Mississauga Indians*
By Donald B. Smith

Grandmother's Grandchild
My Crow Indian Life
By Alma Hogan Snell
Edited by Becky Matthews
Foreword by Peter Nabokov

Blue Jacket
Warrior of the Shawnees
By John Sugden

I Tell You Now
Autobiographical Essays by Native American Writers
Edited by Brian Swann and Arnold Krupat

Postindian Conversations
By Gerald Vizenor and A. Robert Lee

Chainbreaker
The Revolutionary War Memoirs of Governor Blacksnake
As told to Benjamin Williams
Edited by Thomas S. Abler

Standing in the Light
A Lakota Way of Seeing
By Severt Young Bear and R. D. Theisz

Sarah Winnemucca
By Sally Zanjani